WE CHOSE CAPE COD

WE CHOSE

CAPE COD

SCOTT CORBETT

PARNASSUS IMPRINTS
ORLEANS, MASSACHUSETTS

To My Mother

CONTENTS

ARRIVAL

1

NO SNOW ON THE CAPE

As I said to a friend, "We're going to live near the elbow on a neck. That's something not everyone can do."

"It doesn't sound any crazier than the rest of your plan," he grumbled. He was a doubting friend, a tongue-clucking friend, and he had a lot of company.

"It's like our moving—it only sounds crazy. Actually it makes perfectly good sense. We're going to live near the elbow of Cape Cod, on a neck of land. Quivet Neck, to be exact. One of the two necks of land occupied by the village."

"You'll need both of them, with those two heads of yours." My friend went on to raise the standard objections. "It's all right for a summer vacation, but to move from New York city to some little Cape Cod whistle stop—"

"Thanks for the compliment. The railroad doesn't come within five miles of East Dennis. Passenger service doesn't come at all."

"Listen, you're only a free-lance writer! If you were millionaires and could afford to indulge little whims like this it would be one thing, but you two are putting yourselves out on a limb—"

"On a neck," I corrected, though I would not want to give anyone the wrong impression. It was a fair-sized neck, and we would be a good mile back from the water.

"But why Cape Cod? How do you know you'll really like it? How can you be sure you'll make enough to live on? Wouldn't it be smarter at least to wait a few more years?" He saw he was getting nowhere with these sensible questions, so he tried the weather. "Furthermore, you'll freeze up there! Massachusetts must have ten feet of snow all winter!"

I gave my usual patient reply to this standard misconception.

"You're thinking of the North Shore. The Cape doesn't have that kind of New England winter. Remember, it's surrounded by the sea, which gives it a more moderate climate. We'll only get a little cold weather, and no snow to speak of. And if we do get any it won't last. The salt air, you know."

"But what a dismal time of year to move up there! January, for Pete's sake!"

"It'll practically be February when we get there."

"February! If there's one thing worse than January, it's February!"

It was difficult to parry these objections, except with flippancy. How could we explain why we were acting this way— Elizabeth, raised in California, and I, a fellow from Missouri? How could I explain why we felt this powerful urge to move to a spit of land sticking like a coathook off the coast of New England? Both of us had New England ancestry, but neither of us had ever lived there. Nobody in either family had ever lived on Cape Cod. We ourselves had only visited it as vacationers for a total of four weeks. We had seen the Cape for the first time a mere two years ago.

I felt particularly foolish every time I confessed to this

sparse record. It was not an impressive basis for our decision to move there. Something about the Cape felt right to us, but we could not tell anybody why. We could not even tell each other why. Maybe we were all wrong about it. Maybe year-around living there would disillusion us and teach us not to listen to siren calls. It would be a costly lesson.

Our move did not even have the slight logic of taking us to the one small section of the Cape we knew. Our vacations had been spent in a beach cottage near Provincetown. Chance took us to a mid-Cape real-estate agent who happened to produce the kind of house we wanted and could afford—and the house happened to be in East Dennis, a village we had never even visited before.

The village happened also to be a particularly charming one, however. It was on the bay side of the Cape, and occupied those two necks of land I mentioned, Quivet Neck and Sesuit Neck. The village sat on a gently sloped hill overlooking a wide stretch of marsh which separated it from the highway. Though it really contained a variety of architectural styles other than that of the Cape Cod cottage, captain's house, or mate's house, it gave an impression of being all Cape Cod because even those houses which were not Cape Codders were white-trimmed and weatherbeaten and had an air of belonging. The white spire of a New England church rose from the center of Quivet Neck, and even the ridiculous architecture of the village hall had somehow weathered and blended into the picture and become an acceptable part of it.

The house we decided to buy was one of no special distinction, but well situated on two and a half acres of property overlooking the marshes. It had new plumbing, a new heating plant, and a new modern kitchen, all things we were looking for after coping with ancient facilities in an old New York brownstone for five years.

"Of course, this will be the final blow for some of our friends," I reminded Elizabeth, and did not have to explain.

5

In the eyes of many, one of the few excuses for moving to a place like Cape Cod at all was to buy an authentic old house with lots of charm. Nothing less than a 200-year-old Cape Cod cottage would do. And here we were thinking of buying a house that was a mere twenty-five years old!

It is always a shock when things suddenly leave the talking stage and become a solid reality, thorny with problems, that must be dealt with now or never. Should we actually commit ourselves to move halfway out on a narrow strip of land and live among conservative, hidebound, crusty New Englanders, people whom we had scarcely laid eyes on as yet? Had we really thought this thing through? Why were we so sure of ourselves?

Even while these last-minute doubts were racing through our minds, something that could not be put with equal facility into words was making me reach for my checkbook.

After my first night in our new house I woke up on the dining-room floor.

Lots of people have done that after a good rousing housewarming, but we had not had any housewarming and I was better off than most people who wake up on dining-room floors. I had a mattress under me.

Our terraced sleeping accommodations looked like a good location for planting grapes. We were sleeping on three levels, having split up the two studio couches which were the only articles of furniture that as yet graced our new home. Elizabeth had the box springs my mattress went with, and our eight-year-old daughter Florence had a complete couch—or at least she had had until she followed the covers down to her mother's level.

The light that entered the bare windows from a hazy morning sky was subdued enough to have allowed us to sleep till nearly eight. Elizabeth, without setting us an example, remarked that we really ought to get up because the moving van might arrive any minute.

"I am anxious to talk to that real-estate woman. Also that fellow in the gas station," I declared. "In fact, I am anxious to have words with everyone who told us they didn't have snow on Cape Cod. If that wasn't a snowstorm that had me biting my nails through a thirteen-hour crawl up here yesterday—"

"Well, you must admit there was less snow on the Cape than off it."

"There was plenty *on* it. Yes, yes, and what was that other claim they made? That even if they did get a little snow it was always gone by morning? The salt air, you know." I struggled to my feet. "Well, let's see what kind of job the Chamber of Commerce has done."

I was working up a fine head of cynicism, but it fizzled away as I stared out the window. Every trace of snow had vanished during the night!

"By George, it really *doesn't* last!" My faith in mankind was restored. The day was off to a good start. My wife was cheered. Moving men have large, substantial feet, and the larger the feet the more snow comes in on them.

For two days we lived an isolated existence, too preoccupied with getting settled to wonder much about our new neighbors and what their reaction might be to all the activity down at the "Landry House," as we soon found our place was called. (All the time the Landrys had lived in it, the place had been called the "Baxter House," after the people *they* had bought it from.)

As a matter of fact, for a couple of days we wondered if we had any neighbors at all. Our house was in the southeast corner of the village, on a corner. Across the road to the north was a large field. Catercorner from us there was a house which was obviously unoccupied in that winter season, and the nearest house to the west of us was a hundred yards away.

We scarcely glimpsed another human being, except when a car went by, and not over two or three passed in a day's time. Even on the highway, on the far side of the wide marshes, cars were few and far between. We worked hard and enjoyed our solitude.

My wife was the sort of woman who, when faced with a great deal of work, often started in on it right after breakfast and became so preoccupied with her labors that she forgot to stop and get dressed. On our third day, for example, she was still attired in her robe and nightgown at three in the afternoon. Actually she had put in a good day's work by then, but we still wondered what impression our first caller, the Reverend Oswald Blake, must have received.

The Reverend Mr. Blake was very young, very earnest, and very uncomfortable, and once in the house he did not know how to get out. It took him two hours to extricate himself, but at least that gave Elizabeth ample opportunity to slip away during the second hour and return properly attired, and we were well impressed by his calling on us so promptly.

He invited us to attend church, and while I did not say so, it struck me that we did not even know as yet where the church was located. We had of course admired its spire as we approached the village along the highway, but that was all. However, it was nice to know that the little village church was actually in operation, and I sincerely hoped it was getting good support from the local folk. I might even slip a buck into the collection plate myself sometime, when we got around to paying it a visit.

The next day we had another caller. I think I may have been pouring myself something in the kitchen when she knocked at the front door. In fact, I am pretty sure I was, because I distinctly remember Elizabeth saying, "Here comes someone, put that bottle away."

Being a man of principle, I found this suggestion hypocritical.

"Now, wait a minute. I'm not going to start out around here by trying to hide the fact that I drink. Heavily. Sometimes a highball a day for weeks on end."

8

"You're right. Leave the bottle on the sideboard, but at the same time don't wave it in people's faces. Remember, we're in dry country now."

"There is a package store dispensing liquor in bottles right down at the head of our road on the highway. Don't try to tell me it's staying open during the winter months just to spite the natives."

"No, but it's probably all secret drinking up here," said Elizabeth, and went to the door.

Our second visitor was a large, imposing woman with iron-gray hair and a long, strong New England face. It was plain almost at once that the slight stoop of her shoulders came from the heavy responsibilities Mrs. Luella Sears carried in our little town. Unlike the Reverend Mr. Blake, she took into account the piles of unsorted belongings that still cluttered our living-room, appreciated how busy we were, and made her visit brief. She too invited us to attend church, and uttered a few kind words of welcome. There was something official and decisive about her manner, as when the President throws out the first ball on Opening Day. We were now officially present in East Dennis.

As she turned to go her glance inventoried the furniture and lingered on a pair of Victorian grandfather and grandmother chairs.

"Lovely chairs. Family things?"

"Yes, from my mother," said Elizabeth. Our caller nodded curt approval and took her leave.

"I got the impression that Mrs. Sears is pretty active in local church affairs," I told my wife. "Probably a higher-up in the Ladies' Aid. She didn't miss much around here, either."

"Very busy eyes," agreed my wife. "I hardly think her peek into the kitchen overlooked that bottle. We'd better go to church tomorrow to reassure her."

Something in my mate's tone of voice warned me that I had better lay the law down right now.

9

"Hey, look here, don't think for a minute that I'm going to get involved in running over to the local church every Sunday. Oh, I don't mind going once in a while, and as a matter of fact I'd like to go to several of the churches around here," I said, seeing in my mind's eye the charming picture of people leaving a handsome New England church, myself among them on little more than a tourist basis. Whenever I imagined such a scene with me in it, the people were always *leaving* the church, not entering it. It was the architecture of the churches, their age and history, that interested me. The rest of it—well, I felt myself to be a religious man, but inclined to avoid churchgoing as a regular thing.

"I don't want to get too involved with the local church, either," said Elizabeth, "but we might as well face it that in a village of this size it's a center of things, and we can hardly avoid supporting it to some extent. Remember, Florence will probably want to attend Sunday school there, and—"

"Well, sure. I know we can't very well stay completely clear of it. All I want to get straight is that I have no intention of being drawn into a lot of church activities. As a matter of fact, if we ever attend any place with any regularity at all, we'll probably want to go to that nice little Episcopal church we saw over there somewhere in the middle of the Cape."

As we were talking I was standing at the window with my hands behind my back, frowning into space, when my attention was attracted to something else. A large, fleecy white object was settling to the ground. It was followed by others.

"Well, what do you know!" During our chat with Mrs. Sears the conversation had taken its usual turn to the weather. We had agreed that it looked as if it was going to "do something," but the word "snow" had not even been mentioned. It was too great a strain on the imagination to conceive of more snow so soon.

Florence rushed in from outside with a bulletin.

"It's snowing!"

"Nonsense, child. Someone down in Alabama has been picking cotton in a high wind."

"They have not! I'm going to build a snow fort."

She rushed happily outside, full of a child's optimism. And well she might. Along about suppertime, I looked out the window again and watched her playing in what was undeniably a snow fort. The shades of night were falling fast, and so was the snow.

"You know, if this doesn't stop pretty quick now, it's going to take some mighty powerful melting to get it off by morning," I remarked. "If this were anywhere else, I'd say we were in for a real one."

It was at supper that Florence surprised us with a new decision. She wanted to go to Sunday school in the morning, our very first Sunday in town. She had liked the minister, and besides that she had decided it would be an easy way to meet some of the kids before she started in school on Monday.

"Well, that's fine, but did you decide this yourself or did your mother put a bug in your ear?" I demanded with a sharp glance at Elizabeth. I was unable to pin anything on her.

When we went to bed there were several inches of snow on the ground and it was still snowing. In the morning Florence was first up. Outside it was clear and sunny. She hurried to her window, and then came flying into our room.

"Guess what?"

"The snow's all gone."

"No! There's more than ever!"

This time there had been a slip-up somewhere. There was better than a foot of snow outside now, and it was showing no disposition to melt in twenty degree weather.

"Can I still go to Sunday school?"

"Sure."

"But you promised you'd take me."

"I don't think we can drive," said Elizabeth. "It doesn't look as if any traffic is moving today."

11

The snow was deep in the road, and unmarred by car tracks.

"Who needs to drive?" I said. "It's a nice day, we can bundle up and walk." Having checked the day before, I knew the church was around the next corner on the middle one of the village's three east-and-west streets. We were about the equivalent of five New York city blocks from the church, scarcely as far as from our old brownstone to the subway. "By the way, you're not planning any underhanded moves for getting me to attend divine worship today, are you?" I added.

"You're so suspicious, dear. Heavens, we've still got too much to do. We'll walk Florence over and then come home and get to work."

So shortly before ten o'clock we set off through the snow. The clean white snow, the trees that arched their bare branches over us, and our New England surroundings inevitably brought to mind that well-known print of the Pilgrims heading for church under similar conditions.

"We've got it soft," I pointed out. "Look what they put up with. Arrows through the hat on the way, no heat in a cold church, and several hours of yacking from the pulpit to look forward to. Today the parishioners would fire the sexton if he didn't fire the furnace, and if the minister doesn't compress his message into a snappy twenty minutes they start coughing and shuffling their feet."

"Listen to the authority. What do *you* want—cold feet and four hours of Cotton Mather?"

"Deliver me! No, all I want is to go home and get to work. We've got a lot to do today."

"When Sunday school's over, won't you come and get me, Daddy?"

"Nothing doing. People will just be going into church then, and they might try to drag us in. You know the way home."

"Aw!"

It was only a few yards up Sea Street to Centre Street, which ran through the center of the village on our neck. Through the bare trees we could see the spire of the church up ahead on the right side, and the gables of the village hall on the left. The snow and the square white houses both sparkled in the sunshine, and the Sabbath quiet was emphasized by the way the bell in the church belfry set the clear, cold air to throbbing as it began to count the hour. In New York we had lived back-to back with a church, and had been very fond of the bell that struck the hours there. Until now I had not even been conscious of the village church bell. It was good to get acquainted with it, and with those pleasant houses.

The first house we passed was the one catercorner from us. It was a fine example of a really old Cape Cod cottage in excellent repair, and its location gave us a delightful outlook, for although it was unoccupied during the winter its windows were not shuttered and were neatly curtained. It had nothing of that desolate air that attends the house whose doors are blocked up and whose windows are blanked out.

On the far corner of Centre Street was a new little cottage with its shingles not yet weathered to that silver gray which is one of the glories of Cape Cod houses. Along Centre Street itself the houses were square and solid, with here and there a stained-glass window or gingerbread trim to commemorate our grandfathers' days, or with a handsome simplicity that spoke of even earlier times. There were no garages, but only barns which now served as garages, so that on this snowbound morning there was nothing to contradict the impression that the street as we saw it then must have been very little different from the street as it looked a century ago.

As we neared the church and it became plain where we were heading, doors began to pop open all along the street, heads came into view, and halloos were heard. Though we had noticed no stirring of curtains as we passed by, quite obviously our passing had not gone unnoticed. From across the street

13

a woman called to us, smiling sort of apologetically, and also looking amazed.

"Yoo-hoo! Er—there's no church today because of the storm. People can't get their cars out!"

From around the side of the parsonage, snowshovel in hand, the Reverend Mr. Blake appeared and confirmed this statement. The unexpected snow had isolated the faithful and paralyzed all normal activity. According to old residents, this was the biggest snow in fifteen years.

We thanked the minister and the lady across the way, and doubled back in our tracks. As we passed several other doors opened, and people bade us good morning. They all had that same surprised, caught-flatfooted look.

Walking home, we realized we had encountered a condition that exists every place where cars may be used with ease: people have forgotten how to use their feet. To go two blocks, they jump in the car. Coming from New York, where some people still walk a lot, it was second nature to us to think of walking.

Snow had made our path more difficult on moving day. Now snow, without our realizing it, was in the process of making our path easier.

2

SIGNS OF LIFE

Something was wrong with the melting system. The snow plows came around on Sunday afternoon, and the roads were clear, but on Monday morning we still had pretty much all the snow we started with. It began to look as if Florence's snow fort might have become a permanent installation, had it been better placed.

As I scraped away at our snow-blocked driveway, I was rather short with her about that fort. I pointed out that it might have been more thoughtful to build it someplace other than the middle of the drive. In vain she extolled the strategic advantages of the position. I was angry anyway. All that no-snow talk had taken me in so thoroughly that I had not even thought to have the movers bring our snowshovel from the basement entrance back in New York. All I had to work with was an old board.

"I'm going to buy a snowshovel while we're out," I declared.

"You may never need it again," said my wife.

"I hope not. Stop thinking of it as a shovel! Think of it as a cheap insurance policy!"

Florence had been dreading the change of schools for months, so we had promised to take her to school the first day, rather than have her ride the school bus. On the way over I made one last attempt to reassure her.

"Listen, one day at your new school and you'll probably think it's twice as good as P.S. 33 in New York."

"P.S. 33," Florence murmured nostalgically, and her eyes filled with tears at the dear name. We left her sitting shyly at one of the rear desks in her new class, coping courageously with her extra growing pain. Then after doing a few errands, we drove back across the Cape to check in at the local post office.

Cape Cod post offices are not what they used to be, according to old-timers. They used to be full of retired sea captains yarning all day long. They were the local clubhouse, news center, and forum.

Maybe they aren't what they used to be, but they are still a good deal more than just a place to pick up mail.

Our post office was about the size one might expect in a place where there were less than a hundred boxholders in winter. It was in a nice little white building with a real-estate office next door, and when I looked at it the first time all I could think of was the many times I had walked up Eighth Avenue to a post office so big there was room enough for "Neither rain, nor snow, nor heat, nor gloom of night stays these couriers from the swift completion of their appointed rounds" to be engraved across its front in letters as tall as I was. On our post office there would have been just about room enough for "No Loitering and No Spitting" in headline size.

The postmistress, Mrs. Nora Larkins, welcomed us to town and explained the workings of the local postal system. There was no house delivery. Boxholders paid a box rental of twenty-five cents every three months, and if a person objected to that he could get his mail c/o General Delivery and not have a box.

As for Mrs. Larkins, oddly enough she was not a native. It may have been that the appointment was made under a Democratic administration and the only way they could find a Democrat in East Dennis was to import one, I don't know, but anyway there she was.

While we were talking to Mrs. Larkins, a small, gray-haired lady came in for her mail and the postmistress introduced us. Her name was Mrs. Sears, but she did not particularly resemble Mrs. Luella Sears. She was pleasant and said it was nice to have somebody in the Landry house again, and that they had all liked the Landrys very much and knew Mr. Landry would never have sold the house to anybody who wasn't nice.

A moment later another small, gray-haired lady came in and was introduced to us as Mrs. Sears. She had scarcely left when the first small, gray-haired lady came in again.

"Have you met Mrs. Sears?" asked Mrs. Larkins.

"Yes, two Mrs. Searses ago," I said, and both women laughed.

"No, this is *another* Mrs. Sears," said Mrs. Larkins, and I apologized for having mistaken her for the first one.

The third Mrs. Sears left and we were about to go when another gray-haired lady, this time a little taller, came in.

"Oh," said Mrs. Larkins, "have you met—"

"Mrs. Sears, I presume?" I said.

"No—Mrs. Underhill," said the latest arrival, laughing heartily. Mrs. Larkins verified this change of pace. We shook hands, and Mrs. Underhill went to the door and called her husband. A moment later Fred Underhill ambled in. He was a man in his fifties with a face as comfortable and friendly and as seamed as an old shoe, with a strong mouth and kindly eyes. They explained that they were also newcomers, having moved to the Cape five years ago from a suburb of New York. With-

17

out asking, I knew Fred Underhill to be a Midwesterner like myself.

"We hear you took a little walk Sunday." He chuckled. "You caused quite a stir."

"How's that?"

"Why, the whole town's buzzing about it! You really caught 'em by surprise!"

The Underhills said they would call on us soon, and they promised to fill in a little background for us on the local scene. Fred Underhill said something about having to get back to work, and they went their way with Mrs. Underhill at the wheel.

"I'll be interested to find out what drew them here and what kind of work he's found to do up here," I remarked to Elizabeth on the way home. "Say, wasn't that a funny coincidence having three Mrs. Searses come in one after the other?"

"Yes, especially when they all looked exactly alike."

"It seemed so to me. Now that I try to think back, not only did the third one look like the first one, but the second one looked like both of them!"

"Maybe they were triplets. You know, one of those things where three sisters marry brothers."

"That's the kind of stuff that's supposed to go on in New England," I agreed. "We'll have to ask somebody about it. Do you suppose they're part of Mrs. Luella Sears' family? They must be related, having the same name and all."

Mrs. Luella herself called up later on that day and bestowed a signal honor on Elizabeth, but she got her signals mixed as far as my wife was concerned, because Elizabeth had no conception at the time of what an honor it really was. Mrs. Luella called to say that the Ladies' Aid, of which she happened to be president, met the first Wednesday of every month for lunch and the afternoon, and she extended an invitation to Elizabeth to attend the meeting, which was to be at her house.

We were still too busy getting settled to think of anything but working at it all day every day, and Elizabeth had the audacity to say so and decline the invitation.

After a considerable pause at the other end of the line during which my wife's social fate hung in the balance, Mrs. Sears apparently decided Christian forgiveness was in order and that this untutored newcomer should be given another chance. Well, there was another thing she was calling about, too, she explained. There was to be a baby shower on Thursday evening for the minister's wife and another local lady about to put forth a blossom, and the Ladies' Aid would be pleased to have her attend that. Elizabeth said she would be delighted to come.

Mrs. Sears also had a good deal to say about how nice it was of us to come to church on Sunday and how sorry she was there hadn't been services, and wouldn't it have to be the only time they had been unable to hold services for as long as she could remember, etc.

"It's a funny thing," said Elizabeth when she had hung up, "but I can't seem to bring myself to explain to these people that we were only going to walk Florence to Sunday school. After all, we had no intention of coming back to church ourselves, but . . ."

"Well," I interrupted, "I don't see any point in making an issue of it. It's not our fault if they go around jumping to conclusions. Hand me my halo—I'm going outside for a minute."

Elizabeth called up Mrs. Underhill and told her about the invitation to the Ladies' Aid, and when she told her she had refused it Clara Underhill laughed so hard I could hear her in the next room.

"An invitation to the Ladies' Aid the first week you're here? Why, that's practically unheard of! It's that Sunday walk, all right. And then to refuse the invitation! I'm surprised Luella was able to go on talking to you. I'll bet she really strained herself asking you to something else after that."

19

"She thought a while," Elizabeth admitted.

At 3:21 the school bus appeared and Florence came running home from her first day at school. She burst into the house as full of first names as a lodge president. Fifteen minutes later the telephone rang, and I happened to answer it. A small voice piped a question at me.

"Hello, is Janie there?"

"Who?"

"Is Janie there?"

"I'm sorry, you have the wrong number."

"Wait!" Florence rushed down from upstairs. "Who is it, Daddy?"

"Wrong number. Some kid wanting to talk to 'Janie.'"

"Wait! Let me have it . . . Hello? Is that you, Eddie? Yes. Wait a minute . . . Mommy, can Eddie come over and play with me in my snow fort?"

"Well, I guess so, whoever Eddie is."

"It's Eddie Sears that gets off the bus with me and lives down the road . . . Yes, come on over, Eddie. Good-by."

She hung up, and I collared her.

"Wait a minute, young lady! What's this 'Janie' stuff?"

Blue eyes sized us both up from under straight blonde hair.

"Well, gee whiz, I've always wanted to be called 'Janie.' You know I don't like 'Florence.'"

"I know we've been getting some complaints about it lately, but—what did you do, tell the kids your nickname was Janie?"

"Well, no. You see, when the teacher got ready to write my name down in the records she asked me to come up and give it to her exactly, and I told her it was Janie Corbett."

"*Janie* Corb-b-b—!" My voice lodged halfway between a squawk and a splutter. I was outraged. The name "Florence" was a favorite with me, whereas I had never cared for "Jane" and I actively disliked "Janie." I demanded to know what the teacher had said.

"Oh, I explained that my born name was Florence, but that I liked to be called Janie, and she asked me if you cared which I was called, and I—I said you didn't care."

I put my hand over my eyes and rested a moment, making myself count to ten in French, Spanish, and German. But I could not get past six in any of them.

"You mean to tell us you're *registered* in school as Janie?" I was stunned. She had pulled off a first-class *coup*. She had seen her chance—the change of schools. She had awaited her opportunity. And she had seized it. The worst of it was, her mother thought the idea was funny.

"If she wants to be Janie at school, let her," she said. "Speaking of names, though, what did you say was the last name of that little boy down the road?"

"Eddie? It's Sears. Why?"

When we went to the post office next day we met two more Mrs. Searses, and while we could have sworn they were the same ones we had met before, Mrs. Larkins assured us they were not.

"I notice the local store is run by a Sears, too, and one of the roads running off the highway up the hill there is Sears Road. Is everybody in this town named Sears except you and the Underhills and us?"

"No, there are a few named Crowell," said Mrs. Larkins. "You know, this used to be nicknamed Sears Village years ago, because then it was practically all Searses."

"Are they all related?"

"Well, sort of. Some of them don't claim some of the others that claim *them*. They like to pick and choose their branches, but I guess back a ways they're all connected somehow."

Mrs. Larkins suddenly stopped commenting on the Sears clan as a gray-haired, bespectacled man with beetling black eyebrows came in. He entered with a jaunty bounce that seemed at odds with his stern and weighty expression. How could a light-footed step be so bold as to make those magisterial jowls dance?

His hat brim, too, was at variance. His mouth swept down like a grave roundhead's, but his hat brim swept up like a gay cavalier's. He shot a piercing glance through the little window in his postal box, like a rooster examining a feedpan and daring it to be empty, and after twiddling the combination lock with a little flourish of the hand, he took out several letters.

"Morning, Nora."

"Morning, Asa."

Having acknowledged Mrs. Larkins' presence, he favored us with the smallest possible discernible nod and bounced out again.

"Who was that?"

"Oh, haven't you met him yet?" asked Mrs. Larkins, acting surprised, though I had the feeling she would not have dared introduce him without first being sure he chose to be introduced. "That was Asa Sears. I thought what with living near him you might have met him already."

"We live near *him?*"

"Right down the street!"

"Well, well! I'll bet he's real old Cape Cod."

"I should say he is."

I looked at Elizabeth a bit dubiously as we went out and got back in the car.

We had heard a lot about the Cape Codders' clannishness and lack of warmth toward newcomers, and here we were in a village where most of the people even had the same name!

"Well, we'll just have to wait and see how things go. We'll see if the Searses can find room for a few Corbetts. Actually, they've all been pleasant enough, the ones we've met so far. Even that Asa Sears didn't completely ignore us."

"I wouldn't call him a backslapper, either."

"No—and, of course, you know what some of our friends would have to say about our experience so far, anyway. 'Sure, they'll speak to you and be pleasant at the post office and anywhere else around town you happen to meet them, but wait and see if they really take you into things.' "

Nevertheless, we continued to meet people, both natives and non-natives. At first they all seemed alike in one respect: they were all gray-haired and wore glasses. Those first three Mrs. Searses were only a sample. We met at least ten women who all looked alike, or so it seemed on first impression. After about the fifth day, Elizabeth asked me a thoughtful question:

"I wonder when we're going to meet the first people with their own teeth?"

"Well, I'm sure there must be a variety of ages around. The younger set just hasn't been getting to the post office when we have. Probably busy at this time of day." We knew there would be a good many older people in a community such as the one we had moved to, and we had always liked older people, but we no more wanted to live in a community composed solely of elders than we would have wanted to live in one of those developments full of nothing but young people in their twenties. I remembered the reaction of one friend when he heard where we were planning to move. "East Dennis? Why, don't you know what they call East Dennis? A cemetery with lights!"

Was it? Had we buried ourselves alive?

Only a closer inspection and closer acquaintance would tell that. In the meantime, we had all we could do to get acquainted with our new house.

Although shingles and white trim gave it something of a Cape Cod look at first glance, it was of a style that might be found almost anywhere in the country. The man who built it —man named Sears—must have been full of boom-days optimism, because he built a three-car garage, too. The garage sat on a slope, as did the house, and a large room with a concrete floor had been constructed under part of it. The former owner had raised chickens in this room. It had been kept

23

scrupulously clean, and no sign of fowl tenancy remained. We had no intentions of complicating our lives with chickens, but nevertheless for purposes of identification it became "the chicken room" and was never spoken of as anything else.

The house itself was a two-story affair with a good-sized attic and basement, so there was plenty of space. The upper story, supported by round white wooden columns, jutted out over a completely useless porch that ran the full width of the house in front, but it also jutted out over a magnificent porch that ran the full width of the house in back, sitting high over the slope and looking out across the wide sweep of the marshes.

Our two and a half acres were better than half marshland, but we could not have asked for anything nicer. The marshes, with a tidal creek running through them, meant that no one would ever be able to spoil the view that was spread before us and stretched away in two directions. When we had mentioned this marshland at a party in New York, someone who had visited the Cape a few times declared confidently, "Oh, all that stretch in there used to be cranberry bogs." Greenhorns that we were, we believed this and even repeated it. The marshes were flat; they looked boggy; it all seemed logical.

Once on the Cape, however, we soon learned to know a cranberry bog when we saw one, with its summer green and its beautiful deep cranberry red in winter. We learned, too, that when the bogs were flooded to keep the vines from freezing, or to kill off certain insects in the spring, they had to be flooded with fresh water, not the brackish water of a tidal creek. The reason Cape Cod was good cranberry country was because of the scores of fresh-water ponds which dotted its small area. It was these that provided water for the bogs. True, there were such things as "dry bogs," where the owner had no fresh-water supply but merely gambled on getting enough rain. However, these were not located in marshes that filled up when the tides ran high.

The marshes were of no practical value, then, but as part

of a view we soon learned to prize them. We began to find our-selves wandering out onto the back porch every afternoon at sunset. The sun was far enough south at that time of year so that its last rays came straight down the marshes and turned the straw-colored marsh grass into strands of pink gold, while the low hills on the far side slowly went from blue-green to purple. Even in February flocks of birds would flit across this serene outburst of delicate yet full-bodied colors shading away into dusk, for the marsh drew a rich variety of birds in all seasons.

I began to appreciate more fully the feelings of an old couple I had once met in the Ozark Mountains who sat on their porch night after night all their lives watching twilight come down over the same hills without ever growing tired of the view—because it was never the same twice.

The day after she telephoned, Mrs. Luella Sears came by again. I happened to be having a beer at the time but I was having it in the garage so she was spared any pain. Mrs. Under-hill had split her sides when we told her about how I had been pouring myself a drink when Mrs. Luella called on us the first time. It was as we had suspected: if the W.C.T.U. ever seized control of the Government, Mrs. Luella would be the first to charge into the local package store and start smashing mer-chandise with an umbrella.

Her second visit was occasioned by the fact that she had suddenly realized what she had involved Elizabeth in by ask-ing her to the baby shower.

"I forgot at the time that it meant getting presents, but you certainly shouldn't feel obliged to bring any when you don't even know either of the girls yet," she said. Elizabeth told her she had already purchased a couple of small presents and would be delighted to bring them. She said it with such sincerity that I am sure I would never have known her for the same person who had complained to me that very morning,

"How do you like that? Not in town a week yet and already hooked for two baby-shower presents!"

Before Elizabeth left for the shower we tried to figure up how many women the village might be able to muster for such an event. Counting all the Mrs. Searses we had seen at the post office, and the two prospective mothers, and those Crowells Mrs. Larkins had mentioned, and a few strays we had not met as yet, and assuming that a majority of them would be present, we concluded that there might be as many as fifteen women there altogether.

Elizabeth came home flabbergasted.

"Forty-three! They must be brought in on the tide for these affairs. I never saw anything like it. And they said there were a lot absent."

"Where can that many women be keeping themselves? Do they all live on the other neck?"

"No, from what I could gather they're mostly all right around here somewhere. They were all sizes and ages, too, from nineteen to ninety."

"Ninety?"

"Ninety, and going strong. A wonderful little old lady. She's not a native, either, and took great pleasure in telling me so."

"Well, how long has she been living here?"

"Seventy-two years! She came here as a bride in 1879."

Forty-three women jammed even Mrs. Luella's large old-fashioned house, and Elizabeth found herself sitting in a tiny side room with five other women, knee-to-knee with those across from her, like people in an undersized European railway carriage. All the presents were passed around the entire group throughout the house to be admired individually by everyone, and since each present had been scrupulously duplicated for both prospective young mothers and both presents were eventually passed around, admiration had to be expressed and then re-expressed.

Sitting next to Elizabeth was Mrs. Peyson, a newcomer of several years' standing. Mrs. Peyson was quite modish and was wearing a very chic little hat. Most of the other ladies were wearing what Mrs. Peyson described as their Ladies' Aid hats. She gave Elizabeth quite a rundown on some of the ladies present. She apparently had a keen understanding of who was hard of hearing and who was not—either that, or she did not care—because though she kept her remarks behind her hand, she made them in a rather loud voice. Of course forty-three women all talking at once provided quite a curtain of sound.

"See that woman over there?" Mrs. Peyson would say, pointing at some elderly chatterbox not far distant. "She's quite a character. Nutty as they come. No, I take that back—her sister's nuttier. Honestly, half the women in this town are as dim as a moonless night! Her sister's the one with the floppy hat there. She must pack that hat in the bottom of a trunk between meetings."

Mrs. Peyson was young middle-aged, and was careful to indicate that there was quite a disparity of ages between herself and the colonel, and that she had been something of a Washington belle when Colonel Peyson was still active down there, directing the course of Pentagon strategy from behind a screen of generals. They had retired to one of those "cute little white houses on the Cape," as Mrs. Peyson put it, but she was not too happy about it. She felt dreadfully out of things. Elizabeth got the impression that the villagers had not elected Mrs. Peyson their first lady by acclamation, and that this oversight caused her to look upon them with a mixture of bewilderment and disdain.

"The colonel and I will pay our formal call soon," Mrs. Peyson promised. "That's quite a custom in these parts, you know—the formal call on the new family—though I think you'll find it observed more by us outsiders than by the natives."

At one point in the festivities Mrs. Underhill managed to

get Elizabeth off in a corner and tell her about the reaction at the Ladies' Aid meeting of the day before to our Sunday attempt to go to church. Apparently it could be summed up in Mrs. Luella's own words:

"Well! If those new people can manage to get to church, some of the rest of us certainly can. I know that a few live too far out, and some of our older folks can't be expected to walk —but there are enough of us living close by who could make it. I hope you all agree with me that that should be the *last* time our church's doors will be closed on the Sabbath, *regardless* of the weather."

It was so voted.

The letter postmarked "East Dennis" contained an invitation to a "Newcomers' Party," and was from something called the Recreation Association of Dennis and East Dennis. The party was to be at Jacob Sears Memorial Hall in East Dennis next Saturday night.

"Well! Here's some brave little band trying to fly in the face of tradition. Looks like we're going to be on display at the local hall. A welcoming party for newcomers—who ever heard of such a thing on Cape Cod!"

"What do you suppose it's all about?"

"Can't you imagine? There's probably a small group of well-meaning people here who think the Cape should be friendlier toward new people. Funny they'd bother to use the hall in winter, instead of just getting together at somebody's house."

"There must be another family or two of newcomers around somewhere. It doesn't make sense that they would have a party unless there were several. Maybe it's for all newcomers —everyone who's not a native, that is."

During the rest of the week we saw very few people at the post office or anywhere else, and nobody we did see so much as mentioned the party. Who was behind this so-called Recreation Association? Since nobody said anything about it, we did not ask questions, feeling it might embarrass the persons we asked if they were not planning to go. We decided to wait and see for ourselves.

3

NEWCOMERS AND OLD-TIMERS

When we arrived in February, business was very quiet on Quivet Neck. The sole business establishment there was D.H. Sears' Grocery Store, and D.H. was keeping it open out of pure sociability as much as anything else. After sixty-four years, running the store had become something of a habit with him.

David Henry, who was eighty-six years old, was the first old Cape Codder we really became acquainted with. We dropped in to subscribe to the local newspaper, the Cape Cod *Standard-Times,* and D.H. scribbled our name on a card under one of the pigeon-holes where he stuck the papers. There were about twenty other names, mostly Sears. After that we dropped by every day to get the paper, but we seldom got much else, as there was not much to get. D.H. was carrying only a very small stock. "Just hanging on till the summer people start to come," he said cheerfully.

"You'll be baking bread again this summer, I hope?" The day we first looked at the house, back in September, the real-estate woman had taken us by D.H.'s store to get a loaf of his bread. It was not an unusual-looking store—a plain, flat-fronted, flat-topped building, attached to a Cape Cod house, which looked like a country store anywhere—but neither D.H. nor his bread seemed easily duplicated, and I had been looking forward to a closer acquaintance with both of them.

"Well, soon as more folks start coming down in the spring I may get to baking again," he said. He had a gray brush of a mustache that reminded me of my grandfather's, and he wore steel-rimmed spectacles. D.H. was specially constructed for the long haul—tall, lean, and spry, and of a disposition cheerful and elastic enough to watch with interest and accept philosophically the great changes the Cape had been subjected to since he was a boy. His specialties were baking bread and making ice cream, and there were grandmothers in East Dennis who could remember eating both when they were little girls.

"You were down in September, eh? Did you have some ice cream?"

"No, it was too near suppertime—but it was a Saturday and we got a quart of your baked beans," I said—he had baked beans every Saturday for fifty or sixty years, too.

On the wall in the store was a print of the Sears family tree. The trunk was labeled "Richard Sears," and every limb and branch and twig had a name on it. It was an old print, too; it only came within a couple of generations of the present. D.H. was Cape Cod all the way back, but sixty-four years of dealing with the public and his own natural amiability made him easy to talk to, even though my Midwestern ear could not always grasp his accent.

There was the day, for example, when he got to telling about picking cranberries in the old days, down in a couple of small bogs near the beach. The grower who had a big bog could bring in a gang of pickers, but the man with a small bog had to scratch up help locally wherever he could. So D.H.

31

and some of the other boys used to pick in the small bogs in the fall.

Pickers earn their money. They travel on their hands and knees across the bogs, stripping the berries off the vines with their wooden cranberry scoops, and certainly hands-and-knees travel has never been the easy way. Today cranberry-picking machines are often used in the bogs, though some growers grumble about them and say they are hard on the vines. When D.H. first picked, however, they did not even use scoops.

"We picked 'em by hand, running the vines through our fingers," he said. "Lots of folks wouldn't pick in some of them bogs down there because of the arvey. There was lots of arvey in 'em, but it never bothered us any."

I thought and thought, but could not remember ever hearing of this particular menace, beast or insect or whatever it was.

"Arvey? What's arvey?"

"You know, poison arvey, grows all over the Cape," he said, surprised at my having to ask. "After we finished picking we'd wash our hands in salt water, and I never had any trouble from it. Oh, sometimes we'd have a little ticklin' between the fingers, but it would go right away."

Much of the large-scale picking was done by gangs of 'Portygees' brought in for that purpose—"from the Bird Islands," I thought D.H. said, and figured he meant the Canary Islands until I finally got the straight of it—*Verde* Islands, he was saying, meaning the Cape Verde Islands. A group of them settled nearby in Harwich and the colony was still there today.

In the early days they patronized D.H.'s store, and the young storekeeper laid in a stock of rice for them—something for which he had had little previous call—and special spices. He also put in a line of accordions, harmonicas, and jew's harps for them, and he already had watches and cheap jewelry on hand. He carried more nearly a "general-store" variety of things in those days of sandy roads and horses and wagons because people had to rely more on their local store.

At first the Portygees had to have someone interpret for them when they came down to buy supplies, but gradually they picked up a little English. One of them picked up enough to explain their attitude as customers to D.H. one day.

"He said to me, 'We want everything be cheap. When we get a hundred dollars, we want everything be little better. When we get two hundred dollars, we want everything good as anybody.' Guess that was fair enough, eh?"

D.H. had seen about as much change in merchandising as anyone living. When he started out, packaging was less than in its infancy, it was hardly conceived. Everything came in bulk—but then, so did families. No family would have fooled around with little ten-pound sacks of flour then, even if there had been such things. Flour came in barrels, and families bought a barrel at a time—two barrels, when they had a little money ahead.

"Credit was different, too," D.H. recalled. "Why, when I started out most people charged everything and paid their grocery bill once a year. One man who was well fixed told me he'd pay me twice a year because I was just getting started and he figured I'd need the money. Sight different from today, ain't it?"

There was a time for a great many years when D.H. concentrated on ice cream. He sold ice cream at his store, he delivered it all around for special events, and he had a man from Brewster who drove all over the mid-Cape section selling it.

"He drove a covered wagon, and he had a little bell that he rang whenever he came near a house. The ice cream was packed in ice, of course, but in those days people didn't have any ice boxes to put it in, so they had to eat it right up then and there to keep it from melting. Whatever time of day he turned up, that was the time to eat ice cream if you were going to eat it at all.

33

"That feller from Brewster was quite something, too. One day he turned up with a pitchfork in his wagon, and some of the fellers hanging around the store asked him what he wanted with a pitchfork in an ice-cream wagon. 'There's a bear got loose from the circus,' he said, 'and I don't intend to die 'thout a struggle.' "

We occasionally crossed trails with some of our new neighbors in the store, as well as the post office. Once as I was standing in front of the counter talking to D.H. I was conscious that a hand had appeared off to my right and extracted a newspaper from the cubbyhole marked "A. Sears."

"Evening, David Henry."

"Evening, Asa."

I turned and received my customary tiny nod, and the door closed behind him.

"I guess he's going to look us over good before he commits himself," I said, and D.H. chuckled. "Say, where does he live, anyway? Mrs. Larkins says he lives right up the street from us."

"Why, yes, that's right. You're in Ed Sears' place, aren't ye? Well, there's that vacant lot across from you, and that captain's house on t'other side of it. That's Asa's house."

Mr. Cape Cod was our next-door neighbor! Nothing stood between us except a vacant lot, which doubtlessly suited him fine.

"You left here over an hour ago," said Elizabeth when I got home, "and all you had to get was a loaf of bread and the paper. Where've you been?"

"Talking to D.H."

"What were you talking to D.H. about?"

"Just listening. His stories of the old days are wonderful, but it isn't just that. I like his point of view."

Through D.H. we got our first glimpse of a way of life which had passed over the hill and gone down the other side but which still influenced the Cape Codder's thinking and continued to help shape the Cape Codder's character. D.H. was interested in the new people who had come to the village. He enjoyed seeing new faces. He took life as it came and did not make himself sour and unhappy by inveighing against the changes which were inevitably coming to Cape Cod and which no one could turn back now. But at the same time he could remember a village that was a far cry from what it was today. I could understand what he meant when, after talking about the old days, he gazed out at the village and sighed and said,

"Well, it was a different place then, all right. In those days, every house had a *family.*"

We were scarcely out of sight of our house, around the next corner and into Centre Street, before we had to park. I had not even shifted out of second gear yet. We looked at each other almost in alarm.

"Are you sure you read the date right?"

"Of course! At least— Well, you saw the invitation, too!"

"Yes, but you opened it and read it to me. I just glanced at it, I didn't really read it."

"We'd better ask at the door," I suggested as we walked up the street past the double line of parked cars. "This doesn't look like any Newcomers' Party to me."

But a lady standing near the door with an official greeter's smiling paining her face assured us it *was* the party.

"What do you class as newcomers?" I asked.

"In this case we mean all those who have been living in North Dennis or East Dennis for less than a year."

"Oh. Well, how many such families are there?"

"About twenty, I think it is."

I am sure my mouth fell open at that unexpected number, but she was too busy to notice as she went on to apologize for an oversight.

"Every new family was supposed to have a sponsor visit

35

them before the party, but there was a slip-up on a few and that's why nobody has been to see you before now, but it's all straightened out now, so don't worry."

We promised not to worry and she put us in the hands of another lady to find us seats.

Jacob Sears Memorial Hall was some turn-of-the-century architect's loose translation of a French chateau. On a small scale, that is, and with Cape Cod trimmings. When we entered a community sing was in progress, and the hall was ringing with song. Not that everybody was singing; as a matter of fact, the Cape Codders were sitting unmoved and in a granite silence, and no one was singing except the children and the master of ceremonies, but when he let loose the hall rang with song.

We had gone to a great deal of trouble to line up Eddie Sears' twelve-year-old sister as our baby sitter, and the minute we saw the crowd we knew we were wrong, for despite the evening hour the children were there in force.

The master of ceremonies was a tall, broad-shouldered man with the face of a grown-up schoolboy over which an expression of solemnity was occasionally plastered, but never looked at home there. At the moment his large round chin was drawn back into his face and his complexion was more florid than usual as he did everything a concert baritone does except stay on key.

Nearly two hundred persons were present, which packed the hall to capacity. We were a little late, due to our sitter problem, and there were no two seats left together, so we were ushered to separate seats. I sat my unsponsored bottom on my chair and surveyed my neighbors *en masse* for the first time— and suddenly found myself face to face with a tiny nod. I was sitting right next to Asa Sears. I nodded back jerkily and turned my eyes elsewhere almost as quickly as he averted his.

I was astonished at the number of persons present, and wondered which of them, like us, were newcomers. Twenty new families of year-around residents within a single year changed my picture of our section of the Cape radically.

Of course even twenty new families did not account for a crowd of that size. Unquestionably the natives had turned out. If those were not New England countenances, then I did not know my Nathaniel Hawthorne (he wrote "The Great Stone Face," you'll remember). Had I felt any tendency to become expansive, which I did not, the chilling presence of Mr. Cape Cod next to me would have corrected it; and though there were smiling visages here and there, he had plenty of company in the solemnity department. He watched with bristling attentiveness everything that went on, all without noticeable change of expression.

Most of the rows of chairs faced the small stage, but mine was in a row down the side wall, which suited me fine, because I was most of all interested in the audience. What would be the native's reaction to these goings-on? Not far from me sat a portly and dignified old gentleman whom I had seen at the post office and knew to be Mr. Ezra Newton Sears. I decided to watch him with particular care.

He appeared to be merely enduring the community sing in a stoic silence. Then the songfest ended and the master of ceremonies introduced himself as Hadley Ransom, a newcomer himself who had come to East Dennis and opened an antique shop over on the highway just after the war. In the course of his introductory remarks he ripped off a couple of broad jokes which surprised a laugh out of a good many in the audience, and I knew him at once to be irrepressible. Anyone who could throw off-color stories at that staid gathering would gallop into the mouth of a cannon with a song on his lips, unconvinced to the last that it was really loaded. I was almost afraid to look at Mr. Ezra Newton, and when I did it seemed to me I had never before seen such repressed horror and distaste on a human face.

The introductions began, and each new family rose in turn

to show itself to the multitude. There were a good many older people, men who had retired from business, but there were younger couples with small children, too. Mr. Ezra Newton stared at each family in turn, and dutifully applauded by moving his hands together twice. Several of the newcomers had a few words to say, and each time he frowned as though annoyed. When one of them said some rather foolish and fatuous things about himself, Mr. Ezra Newton shifted in his seat and muttered something to his wife.

His dissatisfaction seemed to lessen a bit when the entertainment began, but I noticed he frowned several times at things that were said, especially when Hadley himself rendered the comic poem, "Albert and the Lion." Apparently Hadley had queered himself good with Mr. Ezra Newton. After some singing, dancing, and a rendition of "Casey at the Bat," all by local children, it was announced that refreshments and square dancing would follow. People began to get up so that the chairs could be moved back, folded, and stacked away in a corner.

Mr. Ezra Newton rose and turned to his wife. My ears stood up hopefully, straining to overhear his considered opinion of the entertainment, the newcomers, Hadley's jokes, and "Albert and the Lion." Maybe I could get the lowdown on an old Cape Codder's true reaction to it all! By pretending to be looking for something under one of the chairs, I managed to edge quite close. Matter of fact, any closer and I would have had my head in his coat pocket.

In a loud, deep voice, he uttered a bitter complaint.

"You know," he rumbled, "I didn't hear *one word* of that program! Why don't people speak up any more?"

Meanwhile Mr. Asa Sears, who up to that point had seemed to be welded to his chair, suddenly bounced nimbly to his feet and began both to move chairs himself and to supervise the over-all operation. I saw my wife and Mrs. Underhill chatting in the back of the room and joined them.

"Did you see whom I was sitting next to?" I asked Elizabeth.

"I certainly did."

"Who was it?" asked Clara Underhill. "I didn't notice."

"Asa Sears. I guess he's real Old Cape Cod, isn't he?"

"Old?" She laughed at the inadequacy of the word. "Why, his family has lived right here for three hundred years. He feels people are putting on airs calling themselves natives if their families have only been here since the Revolution."

I watched his busy peregrinations about the hall. From the way he fiddled with the light switches, inspected the floor registers, poked his head sternly down the stairs to the basement to check on juvenile tomfoolery, and generally exhibited a proprietary air, it was plain he was a person of some consequence around the hall.

"He's one of the trustees of the hall," Clara Underhill explained, when I commented. "Mr. Ezra Newton and Ernest Everett are the others—Ernest Everett Sears, that is. The trustees have an annual meeting, and anybody that wants to can come and vote on anything that comes up concerning the hall—provided they live in the right place. Just to show you the cussedness of some of the old Cape Codders, one of the provisions Jacob Sears made when he left the money for the hall was that only residents of Quivet Neck were to have the right to vote on any questions having to do with the hall. Even the Searses and Crowells who live on the other neck can't have anything to say about it.

"Furthermore, he left the money for educational purposes, and he didn't mean maybe. The town couldn't just build the hall it needed with the money, so it built a library and sort of attached a hall to it. The hall is ten times bigger than the library, but you'll notice the sign over the front entrance says Jacob Sears Memorial Library. And actually, anything that takes place in the hall is supposed to be of an educational nature."

"Well, I'm getting an education."

After coffee and sandwiches we settled back to watch the square dancing, or so we thought. We reckoned without Mrs. Ryder, the president of the Recreation Association. A young couple whom we knew to be natives approached us with a sort of dogged determination, with Mrs. Ryder behind them herding them along and cutting off their avenue of escape. She introduced them as the Bassetts and waited long enough to make sure Mr. Bassett was going to speak his piece. He managed it.

"Wouldn't you like to square dance?"

"Oh, we don't know how," I assured him hastily. We had seen square dancing before, and nobody was going to get me up in one of those rat races.

"That's all right, we'll show you how," said Mrs. Bassett bravely. "I'll be your partner and Arthur will take Mrs. Corbett."

Elizabeth got up, which left me with no choice but to do likewise. Just as we had thought, square dancing was nothing to do a standing broad jump into. You wanted to get a running start. We got out on the floor and two other unsuspecting couples joined us to make up a set. We were suddenly aware that the men's coats had disappeared along with their neckties, and that the women who had looked rather dressed-up a moment before had been wearing full skirts and flat shoes all the time. The floor was crowded and the room was noisy with a babble of animated conversation which only quieted down when the caller began the dance to the accompaniment of records played over the public-address system which had been rigged up for the evening.

"Bow to your partner," he ordered. I bowed to Mrs. Bassett, who hastily curtseyed and then grabbed me and transferred me to her left.

"You're supposed to be on this side—"

"And bow to your corner," said the caller.

"Who's my corner?" I asked Mrs. Bassett.

"Your corner lady. The lady on your left."

"Oh." I bowed to my wife. "You're my corner, dear—"

Whing! whing! whing! whing!—the recorded fiddler set out in earnest, and so did the caller.

"Oh, allemande left and a grand right and left!" he commanded in a singsong voice, and I stuck out my right hand to my partner, who was not there. She was looking back at me over her shoulder and signaling frantically with her free hand:

"To your corner! Your corner!"

"Oh!" I stuck out my right hand to my wife. It turned out to be the wrong hand. By this time Mrs. Bassett had circled around her corner and was coming back my way, and Mr. Bassett had seized Elizabeth and appeared to be Indian wrestling with her. I tried my left hand on Mrs. Bassett.

"No, your *right* hand to me. Your left hand to your— Go all the way around. All the way. No, the other way!" she cried as I started to follow her. I did not want to lose sight of Mrs. Bassett, my only hope. At her command, however, I obediently turned and found ladies coming at me in profusion. I stuck out both hands, mostly in self-defense.

"Keep going!" somebody called, and I tried to work my way around what was rapidly becoming a disorganized circle. On the way I noticed a wild-eyed face, gasping for breath, which looked familiar. Oh, yes—my wife. I could see she was feeling the same way I did as she struggled to cope with the unknown, doubly hampered by a suit skirt and high heels. I might have felt even sorrier for her had I not been preoccupied with my own steaming misery under a suitcoat which was speedily beginning to feel like a horse blanket. All at once Mrs. Bassett reappeared out of the tangle and seized me.

"Promenade back!" she said, and walked me around the circle to our original starting point. By now the caller had gone off into complete gibberish. He was saying something

41

about how the first old couple should lead to the right and circle four hands 'round, except that to my untutored ears it sounded like "Firsol couple lean-to rye and surly foreign row." The Bassetts tried gamely, they pushed and pulled and hauled and shoved, but they had no material to work with. From our standpoint, it was hard to say which was worse, our mental frustration or physical exhaustion, when at last we sat down again.

"Not for me! Never again!" I puffed.

"But up here we'll have to learn how. Apparently they do it all the time."

"I'll watch, thanks. Why, that fellow doing the calling doesn't even speak English. Nothing he has said yet makes the slightest bit of sense."

In between square dances the caller put on records for round dancing, and this time just for relaxation he chose a polka. I saw D.H. get up across the room and approach a lady.

"For Pete's sake, don't tell me he's thinking of dancing a polka!" I said to Elizabeth. "I'd figure at his age he'd stick to slow waltzes. Maybe he's getting her lined up for the next one."

But no. The lady got up and they assumed the position of the dance. D.H. jigged up and down four or five times like a courting heron, getting himself into the time of the piece, and then he took off down the floor with his partner like a jumping jack, giving the polka a run for its money.

"Let's get out of here," I said. "I can't keep up with this crowd. I've got to train a while first."

Having a sitter to pay gave us an excuse for leaving a short time later. On the way out, for the first time during that busy evening, we met the Ransom Hadleys. I complimented him on his reading of "Albert and the Lion."

"Well, you never know. Tonight it got a nice laugh," he said, with the thoughtful frown of an old trouper. "Last week

I did it at a Rotary meeting and it didn't get a thing. Laid an ostrich egg. You never know."

Walking down the dark, silent road to our car, I glanced back at the brightly lighted hall and listened to the square-dance music—the windows had been cracked open a little to release some of the heat generated by this energetic form of dancing. The hall had been built back in the days D.H. had spoken about, the days when "every house had a family." Now there were so many newcomers around that a Newcomers' Party was feasible just for a single year's crop. The make-up of the village was changing, and we were a part of those people who were doing the changing. The trick for us newcomers, if we were to be an asset, was to bring new life to the community without spoiling old ways. Cape Codders might be crusty and clannish, but at least some of them were making a conscious effort, in things such as this party, to accept us newcomers gracefully. And yet . . . Suddenly I got to thinking back.

"Say, how many people came up and spoke to you, outside of a few we'd already met at the post office?"

"Oh, quite a few," said Elizabeth, and named off those she could think of. I listened, and commented on each name.

"They're newcomers. . . . So are they. . . . They've been here several years, but they're not natives. . . . They're newcomers, too. What I want to know is, how many natives came up and spoke to you for the first time?"

We both thought hard for a few steps, and then both came up with the same answer.

"The Bassetts!"

"Yes, and Mrs. Ryder had a gun in their backs!"

Almost none of the native Cape Codders had actually come near us. For the most part the old newcomers had welcomed the new newcomers. The natives, by and large, had sat back and watched. They had been willing to poke their heads out

43

and take a look, but they were not ready as yet to come all the way out of their shells.

The Cape might be changing rapidly, with twenty new families in our two villages inside of one year, but the Cape Codder himself was not going to be rushed into anything, nor was he going to throw his arms open and pretend to be delighted at having a lot of strangers encroaching on what had for so long been his private preserve. The first real inkling, based on our own experience and observation, of how deeply ingrained was the Cape's way of life and how little it had been touched by the outside world for generations on end was borne home to us that night.

It was such a fine afternoon, a few days later, that I had stepped out onto the back porch to admire the sunshine on the meadow. I happened to glance to the west, and what I saw made me catch my breath. A perfectly round column of smoke and fire was rising straight up into the sky.

At the same moment a car came down the street and swung around the corner, and a boy yelled something to Florence. By the time I had run out into the front yard, shouting to Elizabeth on the way, Florence was dancing up and down with excitement.

"Daddy! The store's on fire!"

"Come with your mother," I said, and took off on the run. We had heard no sirens to indicate that the volunteer firemen had arrived from North Dennis. For all I knew, every man might be needed for a bucket brigade.

"Corbett to the rescue!" I sneered at myself, suddenly feeling foolish as I pounded along down the peaceful road. It was not far to the next corner, less than a quarter of a mile, but still I could have walked around the side of the house, got into the car, and driven there sooner. Furthermore, I was beginning to puff.

The column of smoke and flame continued to rise in the

still air, and in that setting it seemed colossal. Its roundness looked solid, as though a steel tape measure could have been drawn around it and its exact dimensions taken. It mushroomed out at the top almost as though imitating an atomic explosion, and filled me with dark dismay. What hope could there be for the store or even the house to which it was attached? An old landmark was doomed.

But I had maligned the local firefighters. We had not heard them come, but they were there, and doing a creditable job. The store was lost, to be sure; they were not trying to do anything about that. They were intent on saving the house, and they were doing it, thanks to the absolute stillness of the air. A mere breath of wind in the wrong direction that day would have taken the house with the store.

A couple of people were fussing over D.H. as he stood on the sidelines helplessly watching his store go up in flames. Someone who was longer on solicitude than body had put a coat on him, and he looked forlorn standing there in that short, inadequate garment, with his store apron showing in front. As I came up, I saw that two Searses were battling for the soul of a third. Mrs. Luella and Ernest Everett, no relation to each other and neither related in recent generations to D.H., were engaged in a tug-of-war over D.H. which had not quite approached the physical but seemed almost to threaten to do so.

"I'm going to take David Henry home and give him a drink," snapped Ernest Everett.

"He doesn't need anything like that," sniffed Mrs. Luella. "I'll fix him a cup of tea at my house."

"We'd better get going, Ernest," said David Henry. "I'd like to set down."

"Tea!" Ernest Everett uttered the word with loathing, and led D.H. away while Mrs. Luella stared daggers at his broad back.

I watched the old man walk away and wondered how he

45

could possibly survive this blow. To lose his store at eighty-six, after all these many years! Elizabeth and Florence appeared, and I joined them. I was feeling very low.

"This is awful. We haven't been here a month, and already an old landmark is gone, and maybe it'll take D.H., too. How can he survive such a shock? It's tragic. Sixty-four years of storekeeping, and now this."

We stood by while the firemen gradually got the blaze under control. A fire truck from the nearest forest-ranger station, over in the middle of the Cape, had also answered the alarm, and the minute things were under control the forest-fire crew jumped on their truck and sped away to their regular post. Presently I noticed that D.H. was back again, standing alone, watching the fire. I walked over to him, wanting to say something, but not knowing just what to say.

He greeted me with a nod that was almost cheery. He looked thoughtfully at the fire for a moment, and then uttered a wry chuckle.

"Well, by golly, I ought to be getting used to this," he said. "This is the third time I've been burnt out, you know."

"*What?*"

"Oh, yes. First time I had a store right here and had a fire, so I built a store over across the street on the corner there. Then I had that one burnt out from under me about fifty years ago, so I moved back here. Well, the boys have been wanting to build on the corner again," he said, referring to his grandsons, "so I guess this is their chance. They'll get one of them GI loans, and— Well, if we get to building right soon I expect we can be ready by the time the summer folks start to come."

During our first weeks on the Cape we kept so busy working away in and around our new home that I had to pull up short one day and remind myself that one of the reasons we had risked moving out onto a limb of land was to be near the sea, and here I had hardly had a glimpse of it.

This happened late one afternoon when I had a little free time before supper. I jumped in the car alone and drove down Sea Street, heading not for the inlet but for the main beach that lay half a mile to the east of the inlet.

There are doubtless some who would not consider mine the best choice of time for visiting the beach—the last moments before darkness of a dead gray dusk on a grim February evening.

I soon left the last lighted house behind, and drove down a road become silent and remote, with boarded-up beach cottages accenting the desolation of the surroundings. A torn screen dangling from a porch, the effects of sea air and winter on paint, and the drifted sand, which here had entombed a front step and there had curved high against the side of a cottage, all managed to suggest complete abandonment and disrepair. The cottages had that chilly, ill-clad, depressing, out-of-place look of anything that suggests summer in winter.

Up ahead, there was no sound of water washing against the shore to indicate that I was approaching the sea. The only sound was that of the car motor and the tires hissing on the sand-sprinkled road. No one was anywhere around, and no one was likely to come near. I parked the car in the hard-surfaced parking area and headed for the beach, and even the sound of my footsteps was all but swallowed up by the soft sibilance of the sand.

The cut through the low dunes to the beach was deep in shadow, and the stillness and gloom were so eerie that I would have started at any sound or movement as I picked my way out onto that unfamiliar beach for the first time.

There was no place for man in the crepuscular seascape of sand and rock and water that greeted me. I felt like a minute intruder thrust unexpectedly into an earlier age, before his-

47

tory. The tide was out, and there was not a breath of wind nor a ripple on the water that spread away darkly far out on the other side of the flats. It was dead low, and dead calm.

The vast flat expanse faded from sight in a way that suggested endless reaches, and the impression of great spaces was only enlarged by the massive boulders which dotted the edge of the beach or sat farther out in shallow pools of still water. Here, it seemed, was Earth before life. The hushed calm caught at the imagination and charged it with an uneasy anticipation, until I half-expected something primeval to break the spell. Had the first prehistoric sea serpent suddenly reared its head out of the water and started undulating toward the beach, I would scarcely have been surprised, though the friction of my feet taking me away from that place would have left a glazed trail in the sand.

For me, the beach in winter was an unexpected dividend of our move to the Cape. I had not previously realized that to visit the beach only in summer was to miss some of the greatest moments it had to offer. The beach was a thing of many moods, some of which were more memorable than its brightest summer mood; it was a place worth knowing in all seasons and all hours and all weather. To enjoy the shore when beach umbrellas dotted its sands and bathers frolicked in the surf was a pretty thing; but to walk alone on a deserted beach, and try to comprehend the sea as the cradle of all life and the shore as that magical and mysterious interspace across which life first crawled to dry land, could be infinitely more exciting.

4

SURPRISE VISIT

One thing we often said in our own defense during our last months in New York—and we were given plenty of opportunities to defend our position—was that if we had been uneasy about having to live to ourselves for a while, we would not have considered moving, unknown, unheralded, unsung, and unconnected, to a place like Cape Cod.

Everybody told us people would scarcely speak to us for at least six months. We believed them and were undisturbed. I was in the midst of writing a book, and Elizabeth had plans enough for fixing up the house to keep her busy indefinitely. We even hoped that, left to ourselves, we would actually get something done for a change.

However, our spurious reputation as ardent churchgoers led to Elizabeth's being invited to the baby shower, and then the Newcomers' Party timed in close behind this event, and these unexpected opportunities to mix with our neighbors led to a series of formal calls.

The custom may have been old, but as Mrs. Peyson had predicted it was observed by the newcomers rather than the natives. The Peysons, the Gainsboroughs, the Doctor Rodgers, and the Smiths called. The Searses and the Crowells did not.

Then one evening the telephone rang while we were clearing the supper table. Elizabeth answered, and as I circulated in and out of the dining room—we had been temporarily forced out of the kitchen and into the dining room for our meals by the fact that Elizabeth had the kitchen table piled high with bric-a-brac—I gathered we were going to have more callers.

"Who is it this time?" I asked as she hung up.

"You'd never guess. Mrs. Sears!"

"Mrs. Sears? Fine, that's a general hint. Now could you narrow it down a little?"

"Mrs. Asa Sears."

"You're kidding!"

"No."

"You mean to tell me Mr. Cape Cod in person is going to call on us?"

"If we can clear a path for him through the debris around here, he is."

"Well, I'll be! It must be his wife's doing."

Elizabeth was not listening. She was wearing that preoccupied look of a housewife whose mind has already withdrawn to deal with pressing domestic problems.

"This place is a fright. Come on, let's start shoveling stuff out of sight."

"Okay, just as soon as I finish wrapping up this cheese."

"Oh, throw it away and be done with it! You know you're never going to eat it."

"No, but I can't bring myself to admit I wasted sixty cents, either. I'm going to keep it a while yet. Maybe I can think of something to do with it that doesn't involve eating it."

Like most cheese lovers, I could seldom resist trying a new kind, and when I had encountered a slice of something called sage cheese in a store, I was intrigued. Here was a good old New England variety I had never met before.

It turned out to be, as far as I was concerned, a nauseating morsel with a taste which was the second worst flavor I had ever encountered in cheese—the worst being its aftertaste. Add a texture the consistency of clammy rubber, and you have sage cheese as it struck my palate.

"Well, if that's the way you feel, put it in the refrigerator and I'll see to it that it quietly disappears one of these days."

"I'd be much obliged," I admitted.

"All right. Now let's get busy on this house."

Elizabeth busily stuffed odds and ends into drawers while I spirited away upstairs those casual piles of stuff which, like a body, were too large to hide anywhere downstairs. The upstairs hall was hopeless, being filled with all the apparatus involved in our painting and paper-hanging operations in the guest room, but at least it suggested industry.

At one point I found myself confronted with a bottle.

"What about this?"

Elizabeth hesitated.

"Better put it away," she decided.

"Agreed. I can't imagine Asa Sears taking a drink, and there's no use causing unnecessary embarrassment. You might decide to show Mrs. Sears the kitchen or something—you women are always showing each other your kitchens. Well, I hope this works out as well as the colonel did," I said, referring to Colonel Peyson. "We thought he was going to be trying, and he wasn't, so maybe . . ."

"Well, remember, a formal call is only supposed to last twenty minutes."

"Nobody has only stayed twenty minutes yet."

"Nobody has been as formal as Mr. Sears."

51

By the time the knocker resounded on our front door—thrice, with measured ceremony—we were in reasonably good order.

"See? Real formality! The front door," I commented—for though we had been on the Cape only a matter of weeks, it was already plain that, as with most Cape houses, it was our back door that would get most of the business, including social calls. "But Mr. Sears would approach the front door, and he would use the knocker, even if they came by *droshky*," I muttered, and opened the door just in time to hear him saying, with a sigh, something like 'Too bad those trees . . .'

"Well, good evening! I'll bet you're surprised to have somebody come to the front door!" said Mrs. Sears with a bright smile. "On the Cape we mostly use the back door but the front door here is closer for us because we've usually walked over so we've almost always come to the front door—my, doesn't this room look different!"

Mrs. Sears was a bright, animated woman with an immaculate look about her that made one know instinctively that her house would be just as spotless as she. Her bright eyes, alert and busy behind her cascade of conversation, made a swift and observant appraisal of her surroundings.

As for Asa Sears himself, he entered giving us his usual bobbing nod of recognition, plus, as a special dividend, a firm handshake. As a matter of fact, he was looking less frosty than I had ever previously seen him look. A small, pursy smile had been twitched into being for the occasion, and his ferocious black eyebrows were not bristling at each other. His well-fitted, conservative attire would have been worthy of a bank director, or a prominent local Mason, or an official of some sort. When he accepted a chair, he settled himself more with the air of a judge preparing to hear a case than that of a man paying a mere social call.

"I was just remarking to my wife," he said, after I had hung up their coats and sat down, "about what a shame it was

52

Mr. Landry felt he had to have the two pines cut down that used to be in front of your porch. It's too bad you never saw those trees. Beautiful things."

The trees he referred to must have been planted by somebody who lived for the moment, with little thought for the future. Originally there had been four pines, one on each side of the central section of the front porch, and another pair set in line with these on each side of the two steps that led down to the road from the front edge of the lawn, about twenty feet from the porch. Four small evergreens might have been passable, but in this case the planter picked a type of tree that soon shot up to a height of thirty feet or so, with a proportionate spread.

"They must have sort of overwhelmed the house, though, didn't they?" I asked in a timid voice. "Mr. Landry said you could hardly see out of the upstairs windows any more."

"Judging from the stumps," said Elizabeth—the trees had been cut off level with the ground, "they must have been jammed right against the front of the house."

"Well, yes, they were, somewhat, but still I always hate to see a tree come down."

"They aren't exactly a gay variety of pine, though. I'm afraid one pair of them is enough for me," persisted Elizabeth. Actually we had done a little speculating on how the place would look without *that* pair, too, but it hardly seemed the time to bring that up. "Maybe I'm wrong, but I'd think four of them would have made it look like the entrance to a well-kept cemetery."

Mrs. Sears burst out laughing and waved a finger triumphantly at her husband.

"There! You see? That's exactly how it *did* look and anyway remember you only had to look at them—you didn't have to live with them," she said, and Asa Sears grinned a little as he offered a few blustery phrases of rebuttal.

His good wife quickly made it plain that we need have no

53

worry about the conversation's dragging as long as her assistance was available. She chattered away spiritedly about a variety of subjects while Asa Sears gradually reached a better understanding with his chair. We joked about the confusion of Searses, of course—a standard joke in East Dennis these past two hundred years or so—and she explained the local system used to avoid first-name confusion among the womenfolk.

Needless to say, in a place where there were three Gertrude and four Esther Searses, for example, something had to be done, so each woman's first name was combined with her husband's first name. Thus Esther, wife of Dean Sears, was called Esther Dean to avoid confusion with Esther Howard, wife of Howard Bailey Sears, who was called Howard Bailey to avoid confusion with Everett Howard Sears.

She herself was called Ruth Asa, to differentiate her from Ruth Daniel. As for the men, most of them were referred to by their two given names, even formally—'Mr. Joe Homer,' for example, with the 'Sears' understood. (We later met a lady who was a Sears herself, who grew up in East Dennis, and who was fifteen years old before she knew that the last name of 'Mr. Isaac Berry' was not Berry. Not once in fifteen years had she heard anyone refer to him as Mr. Sears.)

Presently the ladies got off onto a women's type of conversation, and Elizabeth took Mrs. Sears out in the kitchen to show her something. Asa Sears and I, left to ourselves, carried on a men's type of conversation, in the course of which I learned that he was, among other things, a director of a Cape bank, a prominent local Mason, and a county official. He was rightfully proud of his Cape ancestry, and his hobby was the history of East Dennis families and houses.

"It feels quite natural to be in this house again," he remarked, as the ladies returned. "We have known and visited all of the families who have owned this house—which, of course, is not old. Twenty-five years, to be exact. Before Ed

54

Sears built it, a livery stable used to occupy this location."

"That explains the 1908 date in the cement floor of the cellar," I said, but actually I was not paying as close attention as I might have been. The question of refreshments was bothering me. It seemed to me I should be offering something, and yet—what? With the newcomers who had called I had not hesitated to offer a highball, but that was out of the question with a guest who, in this stronghold of the drys, might well prove to be one who worked shoulder to shoulder with Mrs. Luella in the cause of temperance.

Take Asa's bristling eyebrows, now—they seemed ideally constructed for the business of scowling coldly at a poor sinner with liquor on his breath. I racked my brains for alternatives, as I knew Elizabeth must be doing. Tea? Who wanted tea so soon after dinner? At the mere thought I was threatened with a stomach rumble. A soft drink of some sort? Sounded insipid, and the weather was too cold, anyway. Coffee? Well, perhaps. We Corbetts should have discussed the problem before our callers arrived.

It was the former owner of our house who indirectly came to my rescue. Mr. Landry had sold to us because his wife had died suddenly and unexpectedly. He planned to build a cottage near one of his sons in the Middle West, but it was generally felt that Cape Cod had got its sandy hooks into him and that he would be back.

"He even said so himself," declared Asa Sears. "Just before he left we came over to say good-by. He was all packed up; there wasn't even a chair left in the place, but he had saved out a bottle and some glasses for a farewell drink, and as we lifted our glasses he said, 'I won't say good-by, because you'll probably be seeing me again."

I sprang from my chair.

"Speaking of a drink . . ."

For the first time a really broad smile stretched across Asa Sears' face. Far from scowling, the eyebrows leaped with joy, and his eyes twinkled in a way that showed he had put two and two together and was vastly amused.

Elizabeth rose to get some cheese and crackers when I returned with the drinks, but was urged out of the idea by our guests, who had eaten as recently as we.

"Not that I'd ordinarily say no, because I'm a great cheese lover," declared Asa Sears.

"So am I," I remarked, "but today I really got stuck on a cheese buy. You probably know the kind. Sage cheese."

"Why, yes. It's usually excellent."

"Really? Then maybe mine was spoiled, or something. Let me show it to you."

I brought in the cheese. He sniffed the revolting slab, and even broke off a bit and tasted it before I could caution him. His lips smacked together.

"Just right!"

I made him a present then and there.

"Well, *de gustibus—*"

"*—non est disputandum,*" he agreed, accepting.

What with the drink and one thing and another, Asa Sears' thawing accelerated pleasantly, and he thawed into excellent company. He was entertaining, he was well read, and he was a fascinating combination of the provincial and cosmopolitan. His heart belonged to Cape Cod, and he was vitally interested in every little thing that went on there, with special emphasis on his own neck of land in East Dennis, but he could also see wider horizons with a clear eye. And he exceeded most other Cape Codders we were to encounter in his ability to sit back and look at his own beloved Cape in an analytical way and see it as it was, faults and virtues both.

When the Searses had gone and we were in the kitchen washing the glasses, I said, "I have a funny feeling we're going to get along quite well with Mr. Cape Cod after all. We may not agree on cheese and trees, but still . . ."

I glanced at the bottle, which was back on the sideboard.

"I'll tell you another funny feeling I'm beginning to get, too. I'm beginning to think that Mrs. Luella is fighting a lonely battle in these parts!"

A day or two later we received our first invitation to a private home. It was for Saturday night, at the Rodgers', and we were to play cards.

Doctor Philip Rodgers was not a native, but he had married one, which gave him a prince-consort standing in the community. As it happened, the Rodgers were newcomers of a sort, having moved within the year to East Dennis after some fifteen years in a Boston suburb. They were in our own age bracket, and had three children, including one of the few little girls available as a playmate for our daughter, so that we had come to know each other through the children.

Present that night besides ourselves and the Rodgers were the Asa Searses and Mrs. Hall, nee Sears. Mrs. Hall, who was Mrs. Rodgers' mother, was down from Boston for the weekend.

Asa Sears had sternly renounced bridge several years ago, declaring that people took it too seriously (I suspect he muffed a couple of good hands and probably lost sleep fuming about them afterwards). Since we were only seven anyway, we finally all played canasta, four at one table and three at another. It was a pleasant, uneventful evening—until Mrs. Hall grew reminiscent as we were sitting over refreshments.

Mrs. Hall, born and bred in the village—though she had lived a good deal in Boston and still wintered there—began to recall some of the more notable local eccentrics of the past. Like human beings anywhere, Cape Codders loved to tell stories about their own people. It was a long winter evening of the type that must have been invented for storytelling, and she had in us an obviously delighted audience.

"Oh, my, yes. Everybody knew Aunt Lulie," she was saying presently. "She was a very nervous woman, Aunt Lulie was.

One time she bought a whole new set of dishes, and she scarcely got through one year before she had to buy another set. The trouble was that any time she picked up a dish she was likely to throw it over her shoulder. Right over her shoulder. She was explaining to a friend how she did it one day. She snapped her hands up like this," said Mrs. Hall, flipping her hands up alternately to demonstrate, "and said, 'You know—I'm so quick, I'm so quick!' "

Asa Sears coughed and glanced at us somewhat obliquely, but Mrs. Hall went right on. Another lady she recalled was known for her annual garden parties. The local paper would report that Mrs. Featherstone was planning "a series of garden parties" to take place during the coming months, and giving the date and hour for the first one. Mrs. Featherstone would dart around town well ahead of time inviting everybody. Each time, against their better judgment, a few persons would decide to go, either out of curiosity or to see who else had been foolish enough to come.

The appointed hour would arrive, and so would the first of the guests. Their hostess would greet them with a look of pleased surprise and an "Oh, how nice of you to drop in!"

"Well—er—isn't this the day of your garden party? The newspaper said—"

After a momentary blank look she would laugh gayly.

"Oh, I had forgotten! Well, do come right out into the garden, everything will be ready in just a moment," she would say, and hustle them into the garden and then begin flitting madly in and out of the house. First she would slip into something billowy and frivolous in the way of a garden-party dress.

Then out would come the jelly glasses which served her as punch cups, and the tepid, unfortunate mixture which served her as punch. No matter how many or how few persons appeared, there was always almost but not quite enough punch to go around, so that further sprinting in and out became necessary.

In and out, trailing wisps of organdy, she would go, with an occasional snatch of song bursting from her lips. Limp soda crackers or soggy cookies, long exposed to Cape Cod's mellowing air, would appear on odd platters, and the party would soon be in full swing.

Afterwards these parties would be reported in the local newspaper just as solemnly as they had been announced.

Asa Sears chuckled and looked horrified and burst out in a protest all at the same time.

"Sophy, you shouldn't tell these new people those stories, they'll move out of town!" he declared, waving a hand in our direction. "They'll think we're all like that!"

Mrs. Hall laughed and went on, and the more she told the more Asa Sears fidgeted.

"People went in for simple pleasures in those days. On a nice evening they'd go out after dinner for a stroll around the village to look in other people's windows. They didn't make any bones about it, they just quite frankly stopped and took a good look. I remember one time when my father got up from the dinner table and went over to the window. It was summer and the window was open. He leaned out and said, 'Now, listen, Charlie, you and Minnie go on along home.' They were standing right outside with their chins practically resting on the window ledge. I don't wonder but they were trampling down a flower bed. 'We just wanted to see what you were having for dinner, Tom,' they told him. They weren't hungry, understand, just curious—as a matter of fact, Charlie was picking his teeth at the time."

"Charlie and Minnie!" Asa burst out, unable to control himself any longer. "There was a pair!" he said, and from then on the tentative little smiles which had appeared on his face, only to be shooed away by a stern swoop of his eyebrows, began to come more frequently, and he could not resist supplying a small detail or two the speaker was overlooking. As he became more animated, he sat up straight in his chair and his hands

59

began to move wondrously whenever he talked. His hands directed the orchestra of his voice with forceful little arabesques, and he acted out every word he spoke.

"Yes, sir, I can remember old Cap'n Howes ordering Cap'n Forbush off his property—the wind was right, and Cap'n Howes could really swear—and—by—George—he really let him have it with both barrels! I just stood in the door of my barn and *enjoyed* it—"

As both storytellers pointed out that night, in several cases they were talking about their own relatives. Sears, Crowell, Hall, Howes, Nickerson—all represented clans which went all the way back on Cape Cod, and all were interrelated. We soon learned not to comment freely on one Cape Codder to another. The unlikeliest person was liable to smile and say, "You don't need to tell *me* anything about Sarah Jane Forbush —she's my cousin." Turns out Sarah Jane was a Howes before her marriage and that her maternal grandfather, who married a Sears, was a Crowell.

Where blunders were concerned, we narrowly avoided making a colossal one which was a good example of the pitfalls which threaten newcomers in any community as well encrusted with local pride and tradition as our village.

"Going to the supper at the hall Saturday night?" D.H. asked us one afternoon in the store—this was before the old store burned down, and soon after the Newcomers' Party. He was weighing out a pound of chocolate drops for me. I wanted the chocolate drops, but I was particularly interested in seeing how many were in a pound, because he had a sign on the big open box which said, "1¢ ea., 59¢ ℔." and I had a hunch.

"What supper is that?" I asked.

"The turkey supper."

A supper at the hall, probably for some worthy cause— maybe we should go. If we were going to live in the community we should support community endeavors.

"Well, thanks, I'll look into it."

"I think they probably still have some tickets left. Well, now, that looks like a pound right on the line, so now let's count 'em. You hold the sack. One, two, three, four—"

There were forty-six chocolate drops.

"Forty-six! Well, I declare!" D.H. let out a hearty chuckle. "Well, that's one on *me*. They're worth 59¢ a pound, so I sure can't sell 'em at a cent apiece, can I? Don't seem right, though, for a piece of candy like that to have to be more'n a penny. Why, I can remember when—"

By the grace of God, instead of asking some Sears or other at the post office where we should go to get tickets to the turkey supper, we asked the Underhills.

We learned we had almost trifled with something sacred.

The affair in question was the annual turkey supper of the venerable East Dennis Social Club.

Only residents of East Dennis, or former residents who had kept up their membership, were eligible to attend.

New residents who wished to join were eligible to do so only after a year's residence in East Dennis.

In order to be considered they had to submit a written application, which would be duly noted at the annual meeting which preceded by a week or so the annual turkey supper.

Because membership was limited, there was a waiting list, and some people had been on it for as long as five years. When and if we did apply for membership, we would be at the bottom of the list.

The only way an opening occurred for new members was when old members either moved away or died.

Old members seldom moved away and never died.

The reason the membership was strictly limited was because there was a strict limit to how many persons could sit down together to a turkey supper in Jacob Sears Memorial Hall.

This was the sole annual function of the East Dennis Social Club.

Former residents, members of old East Dennis families, their sons and daughters, often came from far and wide to exercise their privilege of attending the dinner.

This had been going on for seventy-five years.

For us to have bounced blithely up to some old Cape Codder after a few weeks' residence in East Dennis—say, to Asa Sears—and asked where we could buy a couple of tickets to the turkey supper would have been enough to send a shiver of revulsion through the whole village.

"But why did D.H. talk as if anybody could buy tickets?" we demanded.

"He probably never even stopped to think about it," said Fred. "Listen, D.H. has been to these affairs all seventy-five times, I expect, so it doesn't necessarily impress him to be a member of the East Dennis Social Club."

"Sometimes that's the kind that take it the most seriously."

"Not D.H. But you'd be surprised how many people around here *do* take it very seriously, and how many outsiders would like to be members. Once years ago when there were a lot fewer people around than there are now, they let a few people from other towns join. Think they'd drop out now? Not on your life! What is it? It's nothing—and yet it's *something*."

5

CHURCH AND STATE

The trouble with a false reputation is, there's always that temptation to keep it up.

"If we don't show up at church one of these Sundays soon, it may slip," Elizabeth pointed out.

"Get thee behind me, angel," I retorted. "When I'm ready to be converted to Christianity, I'll let you know. Right now I'm siding with the Reverend Ozzie's personal Old Scratch."

"You mean Asa Sears?"

"Right."

Asa's sea captain grandfather of the same name—Cap'n Asa—had once tangled with Cap'n Forbush at Sunday meeting over the way the church was being run and had walked out, never to return. Asa was still loyally keeping up the feud, and probably would continue to do so as long as a member of the Forbush family was still prominent in the church. On special occasions, though, he did "get his marching orders" from Ruth Asa, as he called it, and dutifully accompanied

63

her to divine worship. On these rare Sabbaths the Reverend Mr. Blake invariably blew up in the middle of his sermon and had to drag out the original manuscript and find his place. The strain was too much.

"I'll get around to church in due time, so stop pecking away at me," I told Elizabeth.

"Well, Mrs. Luella keeps pecking away at *me*. She asked me at the post office the other day when they'd have a chance to welcome us at church."

"You tell Sister Luella—"

"I did."

"Not what I'm thinking."

"Well, anyway, I staved her off."

It was one thing to resist Mrs. Luella's efforts, and another to cope with Fred Underhill's. Fred was a salesman by profession and nature. His easy-going, low-pressure methods were difficult to parry, especially when applied to anything he believed in as sincerely as the importance of backing up our own little community church. He never twisted an arm, he merely let drop a few persuasive thoughts and left a person to twist his own arm. Slowly, and with long pauses for thought, Fred hammered out his ideas in the palm of one hand with the blunt, crooked forefinger of the other. It was consistent with his general approach that he should emphasize his arguments with a finger that seemed to be seeking to point the way, rather than with his fist.

He was an active man and yet a reflective one. This fact may have saved his life—for while still involved in New York's high-speed treadmill he began to notice how many of his friends were dropping dead at fifty, and to reflect on the fact. He decided to withdraw to the Cape while he could still do so in good order, while he could still enjoy living there, rather than hang on in the city until he was one of those well-to-do but health-broken men who have waited too long, and whose prosperity is an ironical thing.

64

Still a salesman, he decided a number of things could be sold on the Cape which nobody else thought could be made worthwhile there, and his old company gladly assigned him the territory. With Clara at the wheel, Fred moseyed about the length and breadth of the Cape in his own way and in his own good time, touring the back roads as well as the highways, drinking in the beauties of the scenery, and rolling up sales figures his company had not believed possible.

Concerning the church, Fred was frank—but still a salesman.

"The setup of the church here is far from perfect. There are a pile of things wrong. A lot of old feuds are mixed up in it, so that folks in town won't go to church because of some of the ones who do."

"You mean like Asa," I grinned.

"That's right. Nobody can talk to *his* grandfather like that a hundred years ago and get away with it. However . . . Now, personally I happen to be of the same denomination as you, and I know there are a couple of Episcopalian churches within half an hour's ride of here that are mighty attractive places, with ministers who can give you a first-rate sermon.

"Here we've got a young fellow who's still in school—he and his wife and the baby live here at the parsonage, but he goes to theological school in Boston all week and then comes down here on weekends to try to think of something to say that'll interest his elders. Every week he's read a different book and we get a different set of ideas which are too new for him to express clearly.

"The congregation is small, but not so small it can't find things to squabble about. The choir is gotten together by hook or crook, and the organist has arthritis and an ailing reed organ to contend with. A few years back some group or other was asked to make a survey of the church situation in this part of the Cape, and after looking into things pretty thoroughly they declared that there wasn't even any justification for a church

65

here in East Dennis—said it wasn't practical and recommended the congregation unite with the church in Dennis and go there."

"I can imagine how that must have sat."

"Well, there were only a dozen or so in the church here on an average Sunday then, so it looked like the survey people had a point. The only reason they could operate at all was because a retired minister was giving his services for a nominal fee. If you want to go on cold facts and statistics, those survey people were probably right. At the same time, if the early Christians had gone on cold facts and statistics there wouldn't be any Christian religion today.

"It's all very well to say there's no justification for a church here, but there it is, a nice little church in the middle of our village, and since it is there it certainly wouldn't seem right to have it stand there empty. The only way it can grow and really amount to something is to have those of us who live here get busy and do something about it—and the natives aren't going to do it alone when half of them won't even attend because of something some member's grandfather said to their grandfather back in 1847."

"Do you really see much hope?"

"Why, yes. When we came here four years ago there were only a handful attending church, like I said. The first Sunday we attended we brought the total congregation up to eleven. I couldn't even get my nerve up to sing when the hymns were played, because there weren't enough other people present to drown me out! Why, I've seen bigger groups than that get together in East Dennis for a rummy game!

"This was four years ago, and even though we haven't moved mountains we do have at least twenty to thirty in the church every Sunday now, and we've increased our budget several times over what it was and managed to hire a student minister now that our retired man has left, and we have a

Sunday school where we didn't used to have any, so that's something."

"That's a lot. But let's look at another side of things, Fred. You know Elizabeth and I are sailing under false colors on this church-going deal," I said. By this time the Underhills had made their "formal" call and we had let them in on the shameful truth behind our Sunday walk to church. "I haven't been a churchgoer since my Sunday-school days, and while—"

"Well, now, you've touched on one of the very points I was leading up to. If Janie is going to attend Sunday school here you can't very well have much to say as to how that Sunday school is conducted if you don't attend church yourself, and you ought to have some say. However, you think it over. You're going to be living here for a long spell, I hope; there's plenty of time—except, of course, that the more people get behind the church now the better chance there is to make it something we can all be proud of, not just as a building but as a living church."

It still did not seem convenient to drop everything else and go to church at eleven o'clock on Sunday morning, not with all the work we had to do, so we let another week slip by without going. But Fred's remarks were affecting me nonetheless. My curiosity was aroused by his description of the situation. What *did* go on in that church on Sunday mornings?

"Well, I'll tell you what," I said one morning at breakfast very pleased with my solution of the religious problem, "let's go once and then the next couple of Sundays we'll go to a couple of other churches around somewhere, and give out the story that we're looking all the churches over very carefully. Then if Mrs. Luella or anybody else buttonholes us about showing up the next Sunday we can always claim we're making our survey and have plans to attend some new church that week."

"Well, really! I'm glad the school bus has come—I'd hate

67

to have Florence still here to find out what a snake in the grass her father is."

"You've got to fight fire with fire, and I'm going to out-maneuver these characters if it's the last thing I do," I said complacently. "They're not going to rope *me* into any church. I'm going to make Asa Sears proud of me."

"H'm. I'm not sure he's a good influence on you."

"Well, we'll see. We'll go this Sunday and get it over with."

Inside, the church was as plain and modest as an elderly spinster, with a complexion which also was showing the ravages of time. A speaker's stand served as pulpit in the center of the dais, and against the wall behind it stood an old Victorian sofa flanked by two high-backed armchairs. To the right of the dais was the choir stall and organ, and to the left were side pews which could be used for an augmented choir or for the congregation should the occasion arise. In the center of the church at the rear was a little alcove. It was called the "bowfat," and nobody knew why for sure, though some thought it to be a corruption of the French *"beaufait."*

The pews were painted white with dark mahogany trim. There were two aisles with the center pews between them, these divided by a center partition. There were eight rows of pews, and a hundred and twenty persons would have filled them.

On Sunday, about a quarter of that number were present. The congregation had a tendency to fill the pews from the back forward rather than from the front backward, so that Reverend Oswald Blake found himself talking across a no man's land of empty front pews.

The minister was at the mercy of the organist during the service. She was a woman of great determination and since she could play louder than the Reverend Mr. Blake could talk she always had the final chord. He might direct that the first, second, and final verses of a hymn were to be sung; she paid him

68

no heed, and played all five if it suited her. She also feuded with one member of the choir, who thought she played with too many of the stops out, and who sat next to the organ so as to brace her back against them and hold them shut.

The woman who dominated the choir, however, was an elderly dame who had once been a concert singer and who, at a very advanced age, still had a remarkable voice. She occupied the front corner of the choir stall, and made the most of it. Holding her music well out in front of her during the anthem, she tended to turn more and more to the side and project herself out over the corner, until it became ever more like the prow of a ship, and she the figurehead. Beginning as a member of the choir, she gradually assumed the appearance and mannerisms of a soloist.

"Well, what did you think of it?" asked Elizabeth after the service. We had been given a greeting by Mrs. Luella which indicated her extreme pleasure at seeing the sheep gathered into the fold, and, after visiting with this one and that for a few minutes in front of the church, we were now on our way home. It being a fine day, we were afoot.

"I enjoyed every minute of it," I admitted. "I particularly liked the way that woman in the choir put her shoulder to the organ."

"What a way to talk!" said Elizabeth reprovingly. "You're not supposed to go to church looking for entertainment."

"No, but if you happen to find it there, is that your fault? That reminds me—D.H. told me a wonderful church story the other day. I've been meaning to tell you. He said that one time in the old days there was a bad drought, and the gardeners among the congregation asked the minister to pray for rain. He did so with a will. He had more zeal than gardening experience, though, and after a few introductory supplications he prayed, 'Oh, Lord, send us rain in copious confusion!' Right then a voice in the back of the room interrupted him. 'If it's all the same to you, Lord, just make it frizzly-drizzly.' "

We strolled along enjoying the bright sunshine, and I began to turn over certain impressions in my mind.

"You know, it's a funny thing, though," I said presently.

"What's funny?"

"About that church. For all the foolishness that was going on, that little church had a good feeling about it, and a dignity of its own. It—well, it felt the way a church should."

"It's a nice church," said Elizabeth.

Asa Sears swung around the corner on his way back from a stroll down to the cemetery, of which he was a trustee, and caught us in the act of returning from church.

"Well, so you backslid, did you?" he accused me with a genial waggle of his eyebrows. He was wearing a sweater and blue jeans and an old hat with its brim turned up at the cavalier angle, and was looking remarkably fit and jaunty, as is the way of Old Scratch's personal representatives on a fine Sabbath. "Well, how was Ozzie this morning? Did he bring you a message?"

"He did pretty well," I said.

"He lost me," said Elizabeth.

"Poor boy. He's got his work cut out for him," said Asa indulgently. "Well, I must get home, I've got a million things to do. Up to my neck in extra work right now, what with Town Meeting coming up. I'm moderator, you know, and it takes a lot of preparation."

"You're moderator? Wonderful!"

"Oh, yes, yes. You're coming, I hope?"

"Wouldn't miss it."

"Good. There are a few articles on the warrant which should prove of interest."

"I hope so." I glanced down the road. "How did you find things at the cemetery?"

"Tip-top. Abner and Earl are doing a fine job down there. I don't think you could find a more beautiful and cheerful little cemetery with a lovelier outlook anywhere in the country. Personally, I'm looking forward to being buried there!"

He bade us good-by and went on up the street toward his house with that amazingly light and springy step he had when he was feeling good about life.

"You know," I said as we walked on, "everybody thought it was such a crazy time of year for us to move up here, but it seems to me we couldn't have hit it better. It's surprising what's going on. First we time in just right for that New-comers' Party, and now there's Town Meeting, and then I heard something the other day about a local minstrel show that sounded interesting. At any rate, with Asa Sears as moderator, Town Meeting is a must on my calendar. We won't be able to vote as yet—I understand you have to be a registered voter, and to be that you have to have lived here a year—but we can listen and learn something about our new home town."

Town Meeting involved, of course, the whole township of Dennis, which was divided into five villages: Dennisport, West Dennis, South Dennis, East Dennis, and Dennis, the latter often called North Dennis locally to avoid confusion with "Dennis," meaning the whole township.

The meeting was held in a big old gray frame schoolhouse in West Dennis that was no longer used now that the consolidated school was in operation. The big room was crowded, and its population changed constantly as people attended what they could of the meeting and then went off to work, or came from work to be on hand for the voting on articles of particular interest to them. As we entered we were handed a white pamphlet, which was a copy of the warrant. The warrant consisted of some ninety articles which were to be voted on, as for example:

Article 12. To see if the town will vote to appropriate the sum of $473.56, which is the amount of the County Dog Fund received, for expenses of schools for the current year.

71

In all cases where money was involved, the township's finance committee made recommendations. In this routine instance they were favorable, and the Dog Fund went for education—and not at the expense of canine welfare, either, since the money was surplus turned back to the town from the county on money collected from dog licenses.

A petition signed by ten or more voters was sufficient to put an article in the warrant. A lady had only to rally a few of her neighbors in order to get an article in the warrant "To see if the Town will vote to raise and appropriate a sum of money to install the necessary catch basin to adequately drain Dr. Lord's Road in front of the residence of Miss Daisy Doone of East Dennis."

Most of the articles concerned something which would necessitate the town's "raising and appropriating a sum of money" if the article was accepted. Each article was voted on aye or no by voice, with a show of hands and tellers appointed to take the count if the chair was in doubt about the vote. If the noes had it, the article was "indefinitely postponed." In the case of Miss Daisy Doone's catch basin, the finance committee saw the justice of her request and recommended that $125 be raised and appropriated for the purpose—$125 being the standard catch-basin appropriation that year—and it was so voted.

On the rostrum at the head of the room, Asa Sears was holding forth in fine shape. His deportment would have been the envy of a Supreme Court judge, and was all the more impressive in being accomplished without robes. He was a master parliamentarian, able to quote at an instant's notice and with considerable satisfaction his authority for any action he took as moderator or any decision he handed down. There was never any question about who was in charge of the meeting.

An article to raise and appropriate an extra $25,000 for certain improvements in and around the school brought one old gentleman to his feet.

"Mr. Moderator!"

"The Chair recognizes Cap'n Bangs," declared Asa Sears in tones that were even better than pear shaped. They were urn shaped.

Cap'n Bangs took a bellicose stance and swept the audience with his fierce old eyes.

"It seems we ain't spendin' *enough* money on that new school, we have to have *exter* money, too. I don't see what we needed with it in the fust place. I went to school right here in this very room. All the classes was in the same room. It was plenty good enough for us, and it would still be plenty good enough—"

The gavel hit the speaker's stand four times with increasing intensity.

"Cap'n Bangs, the Chair finds you out of order. The consolidated school was voted on years ago, at which time you gave us your arguments against the idea, and you have been giving them to us all over again each year since then. The consolidated school was voted in, it was built and has been in operation now for four years, so it would seem we can pretty safely say it is an accomplished fact. No purpose will be served in discussing it now, so the Chair must ask you to confine your remarks to the issue at hand."

"Hmf!" Cap'n Bangs sat down with a thump, fuming and frustrated, and the article was voted on and accepted.

Many of the articles were accepted with little or no discussion. The Dutch Elm Leaf Beetle got its annual bad news in Article 16—$800.00 to be expended for the spraying and suppression of his kind. Articles mentioning such sums as $6,500 for the protection and propagation of shellfish, $2,500 for various public libraries (of which our small township had five, besides contributing to the support of one in Harwich), and $49,600 for highways were quickly passed, but when Article 35 came along the best part of an hour was spent discussing it:

Article 35. To see if the Town will vote to allow dredging of scallops in Bass River by outboard motor boats using one dredge only. Dredge not to exceed 3 ft. in width.

Opinions on the kinds and sizes of boats that might be used, the kind and size of dredge, and the kinds and sizes of some of the people who went out for scallops were all freely given by a number of men, professional fishermen and others. We learned something about scallops, and something about people, from those earnest and sometimes heated remarks.

Cap'n Bangs had something to say at this time, too, though not necessarily on this subject.

"Mr. Moderator!"

"The Chair recognizes Cap'n Bangs," chanted Asa, betraying only by the slightest roll of his eyes the fact that he was a man sorely tried in the course of duty.

"Seems to me some people are never satisfied, always got to have a little more," growled Cap'n Bangs. "It's like some people are about schools. I was thinkin' to myself as I sat here in this very school building where I went to school—and it's still in purty good shape, too—"

Bang! went the gavel.

"The Chair finds the speaker out of order. The article under consideration at this time concerns the use of dredges on outboard-motor boats for scallops, and anyone wishing to speak must confine his remarks to that subject. The Chair recognizes Mr. Mills."

Daniel Mills of the finance committee rose to make a point in his role of professional fisherman, and Cap'n Bangs sat down muttering darkly. After a moment he rose and stomped out of the meeting with heavy strides, each step a thumping protest against the way things were being run.

"Don't tell me he's walking out!" I said to Clara Underhill, hating to see the captain go.

"He *always* walks out," explained Clara. "I understand he hasn't got past the first forty articles in ten years."

The hottest question of the day came in Article 50, which proposed zoning by-laws for certain areas in West Dennis and South Dennis. Indeed, it was at Town Meeting we first came to realize that the battle of the North and the South was being fought all over again in the township of Dennis. As an old book puts it, "Dennis is a narrow town, but reaching from sea to sea." Its population was concentrated on the shores, and the interests of the North Shore or bay side were often at variance with those of the South Shore or ocean side.

The lion's share of the tourist trade went to the ocean side because the water was warmer there than on the bay side. In the summer the South Shore was more crowded and commercial; it swarmed with tourist courts, resort hotels, close-packed beach colonies, trailer camps, and hot-dog stands.

Dennisport was the most commercial of the villages and had the greatest population and therefore the most votes. And Dennisport feared any kind of zoning anywhere in the township, for fear that if it got in elsewhere it might eventually come to Dennisport. The zoning proposal seemed to have little chance of being accepted, especially when Daniel Mills of the finance committee rose to give it the *coup de grace*.

Dan'l was a leader in Dennisport, and he was a sincere man who felt strongly that nothing should be set in the way of young fellows if they wanted to start up a business of any kind. He sometimes lost sight of all other considerations, such as that of protecting some of Cape Cod's charm—which was, after all, one of the principal things that drew tourists to the Cape and thus brought business prosperity to Dennisport.

"If our young fellows want to set up a shop any place in town they ought to be able to," he declared. "It's all right to talk how this and that might spoil the beauties of the Cape, but the fact remains that this zoning law that's proposed here

75

has been brought up and backed mainly by some of our aged people who don't have to worry about going into business any more."

Never was there a happier choice of words—for the opposition. One after another, vehement voters over fifty—most of them women—rose and scathingly identified themselves as being among those "aged" people who supported the zoning measure, while Dan'l sat beet red in the front of the room and wished he were well out to sea somewhere on a fishing boat. North and South's aged closed ranks, and the zoning article was passed.

The best laughs of the day were provided by the cemeteries, with the help of Manuel, the merry Portuguese. It seemed that Manuel always began to get ready for Town Meeting the day before it was held and that his preparations consisted of emptying one or two bottles whose contents both relaxed and invigorated. During the course of the meeting he generally had something worthwhile to say. Asa Sears ruled the roost with stern impartiality and his gavel made short work of those who exceeded their rights, but when Manuel rose to speak a twinkle crept into the moderator's eye, and he gave him the floor.

The article before the meeting involved the widening and improving of the road into a cemetery in North Dennis. Crowell Hall of that village was the author of the article. 'Crow' Hall was a tall, lean man who looked as if he could have made a good living hiring out as a dignified chief mourner at Episcopalian funerals—a man of controlled grief. His mild, measured, melancholy vocal delivery always managed to suggest that there had just been a death somewhere nearby. The widening and improving of the cemetery road was a project dear to his heart, and one he had patiently tried to put through for several years.

Manuel, however, felt moved to protest.

"Mr. Moderator, whadda we need for widen the road outa the cemetery, the people in there ain't goin' nowhere!"

When the response to this remark died down, the author of the article rose to defend it.

"People have to get *into* the cemetery once in a while," he pointed out carefully.

"Whadda yah mean?" Manuel jovially swept his arm around to take in all the beaming and healthy "aged" folk who were liberally sprinkled through the assembly. "We don't need no cemetery, nobody ever die in Dennis!"

Whether Manuel hurt the chances of Crow Hall's article or not is uncertain, but at any rate, once again it was indefinitely postponed. For at least one more year, the shades of North Dennis would have to make do with the old road.

By the end of the meeting, the finance committee was able to announce an accurate estimate of the tax rate for the coming year. It was down from the present one, so everyone seemed pretty well satisfied. As we went out the side exit, along with the Underhills and Ruth Asa Sears, we passed near the rostrum. The moderator was gathering up his papers and his notes and packing up his gavel. It had been a long day, and he had discharged his task nobly. As we went by he happened to glance down and catch my eye. His eyebrows waggled questioningly as he tipped up an imaginary bottle.

"He wants you to come over for a drink," Ruth Asa interpreted. "He always needs it after one of these sessions."

Half an hour later, then, several of us were sitting in the Sears living room having one of Asa's special old-fashioneds. These we came to know and respect. I was soon seized by the suspicion that Asa dried his ice cubes in a towel before putting them in the glasses, in order to keep dilution to a minimum.

"Well, what did you think of your first town meeting?" he asked. I told him I liked it, and he shook his head reminiscently. "You should have seen them in the old days. Only the

77

men came to Town Meeting then. The air in the room was blue with tobacco smoke all day long—matter of fact, more than tobacco smoke! Tempers ran high, and so did some of the language."

"I'll bet it did. I'd like to hear Cap'n Bangs get going even now."

"Now, there's a one for you. Why, he even complained when they decided to put electric lights in the town office."

"He was wonderful. I don't know which I liked best— Cap'n Bangs, or Manuel, or Crowell Hall."

"Crow! Ha! You haven't seen anything yet. Wait'll you see him in the minstrel show!"

"*Crowell Hall?*"

"Certainly!"

"What does he do in the minstrel show?"

"Why," said Asa, not without a hint of jealousy in his voice, "he's the interlocutor!"

6

NOTHING BEATS

THE LOCAL JOKE

According to the doctors, Hadley Ransom should have lost a leg as the result of the wounds he suffered as an artillery officer in World War II, but Hadley declared that wherever he went, the leg was going to go too, even if he went to his grave for it. He was not ready to go to his grave yet, so finally the leg gave in and compromised with him. It healed, but it locked at the knee, leaving him with a stiff leg.

If this slowed him down any, it was unnoticeable. Outside of the hundred-yard dash, he could still qualify for almost any activity normal to a man in his upper thirties. He was an excellent dancer, for example. As a matter of fact, had he been able to be any more active, to move any faster, to be any more places at once, to get his nose in any more people's business, and talk them into any more wild schemes and mad situations than he

79

was already doing, I doubt if the Cape could have stood it.

He came hurtling up the walk one morning as we sat at breakfast and burst in saying, "Don't get up, I'll get my own cup. Is the coffee hot?" He was a man who quickly established himself in friendly households.

"I have to go down to Brewster to see a woman who's got some antiques she wants to sell—if I can work it right I hope to latch on to some of the good things without having to get stuck with too much of the junk—but I just wanted to stop in to make sure you're coming to the minstrel show," he said, throwing three or four spoonfuls of sugar into his coffee and stirring it with a briskness that caused little wavelets to break against the brim of the cup and fling their spray over the sides. "It's going to be a great show, if I do say so myself as contributed heavily to the working-out of the skit. I will also sing a number or two, of course."

"Mean to say you're not an end-man?"

"I have enough to do," said Hadley graciously, with a wave of his wet spoon. "How about it, though—you're coming, aren't you?"

"We wouldn't miss it."

"Good. Bring Janie too." He swallowed the rest of his coffee with gargantuan gulps and rose. "Next year we'll have to get you in the show."

"Well, I wouldn't have anything to offer as a performer—I've never gone in for shows—but I'd certainly like to lend a hand with writing the material, if that would be any help, and maybe I could make myself useful backstage or something."

"Um. Well, I've got to be on my way. Get your tickets at Goodspeed's store in North Dennis!"

"I'll bet you'd have fun being in one of those shows," Elizabeth said to me, when Hadley had spun his wheels in the gravel of our driveway and gone tearing away around the corner and down the road across the marshes. A gull flying near

the road wheeled away and flapped hurriedly in the direction
of the sea, as though startled by the precipitous Mr. Ransom.

"Not me," I said, shaking my head. "I've never been in a
show since once in the fifth grade. I rushed on crying, 'A message from Santa Claus!', handed the fairy princess the message,
and rushed off again vowing even at that tender age, 'Never
again!' I can't sing, I can't dance—"

"I'll bet that doesn't stop some of them."

Elizabeth was right, of course. It did not. But we still had
one of the greatest evening's entertainments of our lives. I had
not even supposed that minstrel shows were being done any
more, but we learned they were still going strong not only all
over Cape Cod but throughout many sections of New England. The oldest member of the Dennis Jubilee Minstrels, Mr.
Howard Hall, appeared in his first Cape minstrel in 1898 and
had been singing and dancing and rolling the bones in them
ever since.

It was a time of year when last season's summer visitors
were but a memory and next season's crop hardly more as yet
than a gleam in the Chamber of Commerce's eye. Only the
year-around population was on hand. Every face one saw was
a familiar one—not for us as yet, but becoming so. The resort
atmosphere was gone, only the small-town life remained. The
spirits of Dennis sea captains of yesteryear walked more visibly
abroad in the persons of their descendants, and the flavor of
Cape Cod life became more pronounced.

It was then that fifteen men and their faithful piano-player,
Mrs. Estelle Savage, put on a minstrel show in the darkest
interior of the quiet season for the enlightenment of the few
hundred permanent residents of our two villages. Hardly a
joke but turned on some local person, hardly an allusion that
would have meant anything five miles away. Garagemen, a
contractor, a restauranteur, an antiques dealer, a pharmacist,
an undertaker's assistant, a kennels master, and a hardware
store truck driver who also drove the school bus and was the

best end man I ever saw, were among the cast, and the people they told their jokes about were sitting out in front of them, where they could point them out.

Carleton Hall in North Dennis was older than Jacob Sears Hall and looked it, every year of it. It was battered and scarred from generations of use, and its facilities were antiquated. Heat was provided by an old wood stove plunked in the center of the room toward the rear. The hall would seat about one hundred and sixty people for a performance if a few were willing to roast near the stove. But it had a decent-sized stage, and a curtain that worked whenever Bill Kennedy, the shellfish warden and traditional minstrel show curtain puller, yanked on the ropes. It had an upright piano, too, which responded to tuning, and to Mrs. Savage.

One of the surprising things about all this, perhaps, was that the aforementioned undertaker's assistant was not Crowell Hall—the undertaker's assistant happened to be one of the end men. As for Crow, however, his performance as interlocutor was as unforgettable in its way as Asa's had been as moderator. Straight and stiff, tall in the saddle, Crow sat with his sheaf of papers in his hands and his hands folded in his lap, ready to rise in his own lugubrious way and announce the numbers. He was probably the straightest straight man who ever graced a stage.

"Mr. Interlocutor!"

"Yes, Rastus?"

"Mr. Interlocutor, you know Josh and Amanda Clark, don't you?"

"Yes, I know Josh and Amanda, Rastus."

"They're sitting right down there, you can see 'em there. Well, they went up to Boston for their fortieth wedding anniversary the other day. Sort of a second honeymoon."

"Is that so?" said Crow in a way all his own—a sort of courteously interested tone, coupled with absolutely no animation.

"Yes, they went up there and they stayed at one of the

best hotels in a big room with fine twin beds in it and everything."

"Well, well," marveled Crow.

"Yes, sir, and after a big evening out at a fine restaurant and a show, they came back to their room and went to bed. Well, sir, after Josh turned out the light, he heard Amanda start to cry."

"Is that so? She started to cry, did she? Well, that's too bad," Crow deplored in his slow, measured way. "Well, what did Josh do then?"

"He got up and went over to her bed and said, 'Amanda, what's the matter?' "

"I see. And what did Amanda say?"

"She said, 'The night we were married, you kissed me goodnight.' 'Oh, is *that* what was bothering you,' said Josh, and gave her a kiss. Then he went back to bed, and pretty soon he heard her crying again."

"What was the trouble this time, Rastus?"

"That's what Josh wanted to know. He sat up in bed and said, 'Well, Amanda, what is it now? I kissed you, didn't I?' She sniffled and said, 'Yes, but that's not all you did. That night after you kissed me, you bit me on the ear, too!' "

"Well, well. And what did Josh say then?"

"He said, 'Oh, is *that* it?' and he got up again. Well, sir, Amanda could hear him stumbling around and swearing for the longest time, and finally she said, 'Josh, what in the world are you doing?' "

"And what did he say?"

"He said, 'Dammit, Amanda, I'm trying to find my teeth!' "

The minstrel show surprised us in more ways than one. The jokes were broad, hearty, and earthy to an extent that made us feel New England prudery had perhaps been exaggerated—or perhaps had never worked out onto the Cape in its full force from the mainland. The performances were amateur, simple, and unvarnished, but in that shabby old hall with its wood stove and its paint-neglected woodwork fifteen men in blackface created something wonderful of their own for the pleasure of their own tiny community. There was nothing like the local joke to get a laugh, no joke that was so much fun both for the teller and the hearer.

The minstrel show lasted an hour, and was followed after an intermission by an "oleo," a skit in which the strictly local appeal was if anything intensified. The skit was built around a local situation, each character represented a local person, and every line was charged with local reference. The slapstick was spirited, but it brought down the house mainly because of the people it was kidding.

"What did you think of it—as if I need to ask," said Elizabeth on the way home. "I thought you were going to fall out of your seat every time Frank Embler told a joke."

"I thought so too. For my money it was tremendous. I've been missing a lot all my life—I've been missing smalltown life! These villages are guilty of a social lag—the people here insist on creating some of their own entertainment and activities. They aren't content to sit in front of their TV sets like so many sponges. They seem to like old-fashioned flesh-and-blood events. Yes, sir, it's a social lag—and it suits me fine!"

After this outburst I suddenly fell silent, and finally Elizabeth called me on it.

"What's the matter with you? All at once you aren't around any more."

I roused myself and grinned.

"I know," I said, "but I just got an idea for some lyrics for next year's show!"

THE SEASON

7

RUSTLES OF SPRING

Hadley Ransom's voice boomed at me over the telephone.

"Guess what bird we just had on our bird feeder?"

"I don't believe it," I retorted grimly.

"Hey, I haven't even told you yet! What do you think?"

"I wouldn't be surprised to hear you insist it was a bald eagle. I never heard so many loose and unsubstantiated claims as have been going around bird-lover circles in this town."

Hadley's laugh was indulgent.

"You're just jealous because your bird feeder hasn't been packing 'em in."

"Not much it hasn't! We're loaded with starlings. I can't get rid of 'em. I closed in our feeder. They went inside. I made the openings smaller. I had those big slobs getting down on their wings and knees to crawl inside, but they still made it. Meanwhile, Fred Underhill has his place swarming with purple finches and bluebirds and juncos and evening grosbeaks—"

"Come over here any time and I'll show you all those just for a starter," said Hadley confidently. He had but recently taken up bird watching himself; his feeders had been out even a shorter time than ours; but of course to hear Hadley tell it he was getting more different birds than all the rest of us put together. "Are you going to the post office very soon?"

"Yes."

"Come on up for a cup of coffee. I'm getting my furniture and bric-a-brac set up in one corner of the shop just the way I'm going to have it at the show," he said, referring to a New York antique show at which he was going to be an exhibitor the following week. "I'd like you to see how it looks. Maybe you'll have some suggestions for rearranging it."

"That's not my line, I'm afraid, but—"

"Well, come by, anyway."

I went by after stopping at the post office, and found him hard at work in his shop, which was in one wing of the big, handsome old house he had occupied since the war.

"Well, actually, I haven't quite got the layout of my booth completely set up yet. That buffet over there is going to be in this corner—matter of fact, as long as you're here would you mind giving me a hand with it?" he asked, pointing to a piece of early American furniture that was a little under seven and a half feet tall. In the next few minutes I found myself on one end of several sizeable pieces of furniture as the booth layout took shape.

"I haven't come up with any suggestions yet," I puffed, as we struggled with a substantial Baltimore bowfront chest, circa 1790, "but we seem to be getting along all right in spite of it."

"What are you complaining about?" grunted Hadley. "You're getting coffee, ain't you? And Danish pastry, if you don't scratch anything."

We put the chest down, and he snatched up a fragile-looking candlestick with a nonchalance that made me catch my breath.

"Here's something I'm crazy about. Isn't that a beautiful example of Sandwich glass?"

"My God! The way you handle that stuff gives me the willies."

"Listen, I soon found out in this business that you break a lot more stuff treasuring it with your fingertips than you do if you take a good firm grab." Considering the fact that Hadley was a sleight-of-hand artist and belonged to the Society of American Magicians, it may have been that his hands were considerably surer of themselves than mine would have been in the same circumstances.

We admired the booth layout and then went in to have our coffee and pastry. The Ransom kitchen was a comfortable and much-lived-in place, half Colonial and half General Electric. I gossiped for a moment with Agnes Ransom, who was about to leave to go shopping in Hyannis, while Hadley heated the coffee and produced the Danish pastry. Agnes went her way, and we men fell to.

"Wait till summer comes and I start holding auctions out by the barn under the tent. I've got a big tent I put up and people come from all over the Cape. Everybody loves an auction," said Hadley with a wave of his pastry that broadcast a scattering of crumbs over the entire length of the Colonial table. "If you want to have some fun, you'll have to come over and be one of my helpers. I'll pay you, of course, but the point is you'll have fun. Why, George Bean, the Yankee auctioneer, has college professors who never miss helping at his auctions, just for the fun of it."

"Sounds good. Maybe I can take a day off sometime—"

"Swell! I'll count on you."

"Meanwhile, I'd better get back to work. You know, the country is supposed to be a wonderful place to concentrate and work, compared to New York city with all its distractions, but I'm trying to work on a book and so far I find this place more distracting than the city ever thought of being."

Hadley leaned back and centered a quizzical stare on me for a moment.

"Brother, it hasn't even started. Wait'll you really get into things!"

"You mean, when the Season starts?" I asked, but Hadley shook his head.

"I'm not talking about the Season. You'll find out!"

Having just talked about it, I should have gone straight home and got to work, but instead I sniffed the air and yielded to the temptation to drive down to the beach for a look at the bay. It was a clear, sparkling day. Across the blue bay, Provincetown's Pilgrim Monument and water tower were two clear vertical lines on the horizon.

I yielded further and went for a walk along the clean sand and watched the sea birds investigate the bars that were beginning to show on the ebb tide. That was one trouble, of course —the woods, the marshes, the beach and the water were always there at arm's reach, so to speak, and on a nice day I always got fidgety to be outdoors enjoying them. And it was not going to get any easier, now that fine spring days were coming on.

As I finally returned from the beach with the reluctance of a born beachcomber and drove home, I thought about how the signs of spring were multiplying. Asa Sears was thinking about getting his boat ready to paint, when he was not preparing a speech to be delivered shortly before a chamber of commerce group. Mrs. Luella was having her barn painted. Old Colonel Braintree had been down for the weekend and had been seen greasing up his bicycle out in his side yard—that faithful bicycle which took the octogenarian all over the village. The Reverend Oswald Blake was preparing a prayer for the Easter sunrise service on Scargo Hill, highest peak on Cape Cod (100 feet above sea level). D. H. was thinking about starting to bake on weekends. Mr. Ezra Newton was sorting out fishing tackle with slow, patient fingers. According to the latest, Seth Sears was already threatening to return home from Florida, which he considered a waste of time, anyway. And Freddie Barr was getting his tractor ready for spring plowing.

It was nice out.

"This place is murder," I complained to Elizabeth when I got home. "I wanted to get out of New York because I was getting nervous on nice days and worrying about how I was wasting them in the middle of a pile of concrete. Now we're here where I can step right into the outdoors any time I want to—and the only trouble is, I keep stepping. How am I going to get any work done?"

"Oh, you'll adjust to it."

"I hope so. I think I adjust to not working even better, though. Anybody call while I was gone?"

"Freddie."

I laughed.

"What did he have on his mind?"

"Were you working? Well, why weren't you working? Hadley's? What were you doing over at Hadley's? An antique show? When was Hadley going? Well, what else was new?"

Freddie Barr was a middle-aged businessman, a Cape Codder who had left the Cape to make his fortune and returned to enjoy it on his native heath. He lived with his wife and children in a big rambling house overlooking the bay, and he had two hobbies: one was knowing everything that was going on in East Dennis, and the other was a constant squirrel-like gathering-in of provender of all sorts.

In the pursuit of his first hobby he depended strongly on the telephone. He called up dozens of people almost every day, especially people who might know something about some particular thing that was going on. We met Freddie and his family at some of the local affairs, and it was not long before we were on his list. His telephone conversations always began abruptly,

91

with no mention of who was calling, but his amiable growl was unmistakable.

I had scarcely sat down to work before the telephone rang. Elizabeth was in the basement waltzing with the washing machine—it needed to be bolted down, or something—so I answered.

"Hello?"

"He had you working, eh?"

"What?"

"I just talked to Ransom."

"Oh!"

"He's getting ready for a show, I understand."

"Yes. I helped him move stuff in place the way it's going to be in his booth."

"Going to trim those poor suckers down New York way! Well, we're all in a gawdam racket, one way or another. Seen Squire Sears lately?"

"Not in the last day or so."

"I guess he's getting that speech ready for some chamber of commerce bunch."

"So I hear."

"I called him up last night and tried to get him to give me a little sample of it over the phone, but he wouldn't."

"I'll bet not."

"He couldn't have anyway, unless somebody held the phone for him so his hands could start flying around. Well, I got to get busy. Jeezcrise, got to plant a garden soon. 'By."

Our inclusion in Freddie's telephone club really got going strong at the time of the herring run, in the spring. Every spring the herring came up a number of little tidal streams on the Cape, heading for their breeding places in fresh-water ponds. One of their outstanding routes was up a brook in nearby West Brewster, a swift little stream full of rocky rapids which flowed down to the sea from a series of placid fresh-water ponds.

In the spring the herring began to appear in this stream, fighting their way inch by inch upstream against the strong current, jumping the rapids, resting in the pools between them. In places the water was quite shallow, and there the gulls wheeled and dived.

Sometimes a gull managed to pick up a whole fish, but seldom got far with it. A gull with a fish in its mouth was pursued and harried by all his greedy tribe, and usually the fish was soon dropped, either back into the water or onto the bank, there to be shared ingraciously by a dozen squalling birds. Often a gull managed only to get a mouthful, however, and many a herring's back, when it finally reached the ponds, had a chunk out of it to show where a seagull's beak had strafed it.

Danger beset the herring every inch of the way. Some of them became too tired to wiggle and jump their way through the rapids, and dashed themselves to death on the rocks. Some took a wrong turn in places where the water forked, part of it falling steeply over rocks too high to be scaled, and part of it cutting around on a gentler plane; each time a few fishes tried to go by way of the falls, and were doomed. All along the way, the unlucky ones floated belly up in the quiet eddies or lay stranded on rocks, caught and held there by the force of the current. The gulls saw to it that none went to waste.

When the run was at its height the water boiled with fish. Their backs corrugated the water solidly from bank to bank. Their leaps were not the spectacular midair arcs of the salmon, but they sometimes skimmed clear of the water as their dark backs flashed above the narrow part of the rapids in an unending procession. Unending, but intermittent, that is, as they tended to bunch up into schools and go through each narrow point in a group.

Not far from the ponds which were the herring's goal, the stream went under a road. On the upstream side there was a large pool in which the herring could congregate before making their final effort. Beyond this, a fish ladder had been installed to facilitate the last part of their ascent to the calm waters of the ponds. An old grist mill, with its waterwheel in place and still capable of operating, stood beside the pool. The spot had long been a scenic attraction. There were always onlookers, and crowds on weekends.

Local folk were there to do more than watch. Cape residents were entitled to a barrel of herring if they wanted them, and could come and net them or otherwise catch their quota on certain days of the week. The rights for taking herring commercially—for fertilizer, chicken feed, and herring roe—were sold by the town of Brewster to a company which netted the fish on a large scale in the pool beside the mill. No fish might be taken, however, during certain hours of the day. This policy insured a sufficient number of herring to get through into the ponds to spawn.

Herring roe was highly regarded by roe fanciers, and was the chief blessing of the herring run as far as most Cape Codders were concerned. The meat of the herring is sweet and good tasting, but it contains so many small bones that most people will not bother to cook it.

Not so Freddie Barr. We were just beginning to hear rumors about the herring when, one fine spring day, the phone rang.

"Hello?"

"Been over to see 'em run?"

"Huh?"

"The herring," said Freddie impatiently. "They're running now, you know."

"No, I didn't know."

"Ought to go over and get some. I was over today. Got a barrel."

"What do you do with them?"

"Why, the roe is delicious, and I also corn 'em."

"Corn 'em?"

"Sure. You know—with salt. Didn't you ever corn any herring?"

I searched my memory and could not recall a single instance in which I had corned any herring. I also felt very dubious about the roe, having encountered that of the shad without pleasure.

"No, I never have."

"Well, jeezcrise, get some, and I'll show you how. Be sure to get the ones with roe in 'em."

"How do you know a herring with roe in her? By the twinkle in her eye?"

"You can tell. Tell by the feel. I'll show you."

"Well, I'll see. I want to go over and watch them, though. I may take a few, but—"

"Take a lot. If nothing else you can do like the Indians, put one in with each hill of corn, if you're damn fool enough to plant any corn. Well, I've got to eat supper now. God, I'm worn out—been corning those gawdam herring all day. I'll put down a barrel, time I'm through. 'By."

On the way to the herring run Elizabeth and I debated to what extent we should exercise our herring rights. Unfortunately, Elizabeth was not the rabid fish lover I was, and our daughter took after her mother.

I took along a crab net, and with it we managed to net half a bucketful, which began to seem like a lot of herring right there. They were beautiful little fishes, about a foot long and almost unvarying in their size.

"The man who could breed a boneless herring would have a fortune," I mused as we headed back to the car.

"He'd have an awful floppy fish. By the way, did you feel your herring?"

"Yes. They felt fine."

"I mean for roe."

"I'm playing percentages."

We found quite enough roe in several of them to satisfy

95

our restrained and dubious craving. Elizabeth rolled the roe in bread-crumb batter according to a recipe given her by some Crowell roe lovers. I also pan fried a couple of herring to satisfy my own curiosity. As for Elizabeth, she prepared a supplementary meal which she and Florence planned to eat.

While we were eating, the phone rang.

"Hello?"

"Get any?"

"Yes, a few. We're trying them now."

"Cook some roe?"

"Yes."

"How'd you cook it?"

"Mabel Crowell gave Elizabeth her recipe."

"How is it?"

"Well, it's certainly not like shad roe."

"Oh, no."

"Shad roe tastes like coarse sawdust."

"Yes, well—"

"Herring roe tastes like fine sawdust."

Chuckle. "You must not have done it right. I'll have to fix it for you."

Later on in the evening the phone rang again.

"Hello?"

"Come over tomorrow morning. I'm fixing you a corned-herring breakfast."

I went. Freddie's big white frame house sprawled attractively over the crest of a point which overlooked the bay. The view was remarkable. The setting was unforgettable. The fuel bill was terrible. Freddie growled about it, but loved every square foot of the place, especially the big kitchen.

I found him there in his undershirt and a pair of baggy khaki trousers, looking for all the world like the short-order cook in a waterfront hashhouse. A substantial corporation ballooned the undershirt out over his belt, and his hair fell into his eyes after the manner of an operatic assassin. As a matter of fact, he had a particular talent for looking like a villain most of the time, a fact which, combined with his business success, made it easy for a lot of envious people to consider him one.

"Sit down," he said as I entered. "They're in the oven, and about ready to come out."

The corned herring were delicious, and if one operated properly one did not have to get any bones. Even the roe was worth eating when baked and kept moist inside the fish.

"It's all in knowing how," said Freddie, pleased with his triumph. "Most people don't know how. Why, there are people who have lived here all their life and never corned a herring. Cape Codders are funny anyway. I'm one, but I know. They don't take advantage of half the things that are right under their nose, some of 'em.

"At the same time they don't like to see you get ahead of them. And it burns their guts to see somebody else make a lot of money. If you're not doing so hot they'll be nice and help you out all they can, but if you get more prosperous than they are then they hate you. Well, how about another fish?"

I came home agitating for more herring in the home, and only by demanding to know when I intended to do all the work involved was Elizabeth able to restrain me.

Then, just to make her task harder, the herring closed in on us.

I mean some of those who took the wrong turn. A considerable number strayed up Quivet Creek, the tidal creek which ran through the marsh out on the edge of our property. We were suddenly aware of cars stopping at the culvert from time to time, and of people getting out with nets and buckets, and of fishes gleaming in the nets.

Herring right on our own property! All I had to do was walk across the marsh, or down the edge of the road, and scoop them out.

"I feel like a regular squire," I declared, striding about

97

pouter-pigeon style. "Corbett, member in good standing of the landed gentry, with fishes in his creek!"

Elizabeth had the greatest difficulty in repelling a wholesale herring invasion of her household. Every time I saw strangers taking fish out of *our* stream, and every time I thought about Freddie Barr putting down his barrel of those delicious corned herring, I itched to get at them. Only a lack of time prevented me. My writing was suffering from enough distractions as it was. Not only were there the general delights of outdoor life in the spring to contend with, including our early effort to establish a garden—there was also my basement workbench.

"I've got to stay away from that workbench and get back to my typewriter," I said one day as I came upstairs for lunch. "We certainly can't eat on what I make down there."

"Why not?" said Elizabeth. "Aren't you making a table?"

The table I was making was symbolical of our rapidly enlarging social life. It was an eight-by-four-foot piece of plywood, with legs at the corners, made to go over our rather small dining-room table, so that we could accommodate a larger crowd. The weekend of Easter brought us a visit from my wife's elder brother and his family, and we were convinced they made the effort to come up in uncertain weather because they were sure that by then we would be pining for the sight of a friendly human face. They arrived to find us playing cards with a houseful of people, including four Searses and three Crowells.

It had been a late Saturday night in East Dennis, the second week after Easter. I hated to get out of bed, but after I had taken a look at the clock I began to move faster. Hurrying downstairs I put on a pot of coffee, and busily shaved while it was perking. When I came back into our bedroom, Elizabeth opened one eye.

"What are you doing?" she inquired sleepily.

"I put the coffee on. Better get up, or we'll be late to church."

Her eyes opened wider.

"I didn't know we were going to church this morning."

I squirmed.

"Well, don't you think we ought to? We missed last week—"

"The first time in three weeks! And by the way, how about those other nice little churches we were going to try?"

I sighed. "I'd love to, but we really ought to support our own church and help build it up. After all, as Fred says, if we're going to live here and send Florence to Sunday school here—"

That was the same morning Elizabeth fixed the toaster. When we sat down to breakfast, the bread popped up untoasted. We pushed the handle down again, but the toaster still remained cold and unresponsive. It was perfectly obvious to me that something had burnt out in it, but womanlike, Elizabeth refused to be logical about a mechanical device. She unplugged it and took it to the kitchen.

"What are you doing with that thing?" I demanded.

"Shaking the crumbs out of it."

"Oh, for Pete's sake! What have crumbs got to do with it?"

"I don't know, but they may be causing trouble."

"Listen! Didn't you take any physics in college? Don't you know—"

Elizabeth brought the toaster back and plugged it in again. A minute later I was silently eating a piece of hot toast.

At exactly ten minutes of eleven by the kitchen clock we left for church. ·

"I still don't understand what you did to that toaster," I grumbled. Up ahead, the church clock began to strike eleven. "Hey! What's that clock doing striking the hour now?"

"Well, it says eleven. It's ten minutes fast."

"I don't see why they can't keep it reasonably close to the right time. The town voted $125 to each village at town meet-

99

ing for clock maintenance and repair, and I understand it does so every year."

The service was being run by the church clock. We got in at the end of the first hymn, and everything went along all right until the anthem. The choir was gamely approaching the climax of its selection when the organ went dead. The organist was completely astounded and greatly outraged.

"Drat!" she said, and gave it a spirited kick which it accepted silently. The choir struggled on *a cappella,* and at that moment I finally woke up to what had been going on. The kitchen clock was run by electricity, and so was the organ. We had been having brief intermittent power failures all morning, and Elizabeth had happened to time her toaster fixing beautifully.

"I feel better about the toaster question," I muttered.

"I still think the crumbs had something to do with it," she muttered back.

8

SIGNS OF THE TIMES

It was a beautiful day, and we had been promising ourselves a Saturday jaunt to Provincetown. As we turned onto the highway and headed down-Cape, I looked back at the village, with its gleaming white houses among the fresh spring green of the trees. Asa was right. Even the cemetery wore a cheerful aspect.

"We're lucky," I said. "We've been lucky all around."

As far as that went, nobody had congratulated us more heartily on our good fortune in having landed in East Dennis than did the residents of East Dennis, and nobody applauded more warmly our choice of the bay side over the ocean side of the Cape.

"The South Shore is all right for business, if you're just here to try to make money off the tourists, but for year-around living this is the side to be on, away from all that commercial atmosphere," was the gist of what numerous persons in our village told us, with a delicate but perceptible wrinkling of the nose for the money-grubbing South Shore.

101

Near the corner where we turned onto the highway was a milestone that said, 'Provincetown, 35 mi.' It was a thirty-five-mile stretch that involved driving in every direction except south, as we curved around the bay.

"Well, it's nice to be driving up to Provincetown again—I mean, down," I said, correcting my greenhorn error self-consciously. Since the Cape curves north, down-Cape looks *up* to the map-reading eye. It takes a while to get the concept of driving *down* the Cape to Provincetown—down to the end of the Cape, in other words.

We found Provincetown astir. People were busy everywhere, giving their houses a fresh coat of dazzling white paint, touching up 'Guests' signs, shellacking the treasured weather-beaten countenance of the 'Ye Olde Inne' type of signboard, sweeping out restaurants, beating traditional hooked rugs, placing old dories in picturesque positions, washing shop windows, and generally indicating that ye olde Cape-tip community was not going to be caught napping by the first tourist that hove into sight on Route 6 with his pockets jingling.

"I'll bet the South Shore is getting busy too," I remarked as we drove back. "I expect there are plenty of signs over there by now of the commercial gleam in their eye."

We went on up to the post office before we went home. Perhaps it was because we so seldom came along that particular stretch of the highway—we usually drove through the village, entering or leaving it by way of the road the farthest to the west—or perhaps it was because we had been thinking about all that stir down in Provincetown; at any rate, as we passed one of the roads that led up into our village we noticed for the first time a new sign posted at the corner. "Salt Road Cottages, 500 Feet From Beach," it said in unobtrusive but clear and legible lettering, and a small arrow pointed unmistakably in the direction of our neck.

"Hey, did you see that?" We looked at each other blankly.

We hadn't even realized the cottages were there, but now, come to think of it, down near the beach . . .

As we pulled off the highway, Emma Crowell came bouncing out of the post office and waved a sheaf of letters at us. "Answers to my ad in the Sunday *Times*," she said happily.

"What was she talking about?" Elizabeth wondered.

"I don't know—but maybe that's what Mabel was talking about the other day. She said something about how Jeff and Emma had remodeled their barn into such attractive apartments. I wasn't paying much attention at the time, but . . ."

"Now that you mention it, Sabetha Sears didn't get to last Ladies' Aid meeting."

"What do you mean, now that *I* mention it?"

"What I mean is, you reminded me that somebody said something about how Sabetha was busy 'getting her rooms fixed up.' I thought maybe she was doing some redecorating or something, but . . ."

On the way home from the post office, we were perhaps a little more alert than usual. It may have been that that small sign had been on the big elm in the Struthers' yard for several days, but we had not noticed it before. It said, "Cottage."

"Well! I didn't even know the Struthers had a cottage," said Elizabeth. We craned our necks as we went by and sure enough, there it was, a nice little guest cottage out in the back yard under the trees.

From then on the signs multiplied rapidly—either that or our awareness increased. We learned that So-and-so had a summer job lined up at the Drive-in, and Such-and-such was getting organized to take orders for clambakes. Our social life diminished noticeably—so many people were busy getting "places" ready.

"Well, our village may not have its thumb in the tourist pie," I finally concluded, "but its little finger is certainly busy!"

103

It was the last evening of spring, and a lovely one. Evening was settling in with calm, clear serenity, with a sky that promised a brilliantly starry night. For a moment I turned off my light to enjoy the long view across the marshy meadow to the great bowl of blue sky that came down to meet and outline the low range of dark green hills. After all those years of tiny backyard gardens surrounded by brick walls, of buildings that limited my view of the sky to a small square patch, I still looked at that view with a sense of wonder. I still had a hard time believing that it was right there outside my own window. A mere hundred yards from where I was sitting, birds were circling over a marsh, little fishes were swimming in a creek, small animals were slipping through the tall grass and stirring in the thicket that filled the gully.

Out in the "garden," as we called it when nobody was listening, robins sat on the strings we had crisscrossed futilely over our strawberry patch and pecked at berries through the chicken wire which we had in desperation stretched across our meager crop after the strings failed to impress our feathered foes. When they could not reach the berries through the wire they were very annoyed. Sometimes they had to walk halfway around the wire before they found a place where they could walk in under it. But they never hesitated to do so.

Strawberries are one of the glories of Cape Cod, but not the way we raised them. Not yet, anyway.

The Mosquito Control Squad had not made much impression on their particular enemy. The insects sent wave after wave of their squadrons into our garden to make sure we paid for it not only with sweat and tears. As for woodticks, they were having what would surely go down in tick history as one of their best years.

On the credit side, our weigela bush was receiving visits from a hummingbird, a tough, tiny bit of self-reliance on invisible wings. A flicker hopped jerkily along our back walk, his awkwardness showing that he would have been more at home making his way up the side of a tree, and a handsome bird in a neat Quaker-gray get-up, a catbird, perched on our back porch rail for a moment. I could still enjoy the birds, all except robins. Their personality was beginning to wear a little thin with me. Even when I waved my arms at one, he would merely fly off unconcernedly in a wide circle and soon be back putting the beak to our berries again.

Inside the house, field mice had discovered that the molding around our kitchen floor was made of a material which was more fun to chew up than five-dollar bills.

"If only we could meet up with a nice gentlemanly blacksnake who'd be willing to lie in our strawberry bed all day in return for some of the mice that are mincing up our kitchen molding every night!" I was once moved to remark, casting an accusing eye at Tina, the engaging but inefficient beagle puppy we had by that time taken into the family.

Before I put the chicken wire over the berry patch, her idea of something to do had been to run through the patch and drag the strings after her. She only did this when no robins were sitting on them, however. She was scrupulously careful not to disturb the robins.

The first joke about amateur gardeners was probably uttered during the spring following the ejection of Adam and Eve from the Garden of Eden, and amateur gardeners have been the butt of jokes ever since. Elizabeth and I had both read countless stories and articles satirizing their activities. We had heard dozens of friends recount their first efforts and mistakes as novices. Yet when our turn came we jumped to it with more enthusiasm than planning and made the same old mistakes all over again for ourselves.

The ground behind our garage, between it and the gully beyond which lay the marshes, sloped at a not too gentle angle, but it was sheltered by the hill and the garage and its southern exposure was tilted invitingly toward the sun. The former owner had had a successful garden there. Furthermore, he had raised those chickens, and each time he had tidied up the hen house the soil had benefited.

The one mistake we did not make was to do what inexperienced gardeners, crazed by the sensuous pictures in the seed catalogues, usually do. We did not put in four times the garden we could take care of. We kept ours small and compact.

But we put in tomatoes too early and too close together, and then frantically improvised a stockade of old shingles and scrap lumber and other materials to try to protect them from the raw spring nights. Confronted with that slovenly enclosure, with its plants elbowing one another like a subway crowd, Fred Underhill threw up his hands.

"Do you know how many tomato plants I'd put in a space like that?" he demanded. "Two—and that would be crowding 'em!"

We were proud of our string beans until my wife's Uncle Ken paid us a visit. "You know what the amateur gardener says," he told us. " 'Thank God for beans!' "

We put in radishes, and I suppose we should have been impressed with what we took out. After all, some of them were at least ten times as large as the seed we put in.

On that June night, however, I did not know what the future held for our garden. I only knew it was going to be a fine night for me to resume my struggle with a new interest which living nearer the outdoors had given me.

As a starter, I went and got my copy of the *Old Farmer's Almanac*. Like the tide table, the *Almanac* had become indispensable. Actually it even included the backbone of a tide table—the time full sea would occur at Commonwealth Pier in Boston and the height of the tides.

In my never-ending campaign to install some of my own enthusiasm for Nature's clockwork in my womenfolk, I took the *Almanac* and pencil and paper and figured out a report to give them on the last day of spring. Women, however, are realists and take all such things for granted; at the same time, they are nice about humoring their men, and generally listen indulgently unless there is something more important to be done.

"Well, the sun rose today at 5:03 and set at 8:20, giving us fifteen hours and seventeen minutes of sunshine—"

"It was foggy this morning and didn't burn off until almost noon," Elizabeth reminded me.

"Oh, that's so. I'd forgotten. Well, anyway, that's about as much sunshine as we're likely to see, if we ever should see it, that fifteen hours and seventeen minutes, today being one of several days this week which are all within seconds of the same length and which are the longest days of the year." I licked my pencil and gave my figures a last-minute rechecking. "Twilight will last one minute short of two hours, or until 10:19, it says here, though it never seems to last that long to me. At any rate, at 10:19 complete darkness will have occurred. High tides swept onto our beaches at about 1:00 this morning and 1:30 this afternoon—twenty minutes later than at Boston, anyway—and reached heights of about half a foot more than Boston's, which put them at about twelve feet and ten and a half feet respectively, which is pretty darned high for these parts. Matter of fact, it notes here that right these last few days we've gotten the highest tides of the year."

"We know that," said Florence.

"Quiet. The moon will rise at 10:42 and will south at 2:31, which means it will be due south of us at that time, and I'll bet you never knew *that* before."

"Did you, Daddy?"

"No. The moon is at present in Capricornus—"

"Where's that?"

"That's a constellation. I'll point it out to you sometime."

"When?"

"Sometime after I've located it myself, if I ever do," I said, and continued my report. "Summer will begin at 1:25 A.M. in the morning, but it will do it very quietly so as not to wake

107

any of us up. All times are daylight-saving time, and all figures are questionable, due to the fact that Daddy has had a little trouble mastering the correction tables. All that sun and moon stuff, for instance. The sun rises three minutes sooner here according to my figures than it does in Boston, and sets five minutes earlier, and the moon rises five minutes earlier. Boston gets the edge on sunlight, which just goes to show how the big cities are grabbing everything these days, but at least we've got the jump on the moonlight. Romantic old Cape Cod."

"I suppose all this is leading up to your disappearing for a couple of hours," said Elizabeth.

"It looks like a good night for it," I admitted. "Vega should have risen in the east by now—if she hasn't, the universe has stripped its gears and we might as well not make any more long-range plans. Venus is probably making a fine display in the west right this second. At 10:42 a gibbous moon just two days past the full will rise and put an end to effective star study, but in the twenty-three minutes between complete darkness and moonrise I hope to get straightened out on a few things."

At about 10:25 Elizabeth opened the back door and looked out.

"What on earth do you think you're doing?"

It was a typically silly question such as wives are forever asking husbands. From the way I was holding a book open over my head with one hand while I stared up at it by the light of a flashlight held in the other hand, it was perfectly obvious what I was doing.

"I'm reading," I snapped.

"Well, come in here to do it. The neighbors will think you're crazy."

"I'm trying to read a star chart, and if you'll tell me how else you can get one of these fool things lined up with the stars so's to make heads or tails of it, I'll be glad to follow your instructions." I was having my usual troubles with astronomy.

"All I need is one big eye in the top of my head so I can see the whole sky at once. The trouble comes when I have to turn around to look up and see the other half of the sky. Then everything's upside down. Come here, though—I want to show you the Northern Cross."

By wheedling I was usually able to get my good wife to come out and bestow a patronizing glance on my latest find among the stars, but as I said before it was always just to humor me. Women refuse to get excited about such minor matters as stars which happen to be as big as our whole solar system put together, or a nebula which happens to be the most distant object visible to the unaided eye of man. Early in the game women realized that somebody had to get the meals and tend the house and otherwise keep both feet on the ground, and that men certainly were not going to do it. While I was carrying on about the beauty of Vega, Deneb, and Altair, Elizabeth was glancing away to note the fact that I had not put the clam rakes back under the garage in the chicken room yet.

"Don't forget those rakes."

"Oh, go back inside. You women have no poetry in you. Before you hook a man you're full of mush about how beautiful the moon is, but once you've got him roped and hogtied you're all business."

"I didn't hear any mush from you about how beautiful the moon was going to be tonight. All I heard was about how it would rise at nine or ten something and was five minutes later than in Boston."

"Earlier."

We parted friends, and I went dutifully to put away the clam rakes. What with our first attempt at sea clamming and all, it had been quite a week.

9

SEA-CLAM PIE

When I speak of "clam rakes" I am using the term loosely to designate the rakes which we employed in our search for sea clams, rather than the sort of rake a Cape Cod hardware store man would produce if you asked to see a clam rake.

He would bring out a short-handled rake with six slender curved prongs. All we had were a couple of long-handled gathering-in forks. These were plenty good enough for novices, however, and as a matter of fact one of the best sea clammers we knew did not use a rake at all, but a small, short-handled hoe.

It took us a while to wake up to some of the things that were going on around us. Cape Codders did not sit newcomers down and give them a briefing on all the wonderful produce to be gotten for the getting. We heard about sea clams almost by indirection. We kept hearing little conversations such as:

"Well, Caleb. Go sea clammin' yesterday?"

"Yep. Got a few."

"I got half a bucket. Weren't showing, though."

"No. Wind wrong."

Or we would hear references to "next sea-clamming tide" or "last sea-clamming tide," and to something called "sea-clam pie." When we asked questions about sea clamming we generally got a blank look and vague replies such as, "Have to go out on the Dennis flats. Above Corporation there. Have to get 'em on the lowest tides of the month."

How did one find sea clams? "Well, there's various signs. On good days, that is. Some days they don't show at all. You get to know what to look for."

A sea clam, as nearly as we could gather, was a large clam found far out on the flats only at the lowest tides. It was prized for chowder, for scalloped clams, and for this mysterious "sea-clam pie" we kept hearing about. We were preoccupied with other matters, however, and we had no waders, anyway, so that we could not very well have gone out and ploughed through the icy waters—we at least knew that a person could not walk out onto the flats and go sea clamming without getting his feet wet.

As the weather grew warmer and we grew more and more suspicious that we were missing something, we finally overheard one Cape Codder ask another if he was "goin' sea clammin' termorrer." That was the slip we had been waiting for. As yet we did not even have a tide table and did not know one tide from another, but we at least knew a sea-clamming tide was imminent. We asked a couple of questions here and there about what was the best time to go out next afternoon, and were told, "Oh, about six-thirty."

We had a little trouble finding the right road, due to my insistence on the wrong one, and we arrived at the correct cut through the dunes to the beach at the dusky hour of 6:45. Then we seized our buckets and rakes and hurried toward the cut. We arrived just in time to watch several smug groups pass by, coming up off the beach, lugging sacks and buckets

111

full of clams with bluish shells six to eight inches long. The setting sun had disappeared into a deep cloud bank, darkness was descending rapidly, and it was obvious that the show was over and the crowd was filing out. If we went out now onto those dim and forbidding-looking flats we were going to be very much alone.

Among those making their booty-laden exodus from the flats were the Bassetts, our square-dance instructors of the Newcomers' Party. They stopped and looked at us pityingly.

"Oh, you're too late," they told us, and being Cape Codders were hard put not to appear pleased. It seemed that low tide had occurred at 6:15 that evening, which was the very latest we should have arrived—arrived on the far edge of the outermost sandbars, that is, not on the beach with half an hour's walk ahead of us. Though for that matter, the sea clams had shown early that day, before turn of tide, and not after. Some days it was that way, and some days they showed after, except for some days when they did not show at all.

As things stood now, we were already half an hour late, and would be an hour late by the time we walked out, and with the weather the way it was we would need a flashlight by the time we got out there, and there wouldn't be any sea clams showing anyway. Besides which the tide would be coming in fast by then and we would practically have to run back to keep from getting washed ashore.

We had missed the boat utterly and completely, and we had to stand by and watch buckets of clams waved under our noses while we conceded defeat. Obviously the clamming had been good, and we had missed out because we were greenhorns.

Nothing could have made us more burningly determined to become sea clammers. We had a month to cool off in, of course, but we retained our determination, and when sea-clamming tides rolled around again we were ready for them.

Now as most people know there are two high tides and two low tides each day, and the highest tides of the month are generally followed by the lowest. If a high-course tide occurs at noon, a low-course tide will follow at 6 P.M. That was about the case the second time we went sea-clamming. This time, however, we decided to get out there good and early and to try the Brewster flats.

By then we had come to know a few of the summer people, particularly the Larry Finches. Larry's wife, Mitsy, and their two children stayed down all summer in their cottage a short distance from the beach, and Larry came down from Boston every weekend. Mitsy was small, perky, and energetic, and generally ready to try anything once, so she and her two children joined us and our one child for the expedition.

We set out so early that the tide was still a long way from low and the water was still so deep in a couple of channels between sandbars that it came to our shoulders and we had to carry the children across. Our equipment consisted of rakes, buckets, optimism, and our companion's description of what she had heard the signs were supposed to look like.

"There's a sort of thumbprint-looking mark in the sand with a spit mark beside it, and when you see that you start digging and dig like crazy so the clam won't get away," she said.

"What do you mean, get away?"

"Why, they can push themselves right through the sand with that long whatchamacallit of theirs—they stick it out like a tongue, but I think it's called a foot."

From her description we got a picture of galloping clams which made us see ourselves raking frantically at the sand while our speedy prey burrowed deeper just ahead of our rakes for a clean getaway. The idea, we concluded, was to catch them off guard and flip them up before they had a chance to get going with that long whatchamacallit of theirs.

After about a mile and a half of walking and wading we

113

finally reached the outer bars and began industriously looking for thumbprints and spit marks. The sand stretched smoothly away in all directions, free of any such blemishes. Here and there we came across small holes in the sand; earnest digging brought to light either long, pale, uninteresting-looking worms, or nothing at all. Occasionally a bump in the sand with a trail behind it aroused our curiosity and set us to digging, but we soon learned that we would find only a snail about the size of a golf ball with its green and black shell whorled into a marking like a large eye.

While the kids frolicked up and down the sandbar, we grown-ups stalked back and forth until we were stoop shoul-dered from looking. The shallow water was warm, but the air was cool, and the sun was already low in the sky. Two of the children had not been dressed for more than wading up to the knees, but all three were soaked by now. Our time was grow-ing short. The turn of the tide would be upon us within half an hour, and the sun would soon set, and we knew the minute it set the small fry would be cold. It was time to think about starting that long walk back.

Only three other men were out sea clamming, all of them tiny black figures far off down the flats. One of them gradually came nearer, and we worked toward him to watch him in action and see if we might learn something. He was wearing hip waders—old Cape Codders would not think of getting their feet wet—and he had a fish-net bag tied to his waist. The bag was long and dragged on the sand behind him as he walked. We could see that it had clams in it, but only two or three. He shook his head as he went by.

"Not showing today."

I tried to shake my head just as knowingly.

"Don't seem to be," I agreed.

We noticed that he was doing all his looking out in the water, so we waded out and stared at the rippled sand through the clear water, but the fact that even a man who obviously knew what he was doing was getting such slim pickings gave us very little hope of finding anything.

"Well, here's something, anyway," said Elizabeth. She twisted her rake and brought up a fair-sized crab with one claw caught between the prongs. We had caught lots of crabs that way on our Cape vacations and knew they were good to eat. "Shall we switch to crabs?"

"Might as well make the trip pay," I said, and we soon had a bucketful of crabs. While we were still taking them, Mitsy started back to shore with the children, whose goosepimples had arrived on schedule. They were tiny figures far ahead on the flats near shore when we finally quit crabbing.

We crossed an inlet full of clam shells, and that delayed us, because we had to turn over about thirty of them to convince ourselves they were merely empties—in fact, most of them proved to be only single halves, though in a few cases the ligament still held the top and bottom halves together. They were chalky white in color, too, instead of the dark blue of the live clam; when the shell no longer houses a live clam, the dark-blue "skin" of the shell dries and peels off and leaves the shell white.

We dawdled along, feeling rather disgusted with the whole business of sea clamming. We had tried twice now. Once we had been too late, and this time we had seen nothing that resembled a live clam, except in another sea clammer's sack. We had seen nothing of the signs which were supposed to indicate the presence of a live clam.

"Boy, how I hate to go back and admit we got skunked," I groaned as we trudged along. I was dragging my rake behind me, and every once in a while it would hit something hard in the sand and I would turn back hopefully and dig, but each time it proved to be an empty shell. I even came to recognize the lack of real substance in the bump a mere shell gives a rake.

"For two cents I'd go to the fish market and buy half a dozen," I added.

"Not for two cents, you wouldn't. They cost twenty-five cents apiece."

"Then that's out," I agreed. "I'm not laying out a buck fifty for something other people seem to be able to go out and get for themselves. It wouldn't be any fun to pass off store-bought ones as our own, anyway—but just the same it kills my soul to go back to East Dennis and hear the natives talk about how many they always get and then have them ask us how many we got and watch 'em smirk."

We were just approaching a little channel between two sandbars. As we stepped off into the water from a fairly steep little bank of black, oozy sand, I felt something. My rake bumped something, and there was a difference in that bump. Something solid about it.

"Hey! Wait a minute!" I turned and began to dig. There was weight and form to the object down in that black sand. "I suppose it's only a rock, but— Look!"

Tight-closed, bluish, and nobly proportioned, it was unmistakably a clam. We inspected it eagerly.

"Must be something wrong with it. Guess it's dead," I said, turned pessimist by our previous experiences.

"I can't see the slightest sign of life about it," agreed Elizabeth, and we began to be very dubious about my find. "It must be either sick or dead, to let itself be caught by *us*."

"Well, set it on the bank and let's dig around in here a little. We'll watch it and see if it does anything."

Almost at once Elizabeth found another, and we put it beside the first one. It sat there as lifelessly as the other. Then all at once the first one squirted and stuck out a triangular-shaped foot almost the size of my hand and began to dig itself in. Suddenly the second one squirted, too.

"Look—they're alive! Grab 'em!"

We grabbed them in triumph. Then, watchfully, ready to grab them quickly again if needs be, we checked their digging speed. We found that while they could dig themselves under the sand in perhaps fifteen seconds, they could hardly be said to streak through the sand at the pace Mitsy Finch had indicated.

We went to work in earnest then, looking carefully instead of digging at random, and began to find we could actually see certain signs in the water that indicated the presence of a clam. At first, having two, we agreed that we'd stop if we got four, but when we had four we decided we really ought to try to take home an even half dozen, despite the fact that the tide was beginning to come in fast now.

"Look at that sunset!" said Elizabeth, and I cast a preoccupied eye briefly toward a sensational display which many people, including myself, would have driven miles to see.

"Yeah, it's terrific," I said, and plunged back after clams, and never thought to look again until it was much, much too late.

We had eight clams. It was quickly growing dark, the water was lapping the sandbars around us, and we had damp, cold children in the car waiting for us. It was a terrible predicament to be in. It was like hitting the jackpot on a slot machine and then being hauled away by the cops while you were still holding your hat under the cascade of coins.

"Now I know who first complained about how time and tide wait for no man. It must have been a clammer. We've got to quit and go in and that's all there is to it," I said regretfully. "I can't swim with a bucket of clams around my neck, and that's what we'd have to do if we stayed much longer."

One interesting phenomenon where sea-clamming is concerned is the fact that for every mile a person walks out, he walks five miles coming back. That return trip, especially when your bucket contains a number of heavy clams, seems interminable. The flats stretch out endlessly in front of you, and as you stop to set down your bucket for a moment and rest aching muscles, the distant shore seems no closer than it was when you started. To make things more difficult than

117

usual, we had to cross long stretches in water up to our waist, water which made each step forward twice as hard and made the muscles of our calves ache.

By the time we finally reached the shore we were soaking wet, staggering with fatigue, and miserably cold—but still inclined to swagger as we approached the solitary station wagon with our bucket of clams.

Once home, we telephoned Ruth Asa with great joy and anticipation. She had once promised that if we got clams she would make us the finest sea-clam pie we could ever hope to taste.

"Well, we went sea-clamming!"

"Good! How many did you get?"

"Eight!"

"Eight? Oh, that's not *enough* for a pie. You need at least two dozen for a pie. You have to have a dozen for even a small one."

"Oh."

"You can have a nice chowder with eight, though, or some clam fritters, and next time maybe you'll get more."

The bottom had fallen right out of our clam world. At first, when I reported this news to Elizabeth, we were crushed.

"Well, clean them and get them ready, and then we'll look them over," said Elizabeth finally. "I'm going to get out that recipe book we bought once. I can't believe we can't make a pie big enough for two, or even four, with eight clams."

"All right, you see what you can find out," I said, and went down to the basement sink to open the clams.

Opening and cleaning sea clams is a task best accomplished with a sharp kitchen paring-knife. Scrubbing the shells first gets rid of a good deal of sand that might otherwise end up among the clam meats.

It is not difficult to get one's knife to slide between the halves of a sea clam's shell, as it sometimes is in the case of a quahog or oyster. Unlike the smaller quahog, the sea clam

118

must have its stomach removed. Thoreau, in his travels on the Cape, once found a sea clam, baked it whole, and ate it, to his sorrow.

The true purist washes off the meats in their own juice. This is the most tedious part of the job, as sea clams are very uncooperative on the sand question, and always retain enough minute particles of well-nigh invisible white sand to make the clam-cleaner's life miserable.

When the meats are finally free of sand, they are put through a meat grinder and ground fine. They are always ground, whether they are to be used for pie, chowder, fritters, or in spaghetti sauce. Raw ground sea clam mixed with cream cheese makes an excellent cocktail spread.

When I had finished cleaning the clams and brought them upstairs, Elizabeth was at the kitchen table surrounded by cookbooks.

"Any luck?" I asked.

She looked in my bowl.

"That's not a quart. The only recipe I can find doesn't say how many clams, it just says 'one quart.' "

"Well, let's grind 'em up and then take another look."

When we had ground our eight clams, the results looked pretty respectable.

"I still think that should be enough for a small pie, and I'm going to try it," Elziabeth decided.

First she mixed up and rolled out enough pie dough for top and bottom, and lined a fairly deep pie pan. (Proper sea-clam pie pans vary from deep to very deep.) Then, going by her one recipe and her cook's sixth sense, this is what she did:

First she cut up one quarter-pound of salt pork into little cubes and tried the grease out in a skillet. (To "try out," in this sense, means "to render.") Many good sea-clam pie makers use no salt pork, this being a matter of taste. Where pork is not used the recipe is much simpler.

Then the ground clams are poured into the pie shell, three

119

tablespoons of milk which has been salted and peppered and some clam juice are poured over the clams; a small amount of grated onion is sprinkled over them, they are dotted with butter, the top crust is added, and the pie is ready to go into the oven.

As I said, though, Elizabeth used salt pork. After the cubes were brown and crisp, she removed them from the skillet, put in two medium sized onions, chopped fine, and browned them. Removing the skillet from the fire, she added the sea clams to the pork fat and onions, mixed them thoroughly, and poured the mixture into the pie shell. The top crust was then added and she made several slits in it and poured about a quarter-cup of milk over it. The pie was baked in a moderate (375°) oven. A sea-clam pie should be baked for forty-five minutes to an hour, or until the crust is well browned.

When our eight-clam pie came out of the oven it was a golden brown, juice was bubbling out of the top, and if another clam could have found cooking space in it I would have eaten it—gladly. Gladly, but later, because we both ate heartily and still had half the pie left when we were through. It warmed up very nicely the next day. Sea-clam pie is rich, hearty, and altogether delicious.

Before supper, we had a phone call I enjoyed.

"Hello?"

"Go out?"

"Yes. Did you?"

"No. It wasn't a good tide. Where'd you go?"

"Down toward Brewster. There were only a couple of others out, and they weren't doing much. One fellow got three that I saw."

Chuckle. "You didn't get any, eh?"

"Oh, sure. We got half a bucket. Enough for a small pie. It was tough, though. We really had to hunt around. Well, I've got to go now—got to open our clams while Elizabeth's making the piecrust. 'By!"

120

10

POOR FISH

On Cape Cod there is one sure sign of spring the sight of which stirs the blood of every man who likes to wet a line. It consists of a boat set up on a couple of sawhorses in a barn with a fresh coat of paint on its bottom.

Toward the middle of spring this sight became more and more common, and we began to hear men with a very special gleam in their eyes asking each other, "When are you going to put your boat in the water?"

From that moment on our minister knew that his battle had become more grim. He had a new cross to bear. He no longer had merely Satan to fight—he had to fight the tides, too. It is hard enough to be a fisher of men. The going really gets tough when one has to be a fisher of fishermen. Time after time, during the summer, the tides arranged themselves in such a way that a lot of men found themselves out in boats at 11 A.M. of a Sunday morning instead of in church.

This unhappy condition did not set in before the end of

May at the earliest, but long before then boats were being scraped and painted, and the sound of outboard motors being tuned up sent its sweet music to the ears of anglers and set them to rummaging through their tackle boxes, checking their spoons and eelskin rigs and Cape Cod spinners as they dreamt about the Big One that was going to come along that summer and not get away.

We owned neither boat nor motor, and the only fishing equipment I possessed when we first moved to the Cape was a steel fishing pole my family had given me when I was a boy. I brought it out one night when Asa and Caleb Sears were present and talking about fishing prospects. They were suggesting I ought to get some equipment lined up in case someone happened to ask me to go fishing, so I brought out my one piece of equipment and fitted its limber lengths together in the living room.

"This is the only fishing pole I've got," I said. Caleb cleared his throat in a pained way and Asa rolled up his eyes.

"There are no such things as fishing *poles* on Cape Cod," Asa explained in the fatherly manner Moses would have used in reading off the Ten Commandments to a new and uninstructed member of the devout. "Around here we only have fishing *rods*. A pole is something you run a flag up or string a clothesline from."

"Oh. Well, would this *rod* be any good?" I asked hopefully. What little fishing I had done had generally involved the taking of eight-ounce beauties in a perch pool.

Caleb had throat trouble again, and Asa's mouth puckered as though I had suggested going after moose with a bean shooter.

"Well, for up here you'd better get yourself a regular saltwater rod," said Caleb. "They're shorter and bigger around. That one of yours is a little flexible for these waters."

"Not heavy enough for sea bass, eh?" I asked, and this time they both winced.

122

"*Striped* bass!" corrected Asa. I knew the king of the local fish world was the striper, but coming so recently from New York I happened to be more familiar with the sea bass, which we had cooked a great deal in a special sauce, and it was natural to me, when mentioning bass, to say "sea bass." But to a Cape Codder it was like mistaking a poor relation for a rich aunt.

"I'll never be invited into anybody's boat around here," I told Elizabeth after our guests had gone. "All I have to do is keep talking about catching sea bass with my fishing pole and they won't even let me out on the bay."

Nevertheless, I began to gather together a modest amount of fishing tackle, including the finest salt-water rod and reel and linen line a mail-order house had to sell for nine dollars and fifty cents.

My first expedition on Cape Cod Bay, and my first Sabbath backsliding due to unfortunate timing on the part of the tides, were arranged for simultaneously by Asa Sears. We were participating in a large rummy game at the Ransoms one Friday evening in June, and after the game had finished and before refreshments were served Asa and I wandered outside for a look around.

"Wind and weather permitting, what would you say to Sunday morning?" he purred, casting a speculative eye at the heavens.

Hadley Ransom and his father-in-law immediately decided to inaugurate the season, too, and signed on Fred Underhill as a third hand, so that it quickly became evident that at least two boats were going to be in the water come Sunday morning.

On Saturday we all gathered to put the boats in the water, and after due consultation with tide tables it was agreed that seven o'clock would be an ideal starting time.

Saturday night I set my alarm clock for 6:30 A.M., and woke up promptly at 3, 4, 5:30, and 6:10. There is something very strange about all this, but it is the lot of many fishermen. They will go to sleep night after night putting implicit trust in an alarm clock to wake them up in time to insure prompt arrival at their place of business; their bread-and-butter depends on the clock, yet they never worry for a minute that it won't go off; but let them set it to go fishing and they keep one eye on it all night. That was my trouble. I became obsessed with the notion that the alarm clock which had faithfully awakened me day after day for the past ten years would find itself unequal to the task of rousing me to go fishing.

At any rate, I was up at 6:10. Congratulating myself on my get-up-and-go, I crept downstairs to turn the gas on under the coffee before getting dressed, when what did I see pacing up and down the back yard? Not a robin—the robins were all busy down in the strawberry patch. No, I saw Mr. Asa Sears.

This was my first experience with Fishermen's Standard Time, which runs from half an hour to an hour ahead of ordinary standard time.

Asa had been up since 5 A.M. He had already been down to the creek to look the boat over and check his motor. Everything was in order. Wind and weather were right. It was a glorious day. Asa was too full of a fisherman's illogical excitement and boundless optimism to come in and sit down for a minute.

"Had your breakfast?" he asked.

"No," I said. "I'll hurry."

"Take your time, take your time," he said in a reassuring tone that would have fooled no one. So with Asa stalking back and forth outside I enjoyed a leisurely breakfast of some minute-and-a-half's duration and then came flying out of the house with my rod and tackle, lunch and beer.

We drove briskly down to the creek, chuckling indulgently about Hadley and his crew.

"We'll be out on the bay and trolling for bass before they even shove off," said Asa. "Hadley will never get himself organized by seven o'clock. Why, look at yesterday. 'We'll put my boat in the water at eleven o'clock,' says he. Ah-ha! Yes. By the time he got through running to the hardware store for new rope and having his father-in-law splice it and generally fiddling around, it was three-thirty."

Our pleasure was cut short by the sight of Hadley's station wagon in the parking space. Worse yet, they already had their motor on their boat, and had carried most of their gear down from the car. Hadley waved and urged us on boisterously.

"What kept you?" he demanded. "Don't take all day getting out!"

We waved back rather shortly. Asa and I were both thoroughly annoyed.

"That's Hadley for you," grumbled Asa as we quickly dragged our gear out of the car. "No logic to him at all."

There is an air of urgency about the way fishermen load their equipment into boats at the start of a fishing trip. Each man hurries back and forth, silent and dedicated, with his loads, putting aboard the rods, tackle boxes, cushions, bait boxes, lunch boxes, filthy jackets, wrinkled raincoats, gaffs, bailing cans, and oars. They load the boats with the pressing haste of men fleeing from a land disaster. In this case, there was added the unexpressed competitiveness of two boats.

We were a hopeless second, however, and had to endure Hadley's grand wave as he started their motor and putt-putted away down the creek. They were rounding the west jetty and heading for open water by the time we put our last bits of gear aboard.

"Now, if you can shove us off, we'll get going," said the skipper crisply, and I sprang to my task, scrambling aboard over the bow as my shove took us away from the bank. We swung out into the basin, and Asa pulled on the starting-cord.

Nothing happened.

He pulled it again. And again. And again, while his jowls got as red as a turkey's. I tried to look around with great interest in all other directions, and prayed that I was not about to be

125

involved in one of life's most embarrassing moments. Here was a man with the blood of sea captains in his veins, a man with three hundred years of Cape Cod behind him, who was taking a newcomer out for the first time, and he could not get his five-horsepower outboard motor started. His ancestors had rounded the Horn. How would he feel if he could not even round the jetty?

Then Asa fooled with his motor for a moment. Now that I think of it, knowing a bit more about such things, I think it quite possible that in his exasperation with Hadley and his eagerness to get going he forgot to open the gas line. At any rate, suddenly we were both vastly relieved as the motor took hold. Nothing was said. We began to move down the channel at the three knots per hour specified by the harbormaster, and if we were both being tortured by horrible visions of Hadley snagging a huge bass before we even got out into competition, we did not indicate the fact by so much as a groan.

Of course, the really silly part of all this was that we were planning to troll expensive sea worms through the water in search of a fish which almost never appeared in any quantities in those waters that early in the season, so that all our eagerness was being lavished on a one hundred to one chance. We trolled earnestly up and down for a couple of hours and more without so much as a semblance of a strike, bite, or nibble. All this time a keen eye was kept on the other boat, and Hadley's every naval maneuver was commented on and criticized.

"God knows how they're keeping their lines from getting fouled," marveled Asa, shaking his head with gloomy satisfaction. "Look at the way Hadley makes his turns. You can't turn that short without reeling in, and I'm sure Fred's not reeling in on the turns."

When Hadley made a wider turn, that did not suit Asa, either.

"We'll be lucky if he doesn't cut across our lines, the way he's running that boat. I think I'll make an inshore turn in a minute and try to stay inside of him. If there are any bass around they're likely to be pretty close in by now."

After a while, from eastward, Larry Finch's big dory, powered by a ten-horse motor, came speeding toward us and stopped.

"Any luck?"

"Not a thing."

"I've been down toward Brewster. Nothing there."

Larry trolled up and down in our locality a couple of times and then suddenly gunned his motor and went shooting away to westward.

"Never saw such a fellow for jumping about," said Asa. "Can't stay in one place two minutes. That's why he has to have that big motor. He wants to get places right now. He goes one place and fishes for ten minutes and if nothing happens—zip!—he's off for someplace else. When I come out fishing I come out to relax . . . Look at Hadley now! What say let's reel in and then I'll make a sharp turn and we'll go back on the same course. If he thinks he's going to get on the inside of me this trip he's got another think coming!"

All this plotting and maneuvering took place in a bay which was probably as innocent of striped bass as a bathtub. Fishermen take a lot of convincing, however, and it was quite some time before our two boats stopped alongside each other for a conference.

"Well, I guess the bass haven't moved in yet."

"Looks that way."

"We think we'll troll for mackerel for a while."

"Good idea. We might as well pick up a few mackerel as long as there's no bass."

So out came the mackerel spinners and there was a great deal of industrious changing of rigs and discussion as to whether a quarter-ounce weight was advisable or not. For the next half-hour or so we trolled back and forth at the brisker speed called for when stalking mackerel, but they did not care to come to the party, either. A second conference was held.

"Dad thinks we ought to still-fish," said Hadley, referring to his father-in-law, Mr. Grayson. "What say we anchor off Tautog Rock and eat lunch and then still-fish for tautog?"

It was a quarter to eleven by then, which is definitely lunchtime when one has been sniffing the salt air of Cape Cod Bay since seven o'clock. We searched for and found the big rock, slightly submerged a few hundred yards offshore at that hour, and dropped anchor. The lunch boxes were opened, beer foamed over bottle tops, and bass disappointments were forgotten. A festive air began to prevail.

"Well, I suppose the faithful are beginning to gather about now," said Asa with an unregenerate chuckle, causing Fred Underhill to hang his head as he thought of the empty seat in his pew. "Poor devils, cooped up for an hour with Oswald on a day like this. Why, what could be more fitting from a religious point of view than to be out in the midst of God's wonders of nature the way we are? If these surroundings don't inspire you to a better life, I don't know what will. Hand me that bottle-opener."

To be sure, the weather and our surroundings could hardly have been improved upon. The sun sparkled on the blue waters of the bay, and a gentle breeze tempered its heat to mere pleasant warmth. The great sweep of land that cradles the bay stood out clearly as far as Wellfleet, and across the water we could make out the Pilgrim's Monument and the water tower in Provincetown. We congratulated ourselves on our good fortune, and agreed that the only possible improvement on our situation would have been to have vile weather and catch a boatload of fish.

When the luncheon period was concluded and everybody began to rig up for tautog fishing, Hadley, the sporting man, made us a flashy proposition.

"Well, what say we all bet a quarter apiece on first fish,

biggest fish, and most fish? We'll only be in seventy-five cents apiece at the most, and we can have a little fun."

This plan being agreed upon, Dad Grayson promptly got a nibble, and managed to bring up something that was small and undistinguished looking, but undeniably a fish. This was immediately identified by three different names. Dad Grayson, for example, had done most of his fishing in New Jersey and Long Island waters, where the local names of fish often differ from those used by Cape Cod fishermen.

In his later years Dad had lost his sight, but a lifetime of fishing experience enabled him to identify the fish merely by the feel of it. He could also get himself in and out of a boat very handily, and take more fish than almost anyone he went out with. He was one of the best and canniest fishermen around.

"Well, it didn't take Dad long to insure his bets," said Hadley briskly. "That only leaves my boat two classes to win," he added, and Asa became grimly determined looking in the vicinity of the jowls.

We all began to get nibbles, and presently I managed to get a fish on my line which turned out to be a one-pound tautog. Dad pulled in another small fish, and I was looking good for biggest fish. Asa and Fred could not seem to get a thing. Then Hadley's rod bent, and he began to reel in.

"Anybody lost an old boot? No, by George—I feel life!"

He had hooked a flounder, and a larger one than I liked to see.

"Boy, look at that! Three pounds if it's an ounce! Well, two pounds, anyway," he amended hastily, before we could challenge this outrageous overstatement. "Tops so far in the biggest fish derby, anyway, I guess you'll agree to that. Now all I have to do is get to work on the most fish class."

Asa's face became grimmer and grimmer, but his expression must have scared away the fish—at least from his line. And Fred's. Fred still hadn't got anything.

129

Larry came whizzing back down from westward, signaled that nothing was doing up in that direction, either, and went on in.

"You can bet he'd never do any still-fishing," said Asa. "Couldn't sit still long enough in one spot to do it."

"He's a regular sand flea, that guy," agreed Hadley.

Asa glanced at his watch.

"It's almost one. We ought to think about going in ourselves," he said, but we were all getting just enough nibbles to tantalize us, and somehow the suggestion went by the wayside. We continued to enjoy the breeze and the sunshine and let small fish strip off our bait. Then we went from the small and insignificant to the big, ugly, and worthless, as Hadley pulled in a skate. I countered with a small sand shark, equally as worthless, and we were in a three-way tie for most fish with two apiece for Dad, Hadley, and me. By that time it was definitely getting late, as far as tides were concerned, and it was agreed that if we were going to get up the creek at all we had better call it a day and go in.

"Okay, let's reel in," said Hadley.

"Well," Fred began, "it looks like a three-way tie for the most fish—"

"Hey! I've got something on!" cried Hadley, and pulled in a tiny tomcod. Tomcod are all small, and this one looked like the runt of the litter, but it was still a fish. Asa glared at it as though he suspected it of being in Hadley's pay.

"Saved by the bell," Hadley gloated blithely. "Looks like we kept it all in the family, Dad. You fellows don't have to shower down now—you can wait till we get in."

We hauled up anchors, started our motors, and headed in. Asa was a glum figure at the tiller, if one may dignify the steering handle of an outboard motor by that name.

"I'd like to see that fellow lose just once," he snapped. "Just once! I never saw such luck!"

As a party, our luck had scarcely been spectacular, with

two of the five of us blanked. Now, however, our luck ran out on us completely. In consulting the *Almanac* for data on tides we had merely checked the time, without noting the height. We had not seen the little note which said, "Highest and Lowest Tides of the Year This Month." The channel, when we reached it, was little more than damp sand for about a hundred yards through the lower basin.

"Oh, damn! Now we're in for it!" said Asa.

"Everybody over the side!" ordered Hadley. "Looks like we'll have to get out and wade, and pull the boats through the shallows."

Off came shoes and socks, pants were rolled up, and various pairs of white and hairy legs made their appearance. We decided to concentrate on one boat at a time, so we anchored Hadley's and all hauled on Asa's. His boat was small and light, but by the time we had reached the deeper water of the upper basin with it, it had occurred to all of us that we had been out on the water a long time, and that we were tired. Our pace, as we went back for the other, heavier boat, had slowed to a crawl. As a hardy band of mariners we had our limitations, anyway. Hadley had a stiff knee; Fred had a slight heart condition; Dad could not see; Asa and I were in fair shape, but tiring fast. The closer we got to Hadley's boat, the more it looked like the *Queen Mary*.

By the time we began to pull, push, drag, and haul the boat up the channel, our wives and various children had appeared on the bank, and all the kids came scampering out into the water around·us.

"Did you get lots of fish?"

"Who caught the most? Daddy, did you catch the most?"

"Hey, can we ride in the boat? C'mon, Janie, let's ride in the—"

"Get out of that boat!" Hadley and I shouted at once, with parental fire in our eyes. "If you want to do something, help push!"

The five of us had been nothing much to look at when we started out, wearing our old clothes and a variety of battered caps and hats, but by now we looked positively villainous. What with the heat and our exertions, our shirts either had their tails out or bagged about us loosely. Most of us had at least one pants leg which had become unrolled and gotten soaked. We were sunburned and we were whiskery. Our slope-shouldered weariness and foot-slogging gait made a vivid contrast to the gamboling of the small fry as they frolicked about us. One of the ladies said afterwards that we looked like five shambling apes being deviled by a troop of monkeys.

At one point in our struggles, Dad had somehow ended up at the head of the procession with the bowline over his shoulder as he strained forward, while Hadley was hobbling along at the stern of the boat, pushing.

"Hey!" bellowed Hadley, when he realized what was going on. "Somebody else take the lead rope for a while! For Pete's sake, Dad shouldn't be doing it—that's a case of the blind leading the halt, as far as I'm concerned!" he quipped, and his nothing-sacred jest gave the five of us the only laugh we had all the way up.

Fred began to look done in, so we sent him off to sit on the bank, and hauled the boat the last few yards to deep water. We poled the second boat into the bank alongside the first one and began to drag our gear out of them while our wives made pitying comments on our catch, and the kids swarmed around under our feet. To a man, we were staggering with weariness.

"Daddy, did you catch the most fish?" said Hadley, Jr.

"Of course, son," said Hadley, causing Asa to move as though under the lash as he handed me another load to take to the car.

"Daddy, take us for a ride in the boat! We want to take a ride in the boat!" said Hadley, Jr.

I bared my teeth at the children in a way that caused them to shrink back and huddle together.

"The next squirt that asks to get in a boat gets thrown in the water and held under with an oar!" I warned gently.

Home at last, I was poised for collapse on the davenport when the phone rang. Elizabeth had not come inside yet, so I dragged myself to it.

"Hello?"

"Get any bass?"

While I'm thinking of it, I want to apologize here and now to the local telephone operator for the reply I made to that question.

Chuckle. "I didn't think you did. I was watching you through the glasses. How did you make out still-fishing?"

"I got a tautog, and Hadley got a flounder. Outside of that, nothing but skates, sand sharks, tomcod, and whatever that other little pest was—Dad Grayson called it a 'bacall,' or something like that, Asa said it was a small scup or porgy, and Hadley assured us it was a small pollack."

"Oh, sure, I know the fish. Most likely it was a cunner."

"Did you go out at all?"

"Naw. I don't waste my time when there's no fish. I went blueberrying. Got four quarts."

Such was my first fishing trip on Cape Cod Bay. God only knows why I ever went again!

11

BORN ON THE FOURTH

OF JULY

It was a warm day. For the Cape, it was downright hot. I went downstairs to get a drink of ice water, and stood looking out into the yard.

"By George, I was just thinking—we haven't had a bridge game with the Underhills for weeks," I remarked to Elizabeth, who was writing a letter to some friends saying but of course, we'd be delighted to have them visit us for a few days in August. It was a type of letter which people who live in vacation areas get an opportunity to write quite often, as we had already discovered.

"Well, the Underhills are busy taking care of their apartments. I'm glad they've had such good luck renting them. I talked to Clara this morning and she said they're both rented right through to Labor Day now."

"That's fine. Seems like everybody's preoccupied with summer guests, paying or otherwise, these days."

The sound of gay laughter passing by outside made us glance around.

"Every time I look out the window, girls in shorts are going by on bicycles," I declared. "Not that I'm complaining, you understand."

"It does bother your work, though, to have to keep rushing to the window," Elizabeth nodded sympathetically.

"Work!" I rolled my eyes up in supplication. "What *doesn't* bother my work? What a place this is!"

I glanced at the calendar on the shelf above the kitchen sink.

"Do you realize that we're trembling on the verge of the Season? That for the first time in our lives we're about to see what the Cape is like in season?" On both of our vacation trips, we had come after Labor Day. "I wonder how many people ever moved here without having visited the place except out of season? Incidentally, are we going over to Chatham the night of the Fourth for the fireworks?"

"I think it would be fun, don't you?"

We agreed to go for Florence's sake—I love fireworks—and I went back upstairs to work again. The Season! It was upon us at last. The Season officially begins on the Fourth and ends on Labor Day. Those eight weeks are the true Season. Already, however, everything was pretty well under way. The beach cottages were all occupied. Each day along the shore a goodly crop of beach umbrellas sprang up like gayly colored mushrooms, sailboats dotted the bay, and fishermen trolled their hopeful way up and down offshore.

The store was a busy place from morning to night, and D.H. was baking bread and making ice cream every day. The Ladies' Aid was getting ready for its big summer fair which always brought in a large slice of that organization's revenue. All the Cape Codders who wintered in Florida were long since

135

back and established for the summer and fall. Ernest Everett and Caleb were managing to go fishing whenever wind and weather permitted.

Almost every time I went to the post office now, it seemed as though I passed Colonel Braintree on his bicycle. The colonel, a retired cavalry officer, was pushing eighty, but eighty was not pushing him any. He still bore his slight figure ramrod straight, and swung on and off his bicycle in Army Cavalry style as though it were a fine full-blooded mount. I often felt like saluting as the colonel swept by, but did not want to see him let go of the handle bars. I am sure he would have returned a salute if it killed him.

Hadley Ransom was charming customers in his antique shop and getting set for the first of his auctions. Asa Sears was very busy down at the county courthouse, which had a seasonal rush along with the rest of the Cape. Freddie Barr hardly knew which way to turn, there were so many fruits of the earth to be gathered in just then from the sea, the garden, and the fields. It was all a person could do to get out sea clamming, what with everything else.

"Hello?"

"Well, did you get any?"

"Yes, a few."

"Where'd you go?"

"East."

"Brewster flats?"

"Yes."

"Liz go, too?"

"Yes."

"How many'd she get?"

"Four."

"How many'd you get?"

"Three."

"Anybody else out?"

"Yes, Ernest Everett was out."

"How many'd he get?"

"He filled his bucket. 'Got his quota,' as he'd put it."

"Caleb out, too?"

"No, he didn't get out."

"He didn't? Why didn't he?"

"He went up to the canal surf-casting."

"He did? Get anything?"

"I haven't heard."

"I'll call him up. So you only got three, eh?" Chuckle. "I went out for a little while. Went down off my point, got a bucketful. Well, I got to get back to work. Fellow brought me fifty pounds of fresh tuna and I've been canning the gawdam stuff all day. Ever put up any tuna?"

"No."

"I can do it so it's just like you'd get at the store. Have to show you how some day. Well, you going to open those sea clams now?"

"Yes."

"You really know how to do it?"

"Certainly!"

"What kind of knife do you use?"

"A sharp-pointed kitchen knife."

"H'm, yes, that's all right. Have to show you the knife I use sometime."

"I'd like to see it. You coming to the dance tonight?"

"There a square dance tonight?"

"Yes, at the hall."

"Oh, jeezcrise I'll be too tired to dance tonight. 'By."

The Cape Playhouse in Dennis, one of the most famous of summer theaters, was getting its season under way. Up on the hill, the Drive-In was drawing nicely. Traffic on the highway was brisk, and the license plates mentioned half the states in the union.

On the Fourth of July we drove to Chatham and sat on the edge of the bluff in front of the Coast Guard Station, looking out over the Chatham Bars, to watch the fireworks. We packed a lunch and went early, to get a place, and watched the twilight fade over the beach to the west.

The size of the crowd testified better than anything else to the fact that the Season was definitely under way. Every square foot of space between the street and the edge of the bluff was soon occupied. Down below us on the beach, so distant that the individuals were mere animated dots of red and blue and green and yellow in their bright summer outfits, people pebbled the scene with charming color. It might have been a scene painted by a French impressionist. Not far from us, on the bandstand, a band added the final summer holiday touch.

Darkness fell upon the ocean and the beach with soft, unhurried grandeur while we chatted and speculated on how soon the fireworks would begin. At last the "Star Spangled Banner" got the program off to the proper start, and then the first sky rocket arced up from the beach and burst a short distance above our heads. I never saw fireworks to more splendid advantage, and I was rather annoyed with Florence for being so scared and wishing they would stop banging so loudly.

The breeze was onshore, which was of course not too desirable, since it caused the flares to drift away over our heads and float down on the town.

"That looks dangerous," said Elizabeth. Typical feminine remark.

"Don't be silly. Those are all burnt out long before they hit the ground," I told her, with masculine assurance that the technicians who were shooting off the fireworks knew exactly what they were doing. Little did I know then that the next day my wife would be cornering me with, "So, I was silly, was I? Well, Mabel Crowell says that while the fireworks were going on, people were beating out small fires all over town!"

The seasonal upsurge in the Cape's population completely impressed itself on us when we went back to our car after the fireworks and tried to drive away along the narrow and crooked streets of Chatham. The streets were choked with cars and crowds of people. It took us half an hour to go a few blocks.

"Well, it was worth it," I declared, when at last we were moving across-Cape, on our way home. "The fireworks were wonderful. Best I've ever seen."

"Too loud," said Florence.

"Here we go to all this trouble to bring you, and then you complain," I grumbled.

"Ha!" said Elizabeth, whose thoughts had turned to other matters. She was thinking about that letter she had written the other day. "You think you've seen some fireworks, do you?" she inquired, and began to tick off the friends and relatives who had already notified us that we might expect a visit from them during the next two months or so. "That's what *I* call fireworks!"

12

I GOT THREE GIMME FOUR

My wife's brother, John, and sister-in-law, Helen, and their two children lived inland, far from the water. They had made a long trek to come visit us and spend their vacation by the seashore. Consequently they were mystified by our attitude toward the beach.

"I never heard of anything so crazy," said John. "You go to all the trouble of moving up here to live near the water, and then you seldom take a dip, and almost never sit on the beach."

"I never did care much for lolling around on the beach," I admitted, "and swimming gets you all wet."

"Then why—?"

"That stuff is for summer visitors like you," I said. "Oh, I enjoy an occasional swim very much, but there's too much else we want to do, plus all the things we *have* to do. Remember, we're carrying on our everyday life here, just like you do at home. We're not here on vacation. If I went to the beach for the day every time visiting firemen turned up, we'd starve to death. We may anyway, but I'll feel better if I at least go through the motions of trying to make a living. Besides, when I go to the beach I like to be doing something, like sea clamming."

The monthly high and low tides had rolled around again, and we were anxious to introduce our visitors to the fine old native sport. Spurred on by the ninth-inning success of our first outing, and stung by the comparatively poor showing of our second, we had visions of really loading up this time. We planned to go out on the flats that afternoon.

About three o'clock I left the writing I should have continued to do and got together the rakes and buckets for our outing. With three children and four adults going, there were not enough rakes to go around, but I hoped the children would be satisfied mostly to play in the sand or paddle in the water. Actually, of course, this was no way to go sea clamming, anyway. In sea clamming, two's company, and three gets pretty close to being a crowd.

"I hope the kids won't get too tired," I told Elizabeth, who had come in from the garden to get ready.

"Oh, I don't think they will. With five of them, they should keep each other amused."

"*Five* of them?"

"Yes. Mitsy Finch wants to go along again, so there'll be her two, also."

Before I had had time to get used to the notion of going sea clamming in a party of two men, three women, and five children, our family came back from the beach, followed by Hadley and his family. He honked gayly as they went on down the road.

"They'll be right back," said John, his face wreathed in an open, friendly smile. "We were telling them about how we were going sea clamming, and they decided to come along."

"Yes, and what's the name of those other people we were talking to?" asked Helen. "The ones with the three children?"

141

By the time we assembled on the beach we numbered four men and five women and twelve children—our own brood having brought along a couple of friends. I doubt if such a sea clamming aggregation has been seen on Cape Cod's shores before or since. Some of us went on ahead, and some of the women and children lagged along behind, until we were spread out over a good quarter of a mile. The Israelites crossing the Red Sea must have looked a good deal the way we did.

Then, with twenty-one persons having expended forty-two miles' worth of walking energy on the hard sands, we still could not seem to find any clams.

"Where is this place where you found all those clams last time?" demanded Mitsy.

"Well, it must be right on ahead here a little way," I replied uncertainly. "After our last time out I was thinking back, and I was sure I could walk right to it this time . . ."

To find an exact spot out on the flats, where one sandbar has a tendency to look precisely like another, takes far closer observation than we had lavished upon our bonanza spot. It took us quite a while to learn that we were not dealing with street corners or highway intersections. We never did locate our special place.

Altogether we had just a handful of rakes and a few buckets between the lot of us, and of course every child wanted a rake and a bucket of his own. This being impossible, each had to be given a chance to dig for a moment with the same rake, while all the others watched hawk eyed and squawked about how everybody else got a longer turn. The complaint department was kept busy the whole time.

"How stupid of me not to bring my stopwatch," I remarked to Elizabeth. "If we have to deal with gangs of kids like this, there's certain equipment I'm going to get—a stopwatch for measuring turns, a set of jeweler's scales for dividing up candy evenly, and vernier calipers and a mitre-box for

142

measuring off and cutting pieces of cake. They're all things every smart parent should have."

"Don't let it get you down," said Elizabeth. "At least if there are any clams around, a herd like this tramping up and down ought to make them show."

There was something to this, of course. When a clam is disturbed he squirts and thus betrays his location. Sea clammers may often be seen stamping up and down the length of a sandbar in an effort to make the clams "show," and old-timers tell of how they used to drive a team of horses out onto the flats and walk along behind digging up the clams that squirted.

No such plenty came our way, however, despite all the big and little feet that trampled the sand that afternoon. The tide turned, the day waned, the children and some of their elders began to complain about being cold, and we gave it up.

That evening Elizabeth and Helen had occasion to go down to D.H.'s for bread. They came back with news.

"Caleb Sears was there and I heard him say something about sea clamming in the morning," Elizabeth reported. "I asked some questions, and it seems that we weren't even out on the right tide. The *morning* tides are the good ones now. This time of year, they change over."

In true Cape Cod style, of course, nobody had told us this, and I had not had sense enough to deduce it from the *Almanac's* tide table.

"Well, that's interesting. I'll file that away for future reference. I imagine John and Helen have had enough sea clamming to last them forever," I said, but I had underestimated them. They did not intend to be outwitted by a mere clam.

"You mean to tell me you're ready to get up at an ungodly hour in the morning and walk all the way back out there?" I asked, and saw that they were.

"I'll stay home and take care of the kids, and incidentally sleep a little later," said Elizabeth. "Do you think you can do

143

it all right, though, Scott? Remember, you're helping Hadley at his auction tomorrow, too."

"Don't worry about me," I said confidently.

We were up before there was a crack of light, and had to use our headlights on the road down to the point. Dawn was just breaking as we started down the hill to the beach, and the vast flats stretched away below us in eerie desolation into the murk. We were barefoot and wearing the same shorts we had worn the afternoon before. The chill and forbidding look of the flats made our clothes appear pitifully inadequate. A raccoon coat and fur-lined boots seemed more in order. As an inlander it was hard for me to get used to the fact that the flats were seldom as cold as they looked. Nothing seemed less inviting than to go out into the gloom and cross all that cold sand and wade through those steel-gray pools of frigid-looking water in our bare feet, but appearances were deceiving.

Both sand and water were no more than cool, and for all its gloom the atmosphere of the flats was very pleasant once one was a part of it. Then the light began to strengthen in the east and gloom gave way to new-day cheerfulness. A little morning breeze cleansed the air like a good housewife sweeping off her front stoop, and sea birds began to bustle about and chatter to one another. We could see, too, that we had a real sea-clamming tide this time, one that was far lower than the afternoon before.

Once on the outer bars, John and I pressed forward eagerly, anxious to get at it. Helen lingered behind, dawdling along the edge of the bar as it ran back toward shore. John stopped once and looked back, but I urged him on.

"Let her be. Good for her to fool around alone. You and I can concentrate on finding the clams, and let her have her fun," I said indulgently. Helen was a honey-haired little Southerner who had not seen much of the seashore, and needed a chance to get acquainted with it.

"Well, now, let's find some of those thumbprints and spit marks," said John, as we put our buckets down and began prowling along the edges of the bar.

"To hell with spit marks, let's find a likely looking spot and start digging around," I said. "If only I could locate that place where we got 'em last time . . . This looks like pretty much the same sort of sand here—black and oozy. Let's give it a try."

We dug and probed and prodded around for a few minutes with no success. I glanced back at my sister-in-law. She was walking around with her rake behind her back, looking down at the sand.

"Helen's no fool. She's not wasting her time digging for any stupid clams," I remarked. It was beginning to look like a repetition of the same old story—no sea clams!

We were walking back and forth dragging our rakes through the sand, hoping to hit something—that being one way to find sea clams, if a person doesn't mind breaking his back—when we heard Helen calling. She waved to us and we waved back. She waved again, more insistently. We could not hear what she was calling, but then she stooped down and picked up something large in each hand.

"What's she holding up those rocks for?" asked John.

"Judas! Those aren't rocks—those are sea clams!" I cupped my hands and yelled, "How many have you got?"

"Three-e-e!"

John and I looked at each other sideways.

"Looks like we'd better go take a lesson."

Man and boy I had lived on the Cape pretty close to six months then, but it took a little Southern gal to show me how to really find sea clams. While we had been using our backs, Helen had been using her eyes and her head.

"I don't know how it is on the other days, maybe other days you see spit marks, but today it's *tufts*," she explained.

"Tufts?"

145

"Yes. They seem to push up the sand into a little mound, and then as the tide drops the sand falls away on the sides of the mound and leaves a little tuft of sand sticking up." She hunted around, and her sharp eyes spotted a sample tuft. "Here. See this one? That's a clam," she said with complete confidence, and proved it.

At last John and I began to use our eyes, too, and we began to discover all sorts of signs—everything but spit marks. Pretty soon we got into such a bank of clams that we did not even need signs. We found them on the bank and on the water's edge and out in the water. We even found them sticking out of the sand upside down or lying in shallow pools completely exposed. I found at least ten with my feet as I walked through the soft sand out in the water, and more than once I put my rake aside and picked up one with each hand while keeping my foot on a third. We had the sort of abundance old-timers tell about, and the only fly in the ointment was that every one of those heavy sea clams had to be carried in on our backs. Finding sea clams is like eating peanuts, though—"just one more." Our haul overflowed our buckets and a pile grew on the sand. If Helen had not worn a short terrycloth robe that morning, I don't know what we would have done. It held a lot of clams.

The trip back was a sort of joyful agony. The backache one gets from a good catch is the easiest to bear.

"Wait'll Elizabeth sees these!" I gloated as we got out of the car and carried our haul up onto the back porch. But her reaction was not quite as expected. She took one look and gasped.

"Pick them up and get them in out of sight. Mabel Crowell came by a few minutes ago and I told her where you were. She happened to say something about the shellfish warden, and one thing led to another, and I found out we're supposed to have a permit to go sea clamming. And not only that, but

146

the limit in summer is half a bushel weekly per family—and look at you!"

Again we had run into the Cape Cod tendency not to volunteer information. Nobody had ever said a word to us about shellfishing permits. We hastily gathered up our clams and ushered them inside.

"I wonder what the warden would have said yesterday if he'd come along and found twenty-one of us sea clamming without one permit among the lot of us?" I mused. "That's about two hundred bucks worth of fines right there, I expect. Then add another fifty for the three of us exceeding our quota today while clamming without a permit—"

"Yes, and that's not all."

"What? Is there more?"

"Yes. Where we went is on the Brewster side of the line!"

It was eight o'clock by the time we got home from clamming. I was due at Hadley Ransom's auction at nine sharp. It was all I could do to eat some breakfast, shave and wash up, show John how to open and clean the sea clams, and get over to Hadley's half an hour late.

The red auction flag was hanging out on a post by the driveway, and the tent was up and ready, by the time I arrived. It seems as if wherever one finds a resort area one finds an auction, and Cape Cod is no exception. Auctions are a regular part of the summer scene, and Hadley was our leading auctioneer. He was always looking for people to help at his auctions, and had reminded me of what he now referred to as my "solemn promise" to lend a hand. I decided it was an experience I should not miss.

The auction took place under a large tent outside Hadley's barn. It drew summer people from all over the Cape, but not many of the local folk missed the auctions, either. Hadley would have starved on the money the Cape Codders spent, however. They came and watched everything with their special brand of poker-faced amusement, but they seldom bid very high on anything. They could not compete with summer visitors who took a vacation attitude toward their pocketbooks.

The largest number of items in that day's sale came from the homes of a couple of old families who had decided to clear out their attics. There were also various pieces of furniture Hadley had picked up here and there on the Cape, and assorted bric-a-brac which had come his way in his role as an antiques dealer.

Under the influence of Hadley's magic prose all these things took on considerable significance as Americana. As an auctioneer, Hadley was in his element. In his checked sports coat which framed a green plaid vest festooned with a gold watch chain attached to a hunting-case watch which even went so far as to strike the hours, he was every inch a showman. His knowledge of Early American furniture, art objects, and curios was voluminous and impressive, and he was consulted by some of his well-heeled customers with all the deference and acceptance with which they would consult the *Encyclopedia Britannica*. The assurance with which Hadley replied to their questions approached the pontifical.

He was constantly engaged in conversation, and his other assistants were busy with last-minute arrangements, so that it was not until just before the bell was rung to announce that the auction was about to begin that I was finally given a bare outline of my duties by Hadley's chief assistant. Mainly, my job was to hold up the various objects to be sold, first handing each to Hadley so that he could read off the number of the item for the bookkeepers and see what it was. I was also to watch for bids on the left side, where he might miss them because of the wide angle.

The bell rang, and I began to learn about auctions. From out of the barn a steady stream of lustreware, gaudy ironware, milk glass, Sandwich glass, iron-frog doorstops, carved wooden bears, Boston rockers, Kate Greenaway figurines, Tiffany vases, copper teakettles, handblown glass bottles, mirrors, plates, and various other strange and wonderful objects began to flow through our collective hands while Hadley described them expertly, threw in quick little jokes, and chanted, "I have two, gimme three, three, gimme four—three-fifty?—that's a losing bid—three-fifty gimme four, I have four—see, what did I tell you, lady?—four, gimme five, four, gimme five—This is ridiculous! Do you realize what we're selling here? A jug like this, if it were perfect, would sell for a hundred and fifty dollars anywhere! Partridge lists it in his book at two hundred! Four, gimme five, four, gimme five; I've got five—six—new fire broke out!—six, gimme seven, six, gimme seven. Six going *once,* six going *twice,* six going THIRD AND LAST TIME AND . . . All done? SOLD six dollars to Mrs. W.! Put it back in the barn, boys," and if another item was not immediately thrust into his hands Hadley would practically stretch his neck into the barn to see why everybody was leaving him standing there with nothing to do.

Since Hadley, being Hadley, had never bothered to give me any advance inkling as to exactly what I was supposed to be doing, I had to fall in step as best I could after the parade had started. I held up objects for the crowd to admire, hoisted up the rear end of pieces of furniture, and watched for bids on the left-hand side. What nobody had told me, however, was that there were special ways to hold up things when they were being offered for sale. A plate, for example, I would hold up with the same grip I would use on the brim of a straw hat.

"Nobody is buying fingers today, Scott," Hadley would inform me in stentorian tones. "Hold that by your fingertips, man!"

The numbers on items sometimes eluded me, too, and I had a considerable knack for turning them into awkward positions as I searched.

"Hold it up intelligently!" Hadley bellowed as I held up a copper teapot upside down. "Nobody wants to buy a teapot that looks like that."

"I'll teach you to look for bright young men," I retorted in an undertone.

Catching the bids was not as easy as it seems when one is sitting in the audience. Some woman would wave to a friend, catching my eye as she did so, and in that same split second someone else would make a real bid.

"Scott!" Hadley would yell, leaning over and breathing fire down my neck from his perch. "Are you watching?"

Since the help is catch-as-catch-can, I suppose there is also One At Every Auction like the teenager who was a member of the staff that day. I think young Albert must have fallen in with the Boy Scouts and gotten pumped full of that propaganda of theirs about being honest, trustworthy, and brave.

At any rate, he would often remark in a clear, carrying voice as he handed a cup or vase or pitcher to Hadley, "It's got a crack in it," or, "There's a little chip out of its side. See? Right there." Hadley never tried to pawn off anything as perfect that had a flaw in it, but sometimes what Albert thought was a crack would turn out not to be a crack, but by then it might as well have been.

Hadley would look down and pass a lambent glance through Albert's innards like a flaming sword, all without making the slightest impression on that pure young man. Two minutes later, as we held up a Boston rocker, he would be carefully pointing out the fact that one of the rungs was loose. Finally Hadley stopped and leaned down.

"Albert. Whose side are you on?" he inquired gently, but Albert only smiled as the innuendo bounced harmlessly off his hard young skull.

Many of the objects in the auction were beautiful things, but some of them were really frightful. Part of Hadley's stock in trade, however, was an ability to hold up almost anything

150

for sale and keep a straight face. It was just as well, for it was a never-failing source of wonder to me to discover that there was nothing in this world so unattractive that someone would not bid on it.

"Now, here we have a lustre vase with Nottingham finish," announced Hadley, holding up a bulbous object with sand stuck in the lustre so that the finish of most of its surface resembled coarse sandpaper. It looked like a very handy gadget to strike kitchen matches on, but as a vase it would have been unnecessarily grotesque as a target in a shooting gallery. Nevertheless, it fetched a good price after brisk bidding.

No artistic mistake of our forefathers, and they made plenty, seemed too bad to be labeled "quaint" and sold for some surprising sum. A very worn large rug which must have been a dismal eyesore to begin with, and for which Hadley had refused to pay $25 when it was offered to him, brought $82.50 at auction as two women got to bidding against each other.

At one point I was holding up an ironstone pot on which the bidding had started, and I caught a hand up near the back of the tent.

"There!" I cried, pointing it out to Hadley, and then took another look as I realized who had been on the other end of that hand.

Hadley chortled. "I have four dollars from Mrs. Corbett! I have five, gimme six; five, gimme six; I have six, gimme seven —seven, Mrs. Corbett? Hold it up high, Scott!"

"I'm holding it high enough!" I snapped.

"Sold for seven dollars! Take it down to the lady, will you?"

Amid the laughter of my friends and neighbors I delivered my wife's purchase.

"Don't be silly. It's just the thing for Louise's birthday," she declared.

Around one o'clock we took a short break. The weather was threatening.

"Not a very nice day," I commented to Hadley.

"What do you mean? It's perfect!" he declared, rubbing his hands together. "Keeps 'em off the beach!"

The pace of the auction seemed fast and furious to me, but it was not nearly fast enough to suit Hadley, and we went on until six o'clock before we stopped. By then the crowd had thinned out considerably and so had I. It was all I could do to stagger home. The past twenty-four hours had been a busy little time for me, with two trips out onto the flats and back totaling eight miles or so, and then eight hours of auction. I had been on my feet almost constantly for the past thirteen hours. The davenport received my aching bones while the ladies got supper on the table.

"Now do you see why we don't get to the beach too often?" I asked John.

I was just getting comfortable when the phone rang.

"It's Freddie," Elizabeth reported.

"Tell him we got some."

She told him. After a while the phone rang again. Elizabeth answered, and came in grinning.

"That's Mabel. There's a square dance down in Eastham tonight. What do you say?"

I started to yell, "Hell, no!" as she expected me to, but then I hesitated. Supper always did wonders for me, and I did enjoy those square dances of Jay Schofield's down in Eastham, and John and Helen didn't get many chances to go to them . . .

"Tell her we'll call back right after supper," I said, and lay back to rest up while I could.

13

THE SCROD MAKES PORT

It took eyes used to picking out objects on the water. Mine had to be instructed where to look. The afternoon sky was a light hazy gray, the bay was a smooth sheet of gray-green glass, and the tiny speck of gray on the horizon was only the slightest shade darker than the sky behind it. It looked translucent and of no more substance than a cloud—but it was square.

"Can't be a freighter," said Larry Finch. "A freighter heading down the coast toward the canal would be side-to, and even head-on it wouldn't look like that, anyway."

About then we ran through some weed and both fouled our hooks and had to reel in to clean them off. When we looked at the gray square again it seemed more like a box than ever. We could make out a speck in front of it and a shadowy trail behind it.

"I'll bet Freddie Barr's put his glasses on that craft by now," said Larry, and we both glanced up at Freddie's big house on the point above us, but I shook my head.

"I don't think Freddie's home. He had some kind of meeting to go to. Something about the new harbor we're supposed to get."

"The harbor! Of course! What's the matter with us?" Larry jerked his head toward the gray square in the distance. "That's the dredger from Boston—coming here!"

"What else?" I agreed. For the past two weeks, people in our village had been telling each other they heard the dredger was due to arrive any day now.

I eyed the gray square with new concern. Change was coming our way, moving in on our village, and nothing could stop it now. Change. Living in an unspoiled little Cape Cod village, we had soon learned to fear change, especially when it came along masquerading as "progress" and "improvement."

We puttered slowly westward in Larry's big dory, from Tautog Rock toward Corporation Beach, trolling for striped bass which seemed to have urgent business elsewhere on that lazy midsummer day. The sea train came slowly eastward, stretching out a little more. It enlarged as a flower opens: when we were not looking at it. Now we could see the big tug that was heading the parade, pulling everything else, and now we could see that the strange menagerie strung out behind it were a crane, a couple of barges, a dredger, a houseboat, and a small tug.

The whole procession could still have been no more than modern engineering's answer to the *Flying Dutchman,* a mere phantom tugboat towing the skeleton of a crane and the ghost of a houseboat. Everything was as two-dimensional as a child's painting, only in neutral tones, washed gray by the atmosphere. The string of floating oddities were like a cardboard cut-out propped up against a tilted background of flat gray sea—and not propped up any too well, because the angle of the tug's stack and the tall vertical pipes on the dredger's stern and the crane's great skinny arm, a black pencil-line against the sky now, gave the whole cut-out the appearance of being tipped away from us at an impossible angle. For the whole thing to have toppled the rest of the way over and floated away flat on the water, flat as a playing card, would only have been a triumph of logic.

But logic does not triumph on the sea. On land things sometimes shimmer in the distance and appear to be something they are not, but by peering long enough and hard enough one can generally figure out the trick and shatter the illusion. Not so on the water. I could stare and stare at that slow-moving illusion, but I could not stare it down. The sea train refused to take on the slightest semblance of a third dimension, and the sea refused to level back into place. I stared at impossibility, and impossibility remained.

Then Larry thought he had a touch, and for a while our thoughts were no farther away than our seaworm-baited hooks and what might be nosing around them. When I looked again the sea train was abreast of us, half a mile out, and solid reality. Two dimensions had become three. Gray had brightened into strong red and white.

"For God's sake, how are they going to jam all that stuff into our creek?"

"Well, of course the big tug will cast off and go back. The little tug will take the stuff in."

"Even so, it's going to be hanging over the banks."

"We'll see. They've had enough guys running around here with blueprints lately, sticking up their little flags and painting numbers on the jetty capstones—they ought to know what they're doing by now."

"Hey, look. Here comes Ernest Everett. I'll bet you he'll be one of our most faithful beachfront superintendents."

We watched Ernest Everett run his boat down past us, taking in his handline as he came. Ernest Everett was a Cape Codder born and bred, as Cape-rooted as a cranberry. The pale blue eyes laced into his leathery face with a deep crow's-foot tangle had watched sixty years of struggle between tide,

155

sand, and wind, and his knowledge of Sesuit Creek was that of a boyhood friend with whom he had never lost touch. His mouth had drawn together into its characteristic pucker at the sight of the paper planners.

"They're going to spend the taxpayers' money moving a lot of sand around," he declared, "and when they get through, a couple of good nor'easters will move it right back again for nothin'."

Our inlet was guarded by two jetties, the old east jetty on our neck and the newer west jetty that came out from the other neck. Immediately inside the jetties was one large basin, and up the channel a few hundred yards was a second, smaller basin, where most of the boats were kept, even a good many of the sailboats. It was more protected, and its center was deeper.

Once the inlet had been deep enough and wide enough to permit the building of clipper ships over against the high west bank, a quarter of a mile to the west of the present basins. There, from the famous Shiverick shipyards, had come such proud clipper ships as the *Belle of the West, Webfoot, Kit Carson, Ellen Sears,* and *Christopher Hall,* all built a hundred years ago.

The great storm of 1898 reorganized things according to its own ideas. Since then the whole layout of the inlet had changed radically once or twice, as when the building of the new west jetty altered the entire course of the channel. In recent years sand had been allowed to do its work unchallenged, and the channel was badly choked. The small upper basin had water enough, but the lower basin had filled in so badly that at low tide half of it was out of water entirely and a child could wade the channel there without getting wet much above the ankles.

By the time the sea train neared the entrance to the creek —or the channel into "Sesuit Harbor," as the newspaper articles more impressively referred to it—it was well past us, but
156

seemed to grow larger instead of smaller as it squared off to go in.

For one thing, the sky was clearing, and the sun was sparkling on the water there now though we were still shaded by a haze of clouds. The houseboat and dredger both looked bulky and high out of the water, and the arm of the crane was silhouetted against open sky, far above houses and trees and dunes, challenging even the hill the village sat on.

"Get out the shoe horn," I said. "Here we go!"

The big tug cast off and left the other vessels to the smaller tug. Freed of its ungainly charges, the big one seemed to shoot away and in no time at all was a puff of smoke on the horizon. Nothing daunted, the little tug began its perilous ascent of Sesuit Creek. With the gawky crane peering over its shoulder like an anxious giraffe, it moved ahead and drew all that massive equipment into the narrow channel.

It drew us, too, just as surely as though a line thrown from the last barge had been secured to our bow cleat. Like Ernest Everett, we did not want to miss anything. As long as it was going to cost him and the rest of us taxpayers more than a hundred thousand dollars, we were at least going to enjoy the spectacle. A water circus had come to town, and we had a season pass.

Nobody knows what preserved our juvenile population from marine disaster. Every boy who had a boat with an outboard motor or could lay his hands on one was buzzing around the front end of the procession all the way. The tug came up the channel like a workhorse pestered by a cloud of gnats.

As for the village, all East Dennis was alerted. Dozens of people were already on the bank at the basin, and more cars were coming all the time down the two roads that right-angled together at the parking place. How everybody knew so soon that the dredger had appeared was not hard to say. At least three village elders who lived at the top of the hill overlooking the inlet had undoubtedly studied the flotilla when it first

157

hove into view—studied it through the telescopes that were never far from their hands. One of them even had his mounted in his barn, trained on the creek, ready to check catches during the fishing season. They had doubtlessly each telephoned one or two cronies, hurriedly, before jumping into their ancient cars. That meant the telephone operators knew, and so on.

Ernest Everett and Caleb and Mr. Ezra Newton and others who had been in and around the creek since they were boys exchanged that peculiarly blank look of the Cape Codder—a look which speaks volumes by its very lack of expression—as they watched how the houseboat was tethered to the south bank, in close. They did not have to say to each other what Larry said to me as we came up the channel and picked our way into the crowded basin: "If they don't slacken off on that houseboat, they're going to be living on one hell of a slant."

The names of the new arrivals stood out in white block letters on their sides. The tug was *Snapper*. The dredger was *Scrod*. The houseboat was *No. 4*. A television aerial protruding from the top of *No. 4* testified to its truly homelike qualities, and a man was already planing the handrails of the gangplank which had been put over the side to the bank.

Among the rapidly growing crowd, all the men were on hand who were free to come, particularly the older, retired men. From where we stood, after we had moored Larry's boat up the creek and picked our way back across the marsh, Cold Storage Road was screened from us by the brush which grew high along its edges. As we paused beside the houseboat, I saw a head with a white cap on it come floating down the hill above the bushes, serene and mustachioed. Colonel Braintree was approaching on his bicycle.

A different type of mount was favored by Caleb Sears. He was standing beside his faithful green jeep. The usual cigar was thrust forward under the shelter of the long green visor of his fishing cap as he sized up *No. 4*.

158

"I see Colonel Braintree is reporting for duty," I remarked. "I'm surprised it took him so long."

"Hell, he's already been home once," said Caleb. "Went back for his camera."

Larry and I climbed into Elmira the Heap, to go round up our wives and bring them back for a look. Elmira was the most gangrenous station wagon on the Cape. Its wooden body, attacked by the salt air, was rotting away by inches. It was necessary to drive rather fast when traveling downwind in order to keep partially ahead of the exhaust fumes. But it ran. It wheezed now to the top of the hill, where we paused to look back at the red-and-white touches which had been added to our pleasant greens and blues and sandy tans. The crowd was increasing by the minute, with summer clothes adding further bright spots of color. The green jeep was creeping around from one parking space to the other, and Colonel Braintree was coming back up the road on his bicycle. (We later learned he had forgotten to load his camera.)

Larry cast a glum gaze over the scene and muttered dire predictions. He had a gift for looking steadfastly on the dark side of things, but still, in this case he might be justified in doing so. Six feet of water at mean low, a chance to get in and out at any time of day or night without thinking of tides— it was a wonderful prospect, but what else would it mean for our village? A good harbor meant change, and change had to be watched, or it could spoil the very things we prized most.

The store had not seen such a quiet afternoon since the Season began. Only two people were eating D.H.'s ice cream in the soda fountain side of the place, and I was the only one in the groceries side.

"Well, it's a good thing for business a dredger doesn't move into the harbor every day," I said to D.H. "I never saw anything like it. Just about everybody you can think of is down there watching."

159

"I'm going to get down for a look myself pretty soon," he said as he sacked a couple of loaves of bread for me.

"What do you think about it?" I asked. "Do you think it will bring in all the commercial fishermen and ruin the village?"

D.H. glanced up mildly over the rims of his steel spectacles.

"When I was a boy there was quite a fleet of fishing vessels operating out of here."

"There was? I didn't know that. To hear some people talk, you'd think the end of the world was coming if any fishing boats started using the harbor."

"Well, this was before their time. Of course, it stands to reason somebody is going to make money out of that harbor, one way or another. People are always looking for a dollar in everything. That's human nature and you can't change it. Years ago there was a feller here went up to Boston to make his fortune, and when he finally come back he was up in years and rich as Croesus. He says to me one day, 'Well, when I started out I said to myself, I'm going to make fifty thousand dollars and then I'll go back to the Cape. And when I got that I said to myself, Well, I'll make it one hundred thousand dollars and then I'll go back to the Cape. And when I made one hundred thousand dollars I said, Let 'er rip, I'm going to make as much as I can!' "

"That fellow's still around, all over the place."

"And always will be. Course it isn't always money, could be other things. Puts me in mind of one time when a couple of women in town that was nurses decided it was their duty to visit a feller that had a farm over there in the hills and give him some advice—feller that had a wife and a family that was large even for those days. Feller wasn't much of a worker and his farm showed it. His pig pen backed right up to the house and it was hard to tell the one from t'other. He had nigh as many young'uns as pigs and the pigs weren't eating much better than the young'uns. Well, the two women gave him quite

160

a lecture about how he shouldn't have any more children because he couldn't take proper care of the ones he had. He listened with his mouth open until they stopped. Then he fetched a sigh and said, 'Well, I'll tell you, ladies, it's hard to give up the fashions of the world.' " D.H. threw back his head and his Adam's apple danced a merry jig as he laughed. "Yes, sir—it's hard to give up the fashions of the world!"

I went on home with my bread, and as I got out of the car Tina, the beagle, met me. She was proudly carrying a huge bone. Our yard was liberally dotted with others of her trophy collection.

"Tina is certainly doing all she can to verify Asa's story about how a livery stable used to stand on this spot," I told Elizabeth as I went inside. "Every day she brings a new prize up out of the gulley. Our lawn is beginning to look like a horse boneyard."

"What I'd like to see from her," said Elizabeth grimly, "are a few woodchuck bones. Fresh ones." My wife was having a little trouble in the garden with a couple of free-loaders.

"Never mind that now, let's get supper going," I said. "As a charter member of the East Dennis Association of Beachfront Superintendents, I've got to get back down to the harbor!"

After supper I had a look at the tide table that hung on the door to the basement. Not too long ago I had scarcely known what a tide table was, but now it played almost a daily part in my existence. Most homes in our village had one hanging on the wall somewhere. Not only sea clamming but other fishing as well was importantly affected by tides, not to mention seaworm digging, oystering, crabbing, and other such activities.

When we wanted to take a quick dip, we could dip a lot more quickly if the tide was in than if we had to walk out half a mile to deep water. Even a walk on the beach or a jaunt down-Cape to Highland Light called for advance consultation with the tide table. Beachcombing was most interesting at low tide, whereas the dramatic view of the open ocean from Highland Light was likely to be at its scenic best when the tide was rolling in.

In this case, low tide was at 8:08 and the sun set at 7:56 Daylight Saving Time, which suited my purpose fine. So I said to Elizabeth, "How's for driving down to the creek? We can watch the sun sink in the west and the houseboat sink in the south. Or at any rate it ought to be on an interesting angle."

From our house to the little harbor was a scant two minutes' drive. I was still exhilarated by the closeness of everything—the sea, the beach, the woods, the marshes. It still seemed a special privilege to have them all but a step away, outside my door. Already, too, they had taught me how half atrophied my sense of nature had become. The marvelously interlocked workings of time, tide, wind, weather, season, day and night, sun and moon, had been all but lost on me for years. The sea was the greatest dominion in the world, for land is cut off from land all over the earth, but the sea is everywhere connected—and yet, until now, the sea had been almost a stranger to me. Now a sense of all these things was constantly with me.

I had even been paying a lot more attention to sunsets and sunrises. I had seen a surprising number of the latter, for me, in the past few months. Time was no longer merely the face of a wristwatch and the cause of my saying, "Gee, we're going to be late to the theater!" Time was something which the sun kept one way and clocks another. Clocks said it was 8:08 in our village when they were saying the same thing in Dayton, Ohio, but people in Dayton were going to have forty-five minutes' more sunlight than we were. They were on the western fringe of the Eastern Time Zone; we were actually not even in it!

From Philadelphia east, a good slice of the Eastern Seaboard including New York city and all of New England are annexed to the Eastern Time Zone only for purposes of convenience. From sixty degrees to seventy-five degrees longitude is called the Colonial Time Zone, and being situated a little past seventy-one degrees long., our village actually lay well within that zone.

We arrived at the harbor about half an hour ahead of our 8:08 date with the sun, and were thoroughly disappointed to find the houseboat riding serenely level despite low tide. Ernest Everett, wiser in the ways of the sea than we, counseled, "Wait till morning."

With men home from work and supper over, new members were swelling the ranks of our beachfront superintendents. Ernest Everett and Caleb, Mr. Ezra Newton and Colonel Braintree were perambulating information centers where new arrivals could go and be brought up to date. They volunteered nothing unless asked, of course.

The little red tug picked up men from the pipe barge, lying alongside the dredger with the crane poised beside it ready to go to work, and took them to the houseboat in a change of shifts. Out over the bay in the direction of the west jetty an enormous red sun competed gamely for a little attention. In a supreme effort it threw open the paintbox and banded the western sky with pinks and light blues and flung shadings of darker blues and purples into the east as it slipped beneath the placid waters of the bay.

Twilight began to fuzz the edges of distant objects, and the evening hush extended even to conversation. It was enough to sit and draw peace into one's soul as the dredger was drawing in fuel oil; something to go on later. A good many people were still there when the last glow faded from the sky and a fringe of lights began to twinkle aboard the houseboat and the dredger.

The next afternoon was as soon as we could get back, but when we arrived a rewarding sight awaited us. Ernest Everett

163

had been right. "Give it time to settle. Wait till the second low tide." With cheerful little smiles puckering their lips he and Caleb and the others sat looking at a houseboat that was tilted at a horrendous angle, and watched with pleasure as the tug backwatered like a bulldog digging its hind legs into gravel, trying to yank it off into deep water. I spoke to a crewman who was sitting on the side of a beached rowboat, watching glumly.

"We ain't had nothing but cold cuts all day," he complained. "Can't use the galley stoves while she's like that."

Cold cuts or not, work had begun in earnest. A pipeline supported by pontoons ran from the stern of the dredger to an elbow which turned it in toward shore on the west side, and sections of pipe were laid out in a way which indicated that the first fill would be thrown up on the Boat Shop's land. There was a great deal of immediate interest in where the fill was going to be thrown and whose beachfront property was going to benefit, at least in height, by it. There were several rumors going around on this score. There were rumors, of course, about everything, from that moment on.

There were rumors about the fishing fleet. Every commercial fisherman from Barnstable to Wellfleet was going to move his boat into our harbor and it was going to reek henceforth and forever with the smell of decaying fish heads. Gimcrack shops were going to spring up in our village, hotdog stands pimple our beachfront, and the entire vast square of rolling sand between the dunes and our present modest parking space was to be filled and flattened and hardened into an enormous parking lot which would draw thousands of litter-spreading transients who would swarm over our beach in an uncomfortably accurate imitation of Coney Island.

On Monday the dredging began in the upper basin, and it was then that our beachfront superintendents really began to put in their hours. Perhaps the crowd that peered down into the hole when they excavated for Rockefeller Center was many times larger, but the interest shown was hurried and casual compared to that displayed by the men, particularly the old men, of our village in the Sesuit Harbor operation. The interest of the crowd at Rockefeller Center was impersonal, nothing like what was being felt by the Cape Codders of our village. When the dredger bit into the sand of the creek, it was touching the scene of their childhood. For them, it was dredging up far more than rock and sand. It was dredging up a thousand half-forgotten memories.

Not that the dredger was changing hitherto unchanged lines of that childhood scene. Ernest Everett soon relieved us of that notion.

"When I was a boy, the channel was over there, clear on the other side of the Boat Shop land," he said, indicating a course around the base of the promontory of Sesuit Neck, a good quarter of a mile west of where the channel was now. This stood to reason, since the west jetty had not been over there then, thrusting out two hundred yards and forcing the ebb and flow to carve out a new channel over on our side.

But even where there were no man-made changes, the shore changed ceaselessly. Winter storms gouged annual variations in its contours. On the beach at Ward's Point, out of water only at low tide, sat an enormous boulder, with the bluff half a dozen paces behind it; comparatively young men could recall when it rested on the top of the bluff, thirty feet above the water. Some people would swear to you that Cape Cod, wearing away in one place and building up in another, had rolled completely over like a roller towel in the course of the past five hundred years or so.

When work began on the upper basin, the dredger definitely took over as the star of the show. It was really nothing more than a great floating engine room, with a lever house on top at the front where the operator, manipulating five hand-brake-style levers on each side plus a few odds and ends in front of him, sent the cutter head chewing into the bottom of the basin at some forty revolutions per minute. He also reeled in and paid out the two cables, secured on opposite banks, which enabled him to swing the front end of the dredger in its wide arc, back and forth, as it loosened sand and mud and rocks for the suction pipe to draw through the long pipeline leading to the shore.

In order to do this the dredger had to pivot on something, and we soon realized that this was the purpose of the two vertical pipes on the stern. Spuds, they were called. One of these was dropped for a pivot, and they were also used alternately, like a pair of underwater stilts, to walk the dredger forward.

The dredger began slicing neat half circles in the west bank, and almost at once the sand gave up its first treasure—the oaken skeleton of a ship's hull. What ship? Could it be . . . ?

Before going into that, I must fill in a little background on a scholarly squabble which, though it has attracted nation-wide attention, may have escaped the notice of some.

A good many persons have devoted a lot of time and effort to trying to unravel the riddle of exactly where it was that the Norsemen landed and camped when they visited our shores back around the turn of the millennium. Where was the "Vinland" their sagas spoke of? Was it Labrador? Was it Nova Scotia? Was it farther to the south?

A retired Brooklyn schoolteacher, Professor Frederick J. Pohl, became convinced it was Cape Cod, and when on a visit to the Cape he found holes driven into boulders near the banks of Follins Pond, at the head of Bass River in our township of Dennis, he felt he had gone a long way toward proving his case. The Norsemen bored just such holes for their mooring irons.

Thirty members of a state archeological society eventually spent two days digging in the area, and pieces of a small dry-dock were unearthed. These were good for a great deal of excitement until they were found to contain machine-made nails.

The finding of the nails only caused Ernest Everett and Caleb and Mr. Ezra Newton and the rest to snort triumphantly. From the beginning they had considered the theory a lot of foolishness. They might possibly have felt differently had the Norsemen's proponent been a Cape Codder (and preferably a Dennis man from one of the more or less respectable old families), but they did not care to have some bookish outlander deciding who had or had not landed on their cape.

Professor Pohl was as stubbornly opinionated as they themselves, however, and stuck to his theory through thick and thin, and as usual most of the outside world, always a willing audience for a romantic tale, was eager to believe it.

The notion that Cape Cod was the Viking's Vinland will never die now. It will be with us forever, unless absolute proof is found that the Norsemen landed somewhere else and then went straight home again. And every time a piece of wooden boat is brought to light that does not have "Made in U.S.A." stamped on it somewhere, there will be a new stir.

The curved timbers had scarcely been laid on the bank by the dredger's men before the rumor began to spread, not only that a Viking boat had been found but that "Eric's boat" had been discovered. Mr. Ezra Newton and Ernest Everett and the others exchanged blank looks, held brief private conversation, and then stood by and listened while the Viking hopefuls gathered, mostly summer folk from all over the Cape. Included among them was a young radio commentator from Connecticut, up for a visit with his family. He diligently collected misinformation and rumor, and took it back with him.

The old Cape Codders, sitting by on the gunwales of beached boats and seeming to pay no attention as they stared out at the dredger, enjoyed their fill of these excited speculations, and watched unprotestingly as the hull fragments shrank under the greedy hands of souvenir hunters. Particularly ex-

167

citing was the fact that the planks were held together exclusively by large wooden dowels. No nails at all this time. Interesting, too, was the fact that the dowels were eight-sided, and that the holes had been made eight-sided to take them.

These dowels were particularly prized, and were pried and pushed and pounded out at a great rate by zealous scavengers. The planks, pickled into ageless antiquity by their long immersion, could certainly have been as old as Eric the Red, and the apparent size of the boat was about right for a Viking ship. Summer visitors, eager to have a good story to take home from vacation, were quick to agree with one another that it all added up to a perfect case for the Norsemen.

After the first flurry had been enjoyed by all, the reaction began to set in. Hadley Ransom brought his knowledge of Americana to the beach, examined the remains, and made a resonant pronouncement. Most of the dowels were already gone, but fortunately the souvenir hunters had had to leave the holes. An inspection of these led Hadley to announce that the boat had been built not earlier than 1700, for the reason that the type of auger used to bore those particular holes had not been invented until then.

Hadley thus brought us closer to the truth, and our Old Cape Codders, in their own good time, finally set us right. They knew exactly what hull that was, and when and how it had got there. Asa had even looked her up at the county courthouse to check the date she was built.

She was the sloop *Star*, built in 1845 and sailed by Christopher Sears. It was good to know that the dredger had dredged up the remains of a local sloop, but many of us were even more grateful to it for having dredged up the memory of as fabulous a giant as was Christopher Sears. For it seemed he was indeed a giant of a man, three hundred pounds without being fat, and with many a tale that could be told of him. The men who had heard them firsthand told us some of them now.

In those days the production of salt through solar evaporation was still a Cape industry, and salt works were operating down near the creek. The process was invented in East Dennis by Captain John Sears, whose house still stands on North Street, good as ever and occupied today by his descendants. In 1776, while stirring events were taking place in Boston, 'Sleepy John' Sears' mind was on salt. He built a long trough, filled it with sea water, and produced the first salt in America by solar evaporation. It was the beginning of a once-important Cape industry, and salt vats soon dotted the Cape from end to end.

Christopher Sears used to carry salt to Boston in his sloop and bring back provisions. He was a pretty sharp apple, too, a true Yankee trader, and not above making a fast greenback if the opportunity presented itself. He often bought cheap butter by the tub in Boston, cut it up and stamped it on the way home, and sold it as homemade butter.

On one occasion he pulled in alongside a fishing boat that was about to dump a quantity of bluefish which were on the tired side and well dried out after about four days out of the water. Christopher allowed as how he'd just as lief have them if they were only going to throw them away anyhow. He set his course for Provincetown, and soaked the bluefish up good all the way. Just before he rounded the point he let several of the blues down into the water on lines, and made a great show of hauling them in as he came around into sight. By the time he tied up, enough people were on the dock ready to pay good money for fresh bluefish so that he had no trouble unloading his "catch."

Christopher was sometimes referred to as "Bachelor Sears," because that was what he was, and considering the number of Searses around today it seems likely that a bachelor was indeed a rarity among them and worthy of special designation. He had a stutter, but whether or not that handicapped him any romantically speaking is not possible to say. Certainly it seems

169

odd that so large a target should have escaped the matrimonial wiles of the Cape's damsels and its many sea-made widows. Perhaps more than one goodwife, when someone commented on her husband's fine physique, may have felt like murmuring, "Yes, but you should have seen the big one that got away!"

As a matter of fact, if Christopher was not married it was not for want of trying to reach that happy state, for he once became enamored of Mercy Crowell and asked her to marry him. He asked her not once but four or five times over a long period of time, and on each occasion she refused him. Then one day they happened to meet on the street, and she stopped him. "I've changed my mind," said Mercy Crowell. Christopher Sears raised his hat. "S-so've I," he said, and quickly went his way.

His strength was as the strength of ten, without the disadvantage of a pure heart, it would seem. He could handle a hogshead of molasses alone. When his sloop grounded on a sandbar he would get out, put his shoulder to her side, and get her off unaided. One time he went to a carnival where there was a weight-lifting machine with a gauge to show how much the customer was managing to lift. Christopher not only lifted the weights, he lifted the whole machine right off the floor, tearing it loose and doing considerable incidental damage. The carnival man told him he would have to pay for the machine. "I w-will if you'll tell me how m-much I l-lifted," retorted Christopher.

By 1887 the *Star* had seen her best sailing days and was dragged up on the bank and over near the road, beached for good. The oak beams in her were still sound wood, however, and she was gradually pulled to pieces by the local blacksmiths, who came down and took wood from her to make axles and whiffletrees.

For eleven years she lay on the bank, subjected to this gradual attrition, and it was during these years that Ernest Everett and the others were boys living in the creek more than out of it, so that they knew the *Star* and her history. Then came the storm of 1898, in which the *Portland* sank off Race Point with great loss of life, and in which much damage and destruction was done all up and down the Cape. The well-plucked skeleton of the *Star* was swept off the bank and jammed into the side of what was now the upper basin, and there it had remained undisturbed, covered over more and more as the basin filled in, for better than half a century.

A week after the find a well-dressed couple in a large car with a Connecticut license appeared on the scene. They had endured Sunday traffic all the way up from Connecticut solely because of an exciting and fascinating story their local radio commentator had told on his program, and by a bit of rare good fortune they pulled in alongside Ernest Everett's car and he was sitting in it.

"Where can we see the Viking ship?" they asked. Ernest Everett was happy to point the way.

No, the sloop *Star* was no Viking ship, but it did date back to a day which once would have seemed almost as distant to me. The Cape, however, was doing things to my time sense. There was a quality in the very air which had altered it remarkably.

When people speak of the "atmosphere" of a place, they generally have in mind something which is pretty easily detected—the visible picturesqueness or quaintness of a village or a section or an island or a countryside, aided and abetted by various appeals to the other senses. The atmosphere of Cape Cod, on those terms, calls to mind fishing boats warping into a pier, fishermen mending nets, glimpses of fresh-water ponds and cranberry bogs, neat white houses with their shingles silvered by the sea air, sand dunes sending out their siren call to the amateur photographer, the whiff of salt in the air, the sounds of the sea, and the blend of all these things into one pleasant impression. This is the atmosphere which can be

171

absorbed during a brief contact, which can even be driven through, so to speak, in the course of a motor trip down the Cape and up again.

There is another kind of atmosphere, however, which seeps into the mind bit by bit, and which had the extra impact of complete novelty upon one of my Midwestern background. It is an atmosphere that comes from the long-established continuity of a way of life, and only in the course of day-by-day living as a resident did I begin to know it and feel it.

When I was a small boy in Kansas City, it was naturally the center of the world as far as I was concerned—and Kansas City only went back seventy-five years. Kansas City began with my grandfather's day, and before that for me there was nothing solid, nothing but mere history-book talk and shadowy generations that came from somewhere out of the dim, unknown regions that lay to the east of our city—from Pennsylvania and New England, places which existed only on paper.

Anything that happened as much as seventy years ago was ancient history. A building sixty or seventy years old seemed very old indeed, and I wondered how it managed to stay up.

I was over twenty-one before I traveled east of the Mississippi. During my formative years I had never known anything but country that was comparatively new. When Kansas City was celebrating its centennial, the year we moved to the Cape, the town of Eastham was holding a tercentenary celebration. There were settlers on the upper Cape as early as 1637. In short, when my home town put itself on the map the settling of Cape Cod was far more remote in time than the Revolutionary period is today.

Living in New York city altered my Midwestern time sense to some extent, but in New York the old is suffocated by the new, destroyed by constant and over-hasty change, and what is preserved generally has a museum-like quality about it. Cape Cod, with its unbroken line of generations and its dwellings still working successfully at their trade of housing people two and three centuries after the dwellings were built, and with their rambling additions showing the hand of those successive generations—it took Cape Cod to bring our Pilgrim Fathers out from behind those stultifying capital initials and make them fellow human beings.

The Cape was their first stop in the New World. The first child of the Pilgrims born in America was born here as the *Mayflower* lay off the present site of Provincetown in November of 1620. And though they went on to Plymouth and others came later to increase the colony there, it was not many years before some of that colony came to the Cape. They came, and their families have been living here ever since. The names that appear in the earliest records are the same names to be found in profusion in the Cape Cod telephone directory today.

We had not been on the Cape long before the 1600s did not seem so very far back in time when I could glance out the window and picture those early settlers not as figures in a painting going through the woods to church or making history with the first Thanksgiving, but as actual men passing through this very landscape with an eye out for good meadowlands and other likely looking pieces of real estate. In many ways Cape Cod has changed far less since the white man came to it three hundred years ago than the Middle West has in its hundred-odd years of settlement by whites. Until fairly recently the way of life here had not changed very remarkably for a couple of hundred years.

It was easy for me to feel that Thomas Clarke, who came over in the *Anne* in 1623, lived only a little while ago when I could sit and look out at the creek in the marsh which is the line between our property and the township of Brewster, and then read that in 1654 Thomas Clarke purchased a large tract of land in Brewster from Experience Mitchell of Bridgewater. There is something about the drama and importance of a great historical event which makes it seem remote, and

173

something about the everyday business transaction of a man who bought land a few miles further down-Cape three hundred years before I did which draws it near. The nine or ten generations of Cape Codders have gone in strongly for everyday living, rather than for history making in the grand sense, and their orderly procession across the face of the Cape has given life here a powerful sense of continuity which I had not experienced before.

One afternoon soon after the dredging operations began, Elizabeth picked up some information when she went around the village collecting Brownie Scouts whom Elizabeth and I had promised to take to see the dredging. To pass on this information to me now Elizabeth had to shout above the clamor of Brownies in the rear of the car.

"Say, a three-man harbor committee has been appointed, and who do you suppose is on it?"

"Asa and who else?"

"Crowell Hall."

"And who else?"

"Freddie Barr!"

I shouted with glee so loudly that I could almost be heard. A couple of the Brownies even stopped wrestling long enough to glance at me briefly.

"Poor Crow! In the middle between those two!"

The Brownies' tour of the dredger was a great success. I had a wonderful time.

14

SKIRMISHES WITH THE

NATIVES

Our tomato plants, all jammed in together as they were, had grown into as unkempt a tangle of vines as one might find this side of some green hell in British Guiana. They had not been properly pruned and they had not been properly staked. Our stakes were an ill-assorted lot of poles and lathes which lurched this way and that and had the awkward air of hastily-gathered recruits. The bits of white cloth which bandaged stake and vine together made it look as if they had not made out too well in the fray, either.

In short, our tomato plants were a disgrace. They broke all the established rules of gardening. The only possible thing that could have been said in their favor was that they were loaded with tomatoes.

"Take some home, Fred," Elizabeth said to a bewildered

Fred Underhill, as he stood looking at them and shaking his head. "It's a shame the blight got yours."

"If I didn't see it with my own eyes . . . My plants were spaced perfectly, I gave them every care . . ."

Elizabeth tactfully changed the subject.

"Have you been blueberrying yet?"

"No, we haven't."

"Know any good places?"

"Well, we've never been over there, but they tell me there are some good places over behind those hills," said Fred, pointing to the low line of hills beyond the highway.

" 'They' have told us all sorts of things," I remarked. "I notice that as the season of fruition advances and more and more of Nature's bounty becomes available, the natives show even more of that old tendency not to give a newcomer a straight story as to where to locate anything."

"You're finding that out, are you?" Fred grinned. "Well, you're right. This is the time of year when you want to watch for the joker in the directions."

When it came to explaining how to get to a good place to go blueberrying, or where to find beach plums or wild grapes, the native would be attacked by fits of vagueness and a tendency to stud his directions with local terms.

"Well, you go up Six to Sand Creek Road and go till you hit Tinker's Hollow there and bear left off onto the dirt road to the first cut-off by the twin cedars toward Wixon's Point and you might find some if the bushes ain't been stripped clean already," they would say, and look elaborately defeated if we admitted we did not know where Tinker's Hollow or Wixon's Point were. "Well, it's pretty hard to give you any decent directions if you don't know the places . . ."

We soon discovered we would learn more by keeping our eyes and ears open than by asking questions. We began to hear that this person and that one had baked a few blueberry pies, but our queries about the best place to go blueberrying still brought us only vague descriptions of distant and inaccessible points.

"By the way, do you notice a funny thing?" I finally remarked to Elizabeth. "Do you notice that the people who have lived here a few years are almost as bad as the Cape Codders when it comes to not wanting to tell you how to find things? It sure doesn't take them long to go native!"

One morning I happened to see a couple of women walking down the road past our house. Women often walked down our road, which led to the cemetery, but generally they carried flowers. These women were carrying little pails. Women on their way to cemeteries do not usually carry little pails, said I to myself.

In the course of the next two days I was outdoors a good deal when I should have been inside working, so I was in a position to notice several more women walking down our road with little pails on their arms.

"What do you suppose they're after?" asked Elizabeth. "Could it be . . . ?"

"Right under our nose! I'll bet you anything!"

"Have you seen any of them come back?"

"Yes. They had pieces of cloth over the tops of their pails, so I couldn't see what was in them, but there was *something* in them. Have we got any little pails? You and I are going to take a walk. Have you ever noticed Christopher Sears' gravestone? And Christopher Hall's—he's the one the clipper ship was named after, you know. I'll point them out as we go past."

At that time we were handicapped by the fact that we did not know a blueberry bush from a clump of sumac. However, we did know footprints when we saw them. And where they turned off the road into the bushes, we followed. We found several kinds of bushes, and on one of them was a small-sized version of the blueberries we used to see in neat cellophane packages in the city. The only trouble with them was their

177

size and the number of visitors the bushes had had before we got there. An hour of picking produced less than a quart between us. We decided there ought to be places a little more off the beaten track where we might do better. We remembered what Fred Underhill had said and after checking with him again to narrow down our search as much as possible we set off on an expedition over behind the hills.

Our path led us definitely away from the beaten track. First off the highway up a paved side road, then off that onto a narrow sand road, and off that onto a mere pair of wheel tracks that curved away into the brush and past little groves of scrubby trees. A pheasant sprang into the air from the bushes in a flurry of color and went rattling away above the low trees, gliding at last smoothly out of sight.

Ahead of us the woods grew thicker, and the road began to dip down into a fold between the hill we were on and the next one. When we had gone about as far as seemed feasible, and had reached a spot we could turn around in, we got out and walked, following the slope of the land down, hoping for water, though we could see nothing ahead through the thick trees.

The little pond came upon us suddenly. All at once, as we topped the last little rise, it sparkled dead ahead of us on the far side of the bushes that rimmed and screened it and under the leaves of the trees that stood high on the slopes around it. If ever there was a little lost lake this one seemed to be it. It was guarded on every side by steep-pitched hills. It was very nearly round, and not much over a hundred yards in diameter, and it was the central jewel in a little Cape Cod Eden—for growing around it were very nearly all of the Cape's special fruits.

The bushes that stood between us and the pond turned out to be blueberry bushes, and they were covered with berries of the large, family economy size. We began a slow tour of the pond's fringe, taking stock. All around it were more blueberry bushes, and some bore berries which even equaled in size any cultivated berries we had ever seen, and had far more flavor.

Overhead on the western slope, clambering over trees and bushes, were wild grape vines dangling handsome clusters of grapes which another month would ripen.

Under our feet, as we went on, crinkled cranberry vines which matted the ground. The half-concealed cranberries were of startling size, and were already beginning to color up. There were not enough of them nor were they in a state to suggest cultivation, but there were ten times what one family would ever need.

On the northern slope, we found a clump of beach plums which, while still green and half-grown, were already as large as any we had ever seen during our one previous experience with them, on our first Cape vacation.

Then and there, we too went native.

"Not a word about this to anyone except the Underhills," I said as we filled our pails with blueberries. "Florence, do you hear? If anyone asks you where we get our blueberries, tell 'em 'off Sea Street.' "

Due to our experiences with natives of our village, this phrase had become a password with us. For a while it seemed as if any time we or anyone else asked an East Dennis man where he had gone to get sea clams or fish or anything else, he had said, "Oh, off Sea Street," which is as vague a direction as one can give locally. Sea Street runs down to the cut through the dunes which opens onto the bay. There were blueberries 'off Sea Street' down our road, for that matter, and we had heard rumors of wild grapes and beach plums 'off Sea Street,' too. Almost everything was actually off Sea Street; it was merely a question of how far off.

We enjoyed our blueberries, and quietly served a blueberry pie or two to Cape Codder friends without comment, and kept our secret well, but naturally it was too much to hope that nobody else would visit our special spot. However, only once did we actually encounter anyone else there. The third

179

time we went blueberrying, we found three gray-haired ladies, unquestionably natives, industriously picking. Two of them merely turned their backs as we walked past, but the third ventured a remark.

"They're just about stripped clean," she informed us in a doleful voice.

"Yeah," I said vaguely, and we kept right on going, around the bend to some particular bushes we favored. There we found the berries even thicker than they had been the last time. When we had filled our pails and came back around the edge of the lake again, the three ladies were still picking. By now, the fact that we had gone about our business with apparent knowledge of what we were doing had changed our status completely in their eyes. This time, as we went past, they nodded and smiled, as friendly as could be, and the comment one of them made was quite cheerful, and somewhat at variance with the earlier remark.

"Never saw them nicer than this year, have you?"

"Nope, I sure haven't," I agreed quite truthfully.

The beach-plum issue had its instructive sides, too. Whenever we asked a Cape Codder when beach plums got ripe, we always received the same answer: "Right after Labor Day." It sounded as if they were trained to let the tourists get off the Cape first. We swallowed this story and made a note to keep beach-plum picking in mind as a Labor-Day weekend activity.

About the middle of August, Elizabeth was talking to Sabetha Sears on the phone one day, and the subject of beach plums came up.

"They'll be ripe before long now, I guess," said Elizabeth, fishing around a little.

"Ripe? Why, they're practically gone," said Sabetha, with native pleasure betraying itself in her voice. "I got some yesterday down near the beach, and I've been making my jelly all day today. Didn't you get any beach plums down there?"

"Why, no. I thought they wouldn't be ripe until after Labor Day."

"Well, they're early this year. The best ones around here are down near the beach, but the bushes have been pretty well stripped by now. Lots of people were picking yesterday."

"Well, I'm sorry I missed out," said Elizabeth, and let Sabetha have her fun. When she had hung up, though, she subjected Sabetha's remarks to searching analysis.

"The way she said it, I think the bushes down near the beach really are stripped. She didn't sound like that old lady who tried to tell us the blueberries were just about gone—she sounded too happy. And the way she said they're early this year makes me think they're early *every* year."

That same day saw us back at our little pond, and when we clambered up the north slope we found our special patch of beach plums intact—and ripe.

"I'd like to break Sabetha's little neck," said my wife, and a few days later she very nearly did. She was in a small social gathering, talking with Mabel Crowell.

"Did you go to the beach today?" asked Mabel.

Sabetha, sitting close by, was talking to someone else, but her head really snapped around when Elizabeth replied, "No, I didn't have time. We picked beach plums yesterday, and I spent today putting up sixty jars of jelly."

Through all this fruitful season nobody was busier than Freddie Barr, of course. When it came to giving out any information, Freddie was not vague like the others—he would simply chuckle wickedly and say, "Hell, I don't know where to find any, I got mine a week ago, but they're all gone where I got 'em." Freddie was always there fustest and came home with the mostest.

Besides his other activities Freddie did a good bit of farming, so his gathering-in problems increased tenfold as the

181

cornucopia season came on. Most of his crops were built around some of his favorite dishes, as for example his potato and beet crops. He had to have potatoes and beets because without boiled potatoes and pickled beets, "Cape Cod turkey" was nothing.

"What? You've never had Cape Cod turkey?"

"I don't even know what it is."

"Well, jeezcrise! You've got to fix some Cape Cod turkey. I'll tell you how you do it. You take a piece of salt cod and soak it and then boil it. You take a piece of salt pork and cut it up fine and put it in a frying pan and try it out until it's cooked down to little crispy brown squares. You take out the crispy squares and make cream gravy with the fat. You boil potatoes, and you have some cold pickled beets. You take your plate and put on it a piece of cod and some of those little salt pork squares and some potatoes and some gravy and pickled beets.

"The way to eat it is to put a piece of cod and some salt pork and gravy on a bite of potato and eat them all together. You have to eat them all together to get the real taste. Then you eat a slice of pickled beet. Then another bite of cod and salt pork and gravy and potato, and so on. That's Cape Cod turkey."

We decided we would have to try it, or rather Freddie decided we would, and the night we tried it Freddie had dinner with us by telephone. In the middle of the afternoon he began calling up.

"Are you going to have that Cape Cod turkey tonight?"

Toward suppertime he called up again.

"Are you fixing it yet?"

"Yes."

"How are you doing it?"

Elizabeth described her efforts.

"That's right. You're doing okay."

We sat down to Cape Cod turkey, and it was delicious. We were enjoying it when the phone rang again.

182

"Have you had it yet?"

"We're just eating it now."

"Well, how is it?"

"Wonderful."

"What did I tell you. There's nothing better than Cape Cod turkey. I could eat it every day. How are you eating it? Are you eating a bite of potato with a piece of cod and some salt pork?"

I assured him we were following instructions, bite by bite. The odd part about it, as was so often the case with Freddie, was that he was right. The combination of the three things was everything. Not only that, but pickled beets were unquestionably the proper supporting cast.

A few days later Freddie's pick-up truck rattled into our driveway one morning as we sat at breakfast, and he presented us with a bushel of his home-grown beets. We thanked him for his unexpected generosity, and urged him to join us for coffee.

"No, I've got more damn work—well, hell, I guess I'll have a cup of coffee. I made myself some coffee this morning and it was lousy. I think someone must have forgot to wash the soapsuds out of the pot," he said, thumping down into a chair. He was wearing various earth-stained garments and looked particularly villainous. "I had breakfast at five-thirty this morning. I've put in a day's work while you were sleeping. Jeez, I'm dead."

"Well, how's the harbor committee coming along?" I asked, and Freddie shook his head heavily.

"My Gawd what I've been through. I spend all my time smoothing things over after Asa says the wrong thing. You know he's no businessman, Asa isn't, and I just get something set up with people about buying some property down by the harbor or something when he says some damn-fool thing—"

"How about Crow Hall?"

"Oh, we *both* had to jump on Crow a little a couple of

183

times." He leaned toward the window and glowered out as another truck swung into the driveway. "Here comes Hadley. What's he doing here?"

Hadley burst in with news of another auction he had lined up and wanted me to help with. Then he got a cup, splashed some coffee into it, and sat down to tell Freddie what the harbor committee ought to do. This long and noisy discussion continued for some time, and then both remembered they had things to do and took off, though not before Freddie had given Elizabeth minute instructions as to how to pickle the beets.

"Who's running this house, anyway, we or Freddie?" I demanded to know a day or two later as I helped peel the beets Elizabeth was dutifully pickling. "My God, we won't eat a bushel of pickled beets in ten years!"

"Well, when he's nice enough to give them to us . . . Anyway, just think of the pleasure we're giving Freddie. He'll enjoy so thinking about all those pickled beets on our basement shelves."

At first the Cape Codders' attitude toward outsiders annoyed us. They could not have lived without the tourist trade; newcomers who became permanent residents tended to increase their prosperity; and yet, even when they tried to conceal it, we knew that they secretly resented every outsider who came pushing his way across the bridge onto the sacred soil of their beloved Cape. There was a saying about the native attitude concerning what they would really have liked to see the outsiders do: "Leave your money on the bridge and go home."

This attitude seemed downright disgusting. Who were they to bite the hand that fed them? It took us awhile to realize the truth—that tourism was still a comparatively new thing on Cape Cod. For nearly three hundred years, Cape Codders had managed on their own. During all that time they had lived, sometimes well and sometimes frugally, with a crusty, salty independence. Good or poor, their living came from the land and the sea, and they had that land and that sea to themselves. No outsiders intruded to pick their beach plums and catch their fish.

Actually, the time came when the Cape could not support all its native sons and daughters, and many of its young men went west. The trend of the population was down, not up, but at least those who remained depended only on themselves. Within the memory of many of our neighbors who were natives, the number of visitors in summer had been negligible. They had not figured heavily in the Cape's economy, nor much affected its life.

In 1904, however, the first automobile poked its brass headlights onto the Cape and jousted with the ruts of its sandy roads, heeling over like a sailboat as it straddled the high crowns. From that moment on, the Cape began its development as a resort area. Even then, it took another ten years before the summer trade was really of major importance, but in the end it became the Cape's largest industry. The Cape, once the private preserve of the Cape Codder, was now overrun by outsiders who made a nuisance of themselves, were patronizing, asked fool questions, stuck their noses into everything—and spent lots of nice money.

The Cape Codder resented the fact that he had come to need these outsiders, and he could hardly be blamed for that. Hence his tendency to be closemouthed about the natural resources of his land, and of his sea. Even a new year-around resident had to give as good as he got for a long time before he could win anything like an honorary membership in the closed corporation.

One evening we had a group in for cards. Caleb and Ernest Everett were among the company. A fine full moon was riding through the sky that night, and a light breeze was stirring out of the south. A good sea-clamming tide seemed likely for the morning, and the conversation took a turn in that direction.

185

"Going out tomorrow?" Elizabeth asked, looking at the two veteran sea clammers. Caleb chuckled wryly and Ernest Everett's face puckered into an extremely dubious look, as though the very idea pained him.

"Well, depends on how late you keep me out tonight," Caleb declared. "Have to get up awful early tomorrow morning to catch that tide."

"Don't reckon I'll make it," Ernest Everett allowed.

When it came to sea clamming we envied Caleb, because he went in style, driving his green jeep right out onto the flats. However, our game ran late and he and Ernest Everett both left looking at their watches and protesting that sea clamming was unthinkable now. They were quite right, too, from the standpoint of getting any sort of night's sleep. By the time we cleared up and were ready for bed it was one-thirty—and to get out on the flats at the right time we would have to get up at four-thirty. I held the clock poised, ready to set the alarm, and turned to Elizabeth for moral support. Bed looked like a very inviting place in which to spend the next eight hours.

"Well?"

If it had not been for Caleb and Ernest Everett I doubt if she could have found the courage to think about getting up again in a mere three hours.

"Well, I'd love to go out on a tide they passed up and come in with a couple of buckets of clams," she admitted.

"I'm game," I said, spurred on by the same pleasant vision. Wincing slightly, I set the clock.

Three hours later it was still pitch dark outside, and the bed had never been more fleecy soft. Nevertheless we pulled ourselves out, crept down the hall to wash ourselves awake, and then I went downstairs to put on the coffee so that we could have one quick cup to hold us together before we left.

It happened that Elizabeth was sitting at her dressing table when the sound of a car motor came to her ears. By the light of its own headlights she could see enough of the vehicle to tell it was the green jeep as it slowed at the corner and came by right in front of our house. She could even make out two bear-like figures sitting in the front seat.

"How do you like that?" she asked, after hurrying down to report this interesting sight. "Those two. Oh, no, they weren't going—and they have the nerve to drive right past our house!"

The road the jeep was taking eventually narrowed down to two sandy ruts. We did not dare take our heavier car on it, so we drove to the Sea Street beach and went off from there with a long, long walk ahead of us and a long, long, long walk back. We felt hopelessly outdistanced.

"By the time we get out there they'll have their buckets full and be heading back in," I complained. "I can just hear Ernest Everett now. 'Well, I got my quota.' "

As we walked onto the beach, we found two strange men with rakes and buckets standing looking out over the flats. We exchanged good mornings, and one of them uttered a melancholy, comradely snort of despair. At least, that was what he apparently intended it to sound like.

"You're too late, too, eh?" he said in a commiserating tone of voice.

"Too late?"

"Oh, yes. By the time we got out there now we'd be 'way too late. Breeze is wrong, too. We've about decided not to go."

There was a time when, with a long walk across the flats staring us in the face in the grim half-light of early morn, we might have let ourselves be turned back by such a pessimistic statement from a couple of strangers who were obviously Cape Codders. However, by now, and especially during the immediate past, we had had a certain amount of experience.

I shrugged, and nodded.

"I expect you're right, but I guess we'll go on out anyway, long's we're here," I said, and Elizabeth made no protest at my

187

decision. We walked on down the beach silently until we were out of earshot of our friends.

"Either those fellows didn't read their tide tables right, which is unlikely, or they're trying to hand us the same old business, which is very likely," I declared then. "Even from here we've got plenty of time, even walking, to get out there before the tide turns. Mighty funny thing to me anybody would climb out of bed at this hour and not be sure of his tides."

"I don't get it," said Elizabeth.

We grasped the situation about ten minutes later. We heard a motor behind us, and in the strengthening morning light we saw a truck bearing down on us across the flats. It passed closely enough for us to recognize our two pessimists among the four passengers. They went by without so much as a wave.

"There's your genuine Cape Cod S.O.B.," I remarked as we trudged along watching the truck roll on ahead. "First they try to give us a bum steer on the tide, and all the time they're waiting for friends to come pick them up in a truck. Then they go by without offering us a lift or even being civil. Of course, they probably don't want to carry any more weight than they can help, but—"

"They wouldn't offer us a lift if they had a tank," said Elizabeth, and of course she was right.

"Well, let's at least follow the truck's tracks," I suggested. "Maybe it will disturb a clam or two."

We walked on and on, seeming to get nowhere. We felt depressingly impotent and overmatched. Our competition was having a field day.

We decided to enjoy the pleasant morning and forget about the lot of them. We struggled with this type of cold comfort for a while. Then Elizabeth happened to glance ahead and notice that the truck had gotten larger instead of smaller.

"What do you suppose they've stopped for?"

"Probably spotted a couple of clams on the way out," I prophesied sourly.

As we got nearer, however, we could see that all four men were out of the truck and that the back end of it was looking very low-slung on one side.

Elizabeth and I exchanged broad grins which held a deplorably small amount of Christian compassion.

"Am I going to enjoy walking by *them*," she said.

"Well . . ."

"Now, listen, if you dare offer to help that bunch—"

"Now, dear, I can't just walk by, not even by them. Unwritten law of the sea, you know. Small craft in distress."

"Since when is a truck a small craft?"

"It's going to be one if they don't get it out of there pretty quick."

When we reached the truck we found a very satisfying situation confronting us. In the first place, the Cape Codders had obviously tried a few shortcuts through patches of shallow water instead of staying in farther on the high parts of the bars, and they had hit a soft spot. Their right rear wheel was halfway to China and spinning freely.

"Need any help?" I asked, and got a blustering reply.

"No, thanks, I expect we can get her out all right."

I stopped and gazed down the flats to the point where I could barely make out a tiny black dot. A wonderful thought had occurred to me.

"Well, there's a fellow with a jeep down there," I said, pointing.

"That so?"

"Yes. If you want me to, I'll ask him to come back and give you a hand."

"Well, no, I don't guess we'll need any."

"Suit yourself," I said agreeably. "Of course, as you said back there, we're pretty late, and the tide will be turning soon. Breeze is wrong, too. Well, good luck."

189

"Well . . . if we need help I'll come up and get him." Our friend was still full of independence, except for that momentary hesitation. We walked on.

"Our morning is improving," I declared.

"Aren't you awful," said Elizabeth complacently.

We were heading for a point considerably inshore of where Caleb and Ernest Everett were, so that when one of our old buddies from the truck went by he was a considerable distance off to the left of us. Still, we had a fine view of him as his step became more and more hurried. He looked like the man I had been talking to. He finally broke into a run. He was a stocky man with a fair-sized corporation and he was wearing waders, which are not to be recommended for cross-country work.

"Well, well. Looks like our friends changed their minds," I remarked. "Let's see, now—by the time he gets to them, the tide's going to be about half an hour from the turn. I hope he has breath enough left to tell them what he wants. By the way, have you noticed how nice the morning is getting to be? There's a special something in the air!"

By the time we had reached the place where we had intended to start looking for clams, the runner was a tiny figure far across the flats. We watched him confer with two other tiny figures, and then all three got into the jeep and started back the way he had come.

Later on that day Elizabeth and Mabel Crowell had occasion to stop by Ernest Everett's.

"So you went sea clamming after all," said Elizabeth.

"Well, yes—"

"How did you make out? Did you get your quota?"

Ernest Everett all but snorted, and then he burst out with, "Well, if you call *one* my quota, I did!"

"*One?*"

"That's all I got, and Caleb didn't get any. They weren't showin' at all before turn of tide, and just when we might have started getting some a feller come and said they had a truck stuck in the sand. So we had to go down and pull them out. Time we got through with them, it was too late to go back."

"My goodness. Well, that's too bad. They certainly weren't showing until after the turn, I *know*."

Ernest Everett blinked.

"You go out?"

"Oh, yes."

"Get any?"

"Oh, yes, after the tide turned we filled our buckets," Elizabeth told him in her best offhand manner. It was not often anyone caused Ernest Everett to change expression when he was not of a mind to, but that was one time when his eyes popped.

"Did, eh? That's funny—I didn't see you out there."

Elizabeth gave him an arch glance.

"Well, we saw yo-o-o-u!"

15

HOOKED!

My dungarees had a certain something about them that hung in the air like a beaded curtain; nobody would have named a rose after my sneakers; my work was in shreds, and my bank account in tatters; I had not been getting enough sleep, and my eyelids were badly granulated; I had a large hook in my shirt pocket, and a sinker in my pants pocket, along with dark glasses, a bottle opener, a rubber cork, and a booklet on "How To Tie Knots in Nylon."

In short, I was a fisherman.

A problem had arisen which I had not foreseen when we moved so confidently to the Cape. I refer to the problem of living less than a mile from a body of water in which, at the very moment I was trying to get some bread-and-butter work done, fish might be biting.

It is one thing to live in the city and have fishing opportunities arise only on vacation or on weekends. In that case a man does not worry too much in between times about whether the fish are biting or not, because he is a long way from them and tied to the office and there is nothing he can do about the situation.

My case was radically different. I was my own boss, with no one to tell me to get to work but myself—and temptation perched on my shoulder and whispered into my ear every day the wind and weather were right from June to November. I got so I would pray for small craft warnings from Eastport to Block Island.

The fact that we owned neither boat nor motor was no protection from this disease. There were several older, retired men who had their own boats and with whom it was a privilege and an education to fish. During the week one or the other of them was frequently looking for a fishing companion.

Just as I would be sitting down to the dull business of working for a living, one of them would call up.

"Everything's in the boat, and ready to go. I've got plenty of bait, and a good lunch packed, and they tell me there's a school of fish in the bay. There's an empty seat in the boat if you'd like to come."

Already that morning it would not have escaped my attention that it was a gorgeous day, sunny and warm, with an extremely personable little breeze making itself useful around the place. Nor would I be unaware of the heady rumors that were going around about several acres of stripers that were supposed to be stationed off Corporation Beach, searching diligently for baited hooks.

The night before, when I had stopped in at the Players Pharmacy, our local drugstore up at the intersection of Highways 6 and 134, I had heard the fishermen who hung out there talking among themselves about how tomorrow was going to be the day if the weather only held.

An old Cape Codder was paying me the compliment of asking me to go fishing with him, an honor that does not come to all men nor is lightly bestowed. I would learn a lot about

193

fishing if I went, and all I had to do in order to spend a glorious day in a way millions of men dreamed about from one annual vacation to the next was to pick up my fishing rod and step into the boat. What was I to do?

Any fisherman will know what I did. Time after time!

One day early in the season, in July, Mr. Ezra Newton came out of the post office as we stopped by to get our mail. He came over to the car and smiled at us benignly.

"Been out fishing lately?"

"Not since Sunday," I told him. "Have you?"

"Got out once. I was thinking maybe we ought to go fishing some day."

"Well, thanks, I'd like to. You let me know when you'd like to go and I'll be right there."

"Well! Wasn't that nice of Mr. Ezra?" said Elizabeth as we drove away.

"It certainly was. Even if he forgets all about it five minutes from now, I feel real flattered that he would ask me. Maybe we can make a date next week sometime, at that," I said comfortably. "I could organize my work so as to set a day aside, and go pick up some bait the night before . . ." I was constantly handing out a lot of high-sounding talk about "organizing my work," and Elizabeth always played right along, but it was just so much mish-mosh, of course.

I thought nothing more of Mr. Ezra Newton's unexpected suggestion until the following morning at 5:45 A.M., at which time the telephone rang. I tumbled sleepily out of bed, wondering what family crisis had arisen. Instead of a long-distance operator's brisk twitter, however, the slow, measured tones of Mr. Ezra Newton's voice came to me.

"Ready to go fishing?"

"F-fishing?"

"I'm all set to go out."

"You mean now?"

"Yes."

"Wh-who are you going with?"

Mr. Ezra Newton chuckled deeply.

"Well, I thought I was going with Mr. Corbett."

Desperately I pulled myself together, at the same time dismissing a nasty little nagging thought having to do with the work that was on my desk.

"Right. I'll be along just as soon as I can. Half an hour all right?"

"No hurry. I haven't had my breakfast yet, and we can't get out for a while yet anyway."

Elizabeth was wide awake too by then, and she decided to get up just to see what it would be like to get a good early start on the day. We went downstairs to fix breakfast, and I checked the tide table to see how we were set for time.

"Ebb tide was at 5:15, and last night was full moon, so it was a good low one," I said. "We've got plenty of time for breakfast."

After breakfast I collected part of my stuff together—rod, eelskins, jacket, and thermos of coffee—and forgot part—hat and dark glasses—and Elizabeth drove me over to Mr. Ezra Newton's. Mr. Ezra had all his stuff in his car and was puttering around in his barn. His motor was sitting in a fresh-water barrel, and when we arrived he was just taking it out. We put the motor in the trunk of the car, Elizabeth wished us luck, and I drove the Newton car to the creek. Due to an illness of a couple of years previous, Mr. Ezra Newton was not allowed to drive.

At the creek, Mr. Ezra walked slowly down to the bank carrying the oars and cushions while I waited to see which boat he went to, as I was not certain which one was his. The tide had indeed been a low one, and most of the boats were still well up the bank from the water. Mr. Ezra stopped beside one which lay cradled in the sand a good twenty feet from the

195

edge of the water. My first impression was that he had taken the masts off an old schooner and made a fishing boat out of it.

So it seemed, at least, when I thought about trying to drag it down the beach and into the water. I could not let a man in his seventies do much pushing, yet I knew that I was not likely to push it far alone. After a couple of futile attempts which confirmed my estimate of the boat's weight I decided I would have to create a channel for it through the sand if we were to get going any time before half-tide.

The only instrument at hand which might conceivably be turned to digging was an oar, so I started working away with one. I shoveled, we pushed, and the stern of the boat moved an inch at a time down the slight slope toward the water, humping sand up in front of it as it went. By the time we reached dampness the feeling in my back was unpleasantly reminiscent of my first fishing expedition. By the time the boat floated free I was ready to collapse across its bow and let my tongue dangle idly in the water.

As I stood panting at the water's edge, gathering my strength to go back and get the motor, Mr. Ezra Newton glanced thoughtfully at a trim, light little skiff sitting nearby.

"Maybe we should have taken my small boat," he said in his measured tones.

When the motor was in place and our gear all in the boat, I shoved us off, and Mr. Ezra Newton turned his attention to navigation. In his slow-paced, deliberate way, he made a couple of adjustments on the motor and prepared to pull the starting cord.

"Hope it runs. It ran up at the house, but it's been giving me trouble."

While I was digesting this news and thinking about what it would be like to arise at the crack of dawn, drag a heavy boat inch by inch down what had seemed like a Sahara of sand, and then not go anywhere, Mr. Ezra pulled the starting cord.

twice without results. Before I could commit hari-kari in the bottom of the boat with a fish knife, however, he tried it again and the motor started up with an unexpected amount of pep and ginger.

With majestic unconcern Mr. Ezra Newton backed us around in an erratic half-circle and our stern swung in toward another boat with a motor on it. He, bending over his motor in the stern, was placidly unaware of this, but I, tensed in the bow, was not. What with the noise of the motor and his deafness, there was little use in waking up a lot of other people by hollering at him, so I shoved my feet hard against the floorboards and waited to see whether we would smash against the other boat's motor or merely shear its mooring-line.

Mr. Ezra Newton suddenly headed us forward, however, and missed contact by a good inch. This was fine except for the fact that we were now ploughing straight across the narrow channel for the opposite bank. It looked as if we were going to climb it for sure, but then at the last possible instant Mr. Ezra slowly swung us around, dug a little gravel out of the side of the channel, and began to head out. In a minute or two we were in open water with only Tautog Rock to think about, and at that stage of the tide it was showing.

Mr. Ezra had a bag of sea worms, but, as he said himself, they had seen better days, and it was certain they would not live to see a worse one. They were as limp as a pixie's wrist, and inclined to come apart at the seams, but we baited up with them and eased them over the side, and for a while it looked as if it were not going to matter what condition our worms were in. There was not a sign of fish to be seen anywhere, nor a bit of gull activity, nor did we get anything resembling a strike or bump or nibble of any kind. It seemed likely that we would have a pleasant but uneventful ride, but on a fine day the mere pleasure of being out on the water was reward enough for the effort involved, and any fish one might get were a coveted but not strictly necessary bonus.

The sea, as always, offered its passing parade of the interesting and unexpected. At one time we found ourselves riding through a thick jellyfish soup, as small clear jellyfish filled the water to a depth of several feet down. Taking a chance that these small fry were not one of the jellyfish that sting, I scooped water and caught several at a grab. Colorless, transparent blobs, they were the nearest thing to nothing at all I could imagine holding in my hand, and yet each in its way was a perfectly formed receptacle of that mysterious and many-formed thing called life. One large patch of thousands upon thousands of tiny jellyfish was a delicate pink—and even "delicate" is a clumsy word to use in describing a color which only the cumulative effect of countless close-packed organisms, layer upon layer, made visible. When I scooped a handful of the minute creatures they seemed as utterly colorless as the others.

We passed schools of beautiful small fish with ragged-looking black tails whose raggedness was pure camouflage—actually their perfectly formed tails were partly black and partly colorless transparencies. Other schools of bait fish—handsome little green fellows about an inch and a half long—went by, and after a while an occasional gull spread his wings above us and soared past in clean white aerial perfection.

Four or five other boats were within sight up and down the shore, and one big party boat was far out on the horizon, probably after tuna. The water was very calm, and nothing was happening anywhere. By then I had been fishing several times and had even caught a good many fish—mackerel and bluefish—but had yet to see a striped bass. Though we were getting into a time of year when an occasional good day was likely to come along, the best bass fishing for boat fishermen came in the fall, if it came at all. Personally, I was beginning to believe the striped bass was a myth.

It was in this doubtful mood that I suddenly saw one of the most stirring sights a bass fisherman can see. All at once, outside us, I saw gulls gather and begin to wheel and dive, and under them I saw stripers after bait fish, chasing them right on top of the water. While the gulls snatched at bait from above, the bass flopped and splashed and flipped and jumped in their effort to feast on their prey. They looked enormous to me.

"Mr. Ezra!" I bellowed, and pointed. He took in the sight and changed course, turning us in a short circle through the school. I gripped my rod excitedly, but no sweet message in piscatorial Morse code sent its short and long jerks up my line. Then Mr. Ezra's rod bent sharply. He had a strike, and a good hard one. He was standing up, and for a moment he had trouble coordinating on the motor problem, but then he cut it off. I reeled in as fast as I could to get out of the way, after first dropping back when Mr. Ezra got his strike in the hope of picking up something myself.

"Is it big?" I yelled excitedly, but he shook his head.

"No, not very. I thought it was at first, though. It hit hard."

Mr. Ezra went quietly to work reeling in his fish. There was not much fight to it, but as it came near the boat I got excited again. Big or not by striper standards, it was still a good three feet long and the biggest fish I had seen caught yet. The only trouble was, it was not impressive in performance. When it was about twenty yards from the boat, it flopped over once on the surface, slowly, sluggishly, sloshing the water like a fat old lady changing position in a rooming-house bathtub. The same sluggish gurgle. I had the gaff ready, but the odd thing about the fish was that by the time it got alongside the boat it was only about two feet long, and I was able merely to take hold of Mr. Ezra's leader and swing it in. It did not thresh around, and only flapped its tail once. Nothing like a good lively mackerel or blue.

By the time it lay in the bottom of the boat it was scarcely more than a foot and a half long, and I scaled my first mental guess of fifteen pounds down to seven or eight.

199

"How much do you think it'll weigh, Mr. Ezra?"

"Oh, it ought to go five or a little better," he said. I silently trimmed off a little more. In any event it was a handsome fish, with its black speckled stripes lengthwise along its white sides. Its presence in the boat was a great satisfaction to me. At last I had been an accessory to the taking of a bass, if nothing more.

We put our lines back over the side and got going again, but we saw no further signs of the school and got no more strikes. After a while, to conserve the few worms we had, I decided to try an eel rig. I had never rigged an eelskin before, but I had watched Larry Finch and figured I could do it. Mr. Ezra was lost in reverie in his end of the boat, and I tried to avoid catching his attention in case I made a mess of rigging my eelskin. I found a piece of wire to tie the top of the skin on with, and borrowed a pair of rusty pliers out of the top of Mr. Ezra's tackle box to twist the wire.

I struggled and struggled with it, and stuck my fingers with the end of the wire, but finally I got the eelskin tied on. Still Mr. Ezra stared into space on his side of the boat, unaware of my efforts. I trailed the rig in the water, and the skin filled out properly and was a joy to behold. I was very proud of it as I let it out. Now we would see! Now I would start taking fish. This was what I had needed all along!

As my line went spinning out, Mr. Ezra finally roused himself and looked at his watch.

"Well, I guess we better call it a day," he said, and started reeling in. And in we went.

I had a lesson in how to clean a striper when we got in. Mr. Ezra laid the fish on the fish board that Caleb had built near his mooring post and went to work on it. His hands no longer possessed the great strength they had once known, but they moved with a gentle persistence that flaked off scales and cut away fins cleanly, and ultimately resulted in a fish artistically cleaned and ready for the oven. In passing, as he worked, he remarked that once he and Caleb brought in over a hundred fish about that same size, of which he himself had caught eighty-four.

"We had to come in. It was getting dangerous. Water was almost up to the gunwales. If we'd taken any more fish we'd have sunk."

We stood there by the fish board, the old man and I, one as baggy looking as the other in our old fishing clothes, and all at once I was aware that a Cadillac-load of tourists had stopped on the bank above us. A stylish-stout middle-aged woman got out, looked around, and spread her hands wide in an exaggerated gesture that took in her surroundings as she asked in a gayly patronizing manner, "Where are we? What is all this called?"

"East Dennis," I said, and considered pulling my forelock. I resented her "What is this little place?" attitude, and realized with some surprise that I was feeling the first stirrings of something that had long been missing in my life: local pride! From the way the woman looked at us, it was quite plain that we were part of the scenery, and that she considered us a couple of picturesque and probably quite smelly Cape Cod fishermen. (That last part pleased me, of course!)

A second car, also large and expensive, drove up, and a number of men, women, and children poured out of both cars. Quite plainly they were nosing around together, a two-car caravan seeking out the quaint sights of Cape Cod, of which I had temporarily become one.

"Wanta learn how to clean a fish? Here's your chance!" one of the men snickered around the cigar he was mouthing, as he turned to the kids. The way he said it sounded exactly the way he might have said, "Wanta feed the monkeys? Here's your chance!" Why was it so many people sounded like oafs when they were tourists gawking around? Camouflaged as I was, I got some inkling of what it might be like to be a Cape Codder and listen to tourists' comments and watch some of

201

their actions. I multiplied this by forty or fifty years, and began to change my opinion a little about some of our gruffer old-timers.

When I finally got home, Elizabeth naturally wanted to know what I was laughing about.

"I've got a couple of interesting bits of news, one of which will make your hair stand on end," I assured her. "First, Mrs. Ezra wants us to come over and have the fish for dinner with them."

"You told me that over the phone."

"Oh, yes, so I did. Well, the other thing is this. Just before I left, Mr. Ezra went out to the shed for something, and she told me how glad she was I'd gone out with him. 'I know he's terribly pleased about having gone out and come in on his own the way he did,' she says to me. 'You know, this is the first time in five years he's run the boat himself!' "

While I struggled along, wrestling day after day with temptation and generally losing the best two out of three falls, and while I was taking the bad days with the good and coming in as often as not with very little in the fish box to show for the day's outing, Elizabeth demonstrated the sensible way to go fishing.

She only went fishing twice during the season. She did not waste her time worrying about striped bass, either. The first time she went out with Asa to troll for mackerel, and they loaded the boat with mackerel. The second time she went out with Larry to troll for bluefish, and they loaded the boat with blues. She caught more blues than I caught all year. They hit such a mob of them that they had three lines out. Larry was running the boat, handling two lines, and taking fish off all three lines as fast as they could pull them in.

Such a day did not come my way, but some good ones did, including the day, the first of quite a few, when the stripers finally decided to reward my persistence.

Once again we had arisen in the dark, and as we started down the channel the sky was a deep rosy red and full of little clouds that gave it a close-quilted effect. All our preparations, our investment, our early rising, were made worthwhile before we were even out of the creek.

We headed up past Tautog Rock, and by that time the sun began to stick his head up behind us. My contemplation of this sight was suddenly cut short by a terrific yank on my line, and I thought I must have snagged on the bottom, the pull was so hard.

"Dammit, I'm hung up," I said, but Larry was watching the tip of my rod.

"That's not bottom you've tangled with there—you've got a striper on!"

For the next couple of minutes I had a magnificent time. Could this be the same breed of fish that had so disappointed me when Mr. Ezra brought his in? This was no old lady in a bathtub I had here. This was a fish that jerked and ran and flipped and slapped the water with his tail when he surfaced. He looked four times as large as the one Mr. Ezra caught, and by the time I got him in the boat he still looked at least twice as large.

"How come he gave me such a fight?" I demanded, still aquiver with the excitement of my first bass. "That one Mr. Ezra caught—"

"It may have been the way his hook happened to set, or because the water was warmer then. At any rate, now you know better."

"How much does it weigh?"

Larry batted the fish over the head with the gaff and then got out his scales, slipped the hook through its gills, and held it up. I looked.

"Nine and a half pounds!"

Larry eyed me coldly.

"Now, listen, knucklehead. There is no such thing as a

203

nine-and-a-half pound fish. Understand? You're looking at the prettiest ten-pounder you ever saw, and don't let me hear you call it anything else!"

In the course of the next three or four hours, Larry and I got six fish apiece, and though two or three of them were nearly as large as my first one, it remained the prize catch of the day by a matter of ounces. Meanwhile the breeze had freshened steadily, and by the time we headed in, the bay was working itself into a decidedly inhospitable mood, especially toward men in small boats. It was a poor time to have to go in—once more, it was nearly low tide—and the tide and wind were having an argument in the mouth of the channel which was nothing to get in the middle of, at least not in Larry's dory, which was a good deal larger than average. Fortunately, he had a mooring set up outside the channel where a boat could be moored until the tide came in again.

"You can drop me on the beach and I'll go get the kids' boat. I can row it out and meet you at the mooring," said Larry.

"But wait a minute," I said, spotting the flaw in that line of operations right away, "how are you going to get this boat back out to the mooring?"

"You can run it back out," said Larry. "You know enough about it now."

I can testify that the first time a landlubber finds himself alone with a ten-horsepower outboard motor and a sixteen-foot dory that is acting like a runaway seesaw in heavy surf, he feels very much alone indeed. However, I headed out, reached the mooring, and got a line on it without mishap. I felt very proud of myself. The only complaint I might have made would have been that the big dory was taking a fairly hard slapping-around while I sat there waiting for Larry, but at least it was not quite shipping any water as the waves banged against the stern.

Presently Larry appeared, rowing down the channel in

what looked like a highly inadequate skiff, but he managed it well and by dint of strenuous rowing succeeded in getting through the shallower parts of the channel. After that he was able to use the boat's little outboard motor. At first I thought the motor was not working, for when he was only twenty yards away I could not hear the slightest sound. Not until he was quite close could I pick it up. It was, by then, that kind of wind.

"Well, I made it all right," I told him proudly as he came alongside. "Been taking quite a beating out here, but I guess that's to be expected in a sea like this."

Larry inspected my job of mooring with a wooden expression while I waited anxiously for a word of praise or censure.

"Is that knot all right?" I asked. "I figured a double reef—"

"Nothing wrong with that," said Larry. "I do have one suggestion to make, though. Never moor a boat by the stern." I had pulled the most landlubberly trick of all!

We transferred stuff from one pitching boat to the other. It was like trying to work on the backs of two charging elephants who were out of step.

"We'll probably drop our whole catch into the bay," said Larry with his usual cheery pessimism, echoing my own horrible thoughts, but actually it was I who came nearer to falling in than the fish.

"Don't fall in yet," said Larry, when I had finally managed to scramble from one boat to the other. "If we can just make it to the mouth of the channel we'll be all right. Then, if you fall overboard, you'll only be in up to your neck."

"Up to my neck? Why, there's hardly a foot of water in the channel now!"

"I know. I figure if you fell in you'd manage to do it head-first."

Wind and wave were forgotten now, however. I had caught my first bass, and five more; we had landed a round dozen between us. No returning Roman hero ever enjoyed his triumphs more than we did when at last we had tied up for the day. Wives were fetched, cameras were loaded, and after a few group pictures of Larry and me and *all* our fish, I had a couple of studies done separately of my first and biggest bass and me.

Then we cleaned the fish, with special attention lavished on my big one, as that one was earmarked. My others I would give to friends, but my big one was for our oven alone, and would grace our table that very night. Florence went flying off on her bike to tell everybody who would listen that her daddy had caught the biggest fish and we were going to have it for dinner.

After a drink, Larry and I put our fish in the old station wagon and set out to spread them around. Along the way we met Alice Lawrence walking down to the beach. She was on our list, and was delighted to hear it.

"No need for you to go clear back home just to stick a fish in the refrigerator," said Larry. "We'll do that on our way by."

We stopped by the Lawrence's cottage and Larry took the fish in.

"Gee, that fish we wrapped up for them wasn't very big for four people," he said when he came back out, "but I guess they'll make out all right. Maybe we should have given them one of the larger ones, though."

We agreed that we would go ahead and see how we made out, and maybe come back later with a larger fish. Soon afterwards, however, we had disposed of all the fish we had except for my special fish and one for the Underhills, who were not home as yet.

I took these to our house, put them in the refrigerator, and went to work for a while, trying as usual to squeeze in a little gainful employment between fishing excursions. At five o'clock I telephoned the Underhills and found them home.

"I have a striper for you, Fred!"

"Say, that's wonderful, fellow!"

"I'll bring it right over."

I rushed downstairs to get the fish, and called to Elizabeth on my way out.

"Going to run their fish over to the Underhills. Be right back."

As I got in the car and put the newspaper-wrapped fish on the floor, I began to think about the Lawrences. Four of them, including two growing boys with ravenous appetites. The fish I was delivering was very good-sized, definitely larger than the one Larry had left for the Lawrences. The Underhills had only the two of them to feed, whereas the Lawrences could really use a larger fish. Matter of fact, a smaller one would be just right for the Underhills. How did I know how much they really liked fish? I *knew* the Lawrences were very fond of it. And they had those two growing boys . . .

Nobody was home at the Lawrences'. Alice was apparently still at the beach. I opened the back door and was greeted by savage snarls and barks from Henry, a small, cross dog who did not care for anything on two legs except Lawrences. I knew Henry and ignored his ferocious antics. This wounded his pride and he retired to a corner to sulk. I opened the refrigerator, found the fish, and switched fish. Then, when I looked around, the dog was gone. I had left the door open, the dog was gone, and our roads were full of careless summer motorists who might clip poor Henry and cut him down right in his surly prime.

"Here, Henry! Come on, Henry! Nice Henry!" I called without much conviction. I could not imagine Henry giving any pleading of mine house room. I went out and ran completely around the house begging Henry to stick his disgruntled muzzle into sight, but my supplications were wasted. I decided to take a chance that he would stay out of the road until I could deliver the Underhills' fish and get back to look for him some more, but all the way back around the corner to the Underhills' I kept thinking about how terrible it would be to have Henry's blood on my head.

When I picked up the smaller fish to take it in to the Underhills I almost regretted having changed fish, it was so much smaller, and when I unwrapped it on the Underhills' drainboard it looked downright unimpressive to me. Clara, however, registered delight.

"Oh, that's wonderful, and it couldn't have come at a better time. I'm having five of us for dinner tomorrow night!"

"*Five* of you?"

"Yes, some of Fred's family are coming down—and they particularly love fish. I was thinking of getting some."

The fish on the drainboard seemed suddenly to become a minnow. What had I done? Here was Clara with five mouths to feed, and I had switched fish on her! I quickly wrapped up the fish again.

"Listen, if you've got guests coming, you need a bigger fish than this, and I've got just the fish for you. I'll be back in two minutes!"

"Oh, now, don't do that!" protested Clara. "I don't want you to run clear back home—"

"I won't have to!" I said hastily, and left them looking understandably puzzled as I hurried out to the car. My hope now was that I would beat Alice Lawrence to her refrigerator. If she had returned from the beach and started getting her fish ready for the oven, I was stuck.

"When will you learn to let well enough alone?" I asked myself as I sped down the hill again. And what about Henry? He was still at large. I had to locate Henry.

There was no sign of life at the Lawrences'. As I slipped in and switched fishes again, however, I was startled to hear footsteps on the stairs. I had forgotten the house had a second floor. Luckily the footsteps were the four-footed type. It was Henry, who had apparently gone upstairs when I thought he had gone out.

"Well, you nasty bastard, am I glad to see you!" I said warmly over his snarls. "Nice old lovable Henry—get away from that door, or I'll bat your brains out!"

Minutes later I was home again and recounting my adventures to Elizabeth.

"Well, once more I'll try to get a little work done," I said when I had finished. "How soon do we eat?"

"I'm going to start dinner right now."

"Good! After all the exercise I've had, I'm hungry!" I was feeling well contented with myself and my efforts. Florence came bursting in just then from making her rounds, spreading the news about Daddy's big fish.

"When are we going to eat it?" she demanded importantly, reveling in reflected glory.

"I'm going to put it in the oven right now," said Elizabeth.

"I want to see it!"

"Yes, let's have a look at it," I agreed, and got it out of the refrigerator. I laid it on the drainboard and unwrapped it reverently.

What appeared from within rather more sheets of newspaper than were necessary to wrap one fish reminded me of a wizened matinee idol after his shoulder-padded coat had been removed. Here was no majestic denizen of the deep. Here was a miserable little striper that even made the Lawrences' fish look good. For one instant both Florence and I stared at it speechlessly. Then I exploded.

"Good God! Elizabeth, do you know what I did? *I gave away the wrong fish!*"

16

SEASON'S END

One of the last of the summer visitors was about to depart. She gazed at us compassionately and it was plain to see that her heart went out to us.

"What on earth will you do with yourselves after Labor Day, when everybody's gone?" she asked wonderingly.

Until I moved out of the city myself, I never realized how wonderfully conceited city dwellers are about the fact that they live in the city. However, the visitor meant well, so I restrained myself. I did not explain to her that summer, as far as we were concerned, had been just about long enough to suit us, and that Labor Day seemed very likely to become one of our favorite holidays as time went on.

Our friends and relations had not failed in their promises to visit us during that brief summer season when outsiders brought life and excitement to Cape Cod, only to take it away with them again in the fall. Our days had been full, and so had our house. Most of it had been fun, but lately there had been times when an odd mental picture of Labor Day's approach sprang to mind: it began to look exactly like the U.S. Cavalry riding to the rescue. We were ready to start living once more in a community instead of a resort.

Summer had been a hard time to get any work done. Visitors on vacation were always surprised and even a little hurt when I did not drop everything and spend my days frolicking in their company; after all, they were only going to be here a few days, and it seemed as if I might spend a little extra time with them . . . Those few days multiplied by ten or fifteen gives some idea of my predicament.

Our visitor's question—"What on earth will you do with yourselves after Labor Day, when everybody's gone?"—had to be answered somehow, so I trotted out one of my milder rejoinders.

"Well, we moved here in February, you know, and managed to survive until everybody got here."

"Yes, but by February the worst of it was out of the way. Within a month or so people were beginning to get ready for the Season. Besides that, you were just getting settled and had a lot to do."

I thought about the date written on the bare wall in our upstairs hall, written there the day we finished stripping off the old wallpaper in preparation for putting on new. "March 12," it read. I thought, too, about the fifteen hundred deferred projects I wanted to get at in the house and in the garage and up in the attic and down in the basement and in the room under the garage, not to mention the fence I wanted to remove, the grove I wanted to clear, and a few other things.

"We still have a good deal to do," I said. "I'm really looking forward to having a little more time on my hands, so's I can catch up on my odd jobs, and maybe even do a little work at my desk."

"Another thing," said our visitor, warming to her subject, "I was wondering about the schools."

211

From her tone it was plain she was prepared for a one-room schoolhouse with twin privies out in back and a teacher who had attended her last Teachers Conference in 1908. Not that Cape Cod did not have its school problems, the same as other places. In fact, Cape Cod had been having them longer than anyplace else in the country. The first public schools in America were established on Cape Cod in 1670, and maintained with funds from the fisheries tax, at a time when there was not so much as a henhouse in the place our visitor came from.

"The school seems to be pretty good," I said. "It's a consolidated township school. Fairly good sized, too. There are two classes each in most of the grades. As a matter of fact, a lot of Cape Codders seem to have quite a few kids. Must be that long Quiet Season."

Our visitor sighed.

"Well, I suppose there must be some interesting people around, here and there, and I hope you find them. I just hope it doesn't turn out to be deadly," she said, and went away convinced that for the next ten months we were either going to hibernate or stagnate. Actually, we did not really know ourselves what we were in for—but we had an idea.

On Labor Day the hum of motors on the distant highway was constant as a steady stream of cars flowed past, leaving the Cape. We thought about what the real-estate agent had told us—"The day after Labor Day you miss the traffic on the roads and things seem very quiet. Two days later you've forgotten all about it. You start seeing your local friends who have been tied up all summer with business or rentals, and the first thing you know you're busier than ever."

Of course the people who really noticed the difference in the traffic were those who lived along the main roads. We had to remember to look over at the highway to see the difference. After Labor Day, the mighty stream of traffic dwindled to a trickle, and it was noticeable that there were fewer cars circulating around the village streets, but the total impact on our section was rather gentle. In fact, the letdown was less noticeable than the pick-up which, right on schedule, followed on its heels. After about a day or so, the telephone began to ring.

"Hello?"

"Been fishing?"

"No, but I may go tomorrow."

"Better get out there. Now that the gawdam tourists are out of the way the fishing ought to get good. Best fishing always comes in September and October, you know. Finest weather, too. Well, I've got to go out and dig some more potatoes. Dug six bushel yesterday. Jeezcrise, it's killing me!"

And, then there was Hadley calling up to say:

"Hey, there's a square dance down in Eastham Saturday night, and we thought it would be fun to get up a set and go—"

And:

"Got your tickets for the men's supper yet?"

And:

"This is Fred. Say, we've been neglecting our bridge . . ."

And:

"Well, I guess we'll *have* to make it Thursday, then— there's something already doing every other damn night next week!"

And:

"Hell's bells, when are we supposed to get any sleep?"

And:

"Listen, how can I be there? I've already got one meeting that night!"

The Quiet Season had begun.

THE QUIET SEASON

17

WE REALLY OUGHT TO

SUPPORT IT . . .

September is the finest month on the Cape—until October comes along. Between them, at any rate, they take top honors. Spring is an uncertain, ill-defined season, with only a moderate amount of the glory that other parts of New England know. It is less positive on the Cape, less assertive. One week winter is holding its final remnant sale, and the next week summer is making its introductory offers, or so it seems.

What spring lacks is amply made up for by autumn, however. Thoreau, writing of the Cape in October, declared: "I never saw an autumnal landscape so beautifully painted as this was. It was like the richest rug imaginable spread over an uneven surface; no damask nor velvet, nor Tyrian dye or stuffs, nor the work of any loom, could ever match it. There was the incredibly bright red of the Huckleberry, the reddish brown of the Bayberry, mingled with the bright and living green of small Pitch-Pines, and also the duller green of the Bayberry, Boxberry, and Plum, the yellowish green of the Shrub-oaks, and the various golden and yellow and fawn-colored tints of the Birch and Maple and Aspen,—each making its own figure, and, in the midst, the few yellow sand-slides on the sides of the hills looked like the white floor seen through rents in the rug.

"Coming from the country as I did, and many autumnal woods as I had seen, this was perhaps the most novel and remarkable sight that I saw on the Cape. . . . What other dyes are to be compared to these? They were warmer colors than I had associated with the New England coast."

Every drive and every walk through that autumnal landscape was a rich experience, though it was not necessary to set foot out of the house to enjoy it. There was no view any finer than the one from our own back porch. Our field above the marshes, the marshes themselves, and the trees that bounded them on the far side, lining the highway and climbing the hills, provided every imaginable brightness and shading of fall tints. They drew us out onto the porch again and again.

At first, where the fine fall days were concerned, our pleasure was unalloyed. We still retained the city-dweller's superficial and short-sighted attitude toward the weather. An autumn rain in the city was a chill and dreary inconvenience, and if a warm southern wind yielded to a sharp northern blow in late September, bringing a sweep of cold air down from the Arctic reaches of Canada, we shivered regretfully.

On the Cape we learned to look at these things differently. One September day Elizabeth came in from the garden, where the sun and a strong southwest wind were combining to make the outdoors delightful. It was no mere breeze we were getting, it was a hard, steady wind that had been blowing for two days, but it was warm and did not buffet unpleasantly the gardener who was working close to the ground.

Elizabeth had occasion to telephone Ruth Asa, and in the course of their conversation the weather drew comment.

"Isn't it wonderful out? So nice and warm," said my wife, who is opposed to winter in any shape or form.

"Yes, but according to the weather report a cold mass is moving down from Canada, so the wind will be switched around by tomorrow." Ruth Asa spoke with what sounded strangely like satisfaction.

"Oh, I hope it doesn't," said Elizabeth, "this warm wind is wonderful. It could stay this way all winter so far as I'm concerned."

"H'm, well, you wouldn't say that if you'd seen it blow up here as hard as I have. It's when a sou'wester like this keeps blowing for about three days that it's likely to bring in a hurricane. There's one off the coast of Florida now, so what we want is a good cold northwest wind that will push that hurricane away from us out to sea if it moves this way. The only thing I wish this sou'wester *would* do is bring us some rain. We sure need rain. If we don't get some soon we're liable to start having forest fires."

Hurricanes and forest fires and drought—not for a long time had we worried about any such things at close range. Actually, some of the old Cape Codders were never free of the canker of worry where the elements were concerned. They knew the fury and the power the wind and the sea could display, and they feared them. They were not only afraid of hurricanes, they were afraid of tidal waves, and perhaps not without reason.

The highest tide on record, in 1815, came close to inundating the Cape. Ships were torn from their moorings, houses damaged, trees uprooted, and saltworks destroyed.

As for hurricanes, such reminders as our own hurricane dump, and those grim sections across the Cape where only jagged trunks remained of acres of once large trees, and the absence of all but a few of the great shade trees that once so

219

proudly lined the streets of Provincetown, bore testimony to the damage done in 1938 and, more particularly as far as the Cape was concerned, in 1944.

In this instance, however, the wind switched around on schedule and brought us its cold comfort, and the hurricane petered out, anyway. Colder weather helped to emphasize how numbered were the days of the beach umbrella, even though it would still blossom sparsely on the sands of the seaside during moments of southerly winds and bright skies. Except for a few newlyweds and an occasional childless couple or older folk taking a late vacation, the tourists were gone. Traffic had dropped to a point where the stretch of highway that came into view beside the marsh would often be empty for minutes at a time before anything—and then it was usually a solitary car—passed along it like a toy pulled by a string. Men and women in shorts were almost a forgotten sight. Wool, flannel, and corduroy began to be seen ever more frequently. So did the large-checked green-and-black or red-and-black wool caps which so many Cape men wore in all seasons except the hottest part of summer.

The rhythm of small-town social life, which the summer season had interrupted and diffused, focused down again into a clear and regular cadence of activities and events. For the most part, the only outsiders still on the scene were the regular summer residents who owned their own places, and they appeared now only on weekends. More and more of the beach cottages were drained of water and of life, and took on their dreary, boarded-up, out-of-season look.

While the golden days of fishing lasted, the Reverend Oswald Blake continued to miss some of us when the tide was running against him, but in due time the fish left for warmer waters, and the annual ceremony of taking up the boats marked the end of another fishing season. This was always a moment filled with gentle melancholy, this moment when the diehard fishermen of the community gathered on the beach of the inlet

220

and, by the decisive act of taking the boats out of the water and towing them on trailers to barns or sheds, finally conceded that the fishing was finished and done with for another year. This ceremony unfailingly took place on a glorious Sunday morning, the sort of morning that would be perfect out there on the water if only a few fish had had the decency to stay around. That same Sunday, some of us would be in church who had attended but irregularly for several months past.

After the boat ceremony, Asa and I finally ended up back at my house to have coffee with Elizabeth. Our talk was all of local affairs, and presently Asa gave us some idea of the struggles of the harbor committee.

"That Freddie!" he sighed, and his eyes rolled expressively under the heavy eyebrows raised into a martyr's arch. "You know, he's no politician, and, well . . . We were trying to argue a man into selling some beachfront property to the town, and Freddie got so mad he had to leave the room. I managed to smooth things over, but it was a trial."

Asa seemed to be on half the committees in town. As we settled into our first full Quiet Season, however, we soon discovered for ourselves that in a small community any willingness and ability to render public service was quickly seized upon, and that since all activities are interlocked—due to the fact that the community's real workers always overlap from one committee or organization to another—one thing led to another with deceptive speed.

Indeed, such acceptance as we had been granted by our Cape Cod neighbors was due in large part to the same thing that had won acceptance for the Underhills and the Ransoms —a willingness to meet them more than halfway, and to serve the community. Actually, certain of the Cape Codders' wives found it convenient to get newcomers to do a lot of the work, and were continually roping them in. However, the end result was still sociability.

On the other hand, many a family who had moved here

221

before us were not a real part of the community and could not understand why some of us were accepted when they were not. It was mainly because they sat at home and expected to be courted; because they went to church suppers and expected always to be the guest; because they really had no respect for the Cape Codder's intellect and attitudes. All of these things were obvious to the Cape Codder, even though the newcomer in question thought he was too dumb to notice.

Children in the family bring on involvements more rapidly, of course. The first three days of Florence's busy week were filled from eight to five, due to after-school activities. There were dancing classes, and the Brownies also entered her life. Her mother took her to the first few meetings, and came home looking amazed at herself.

"Guess what I am?"

"What?"

"A Brownie leader!"

"What? They signed *you* up?"

"Yes. They needed another mother to help, and, well . . ."

After thirteen years in New York city, it took me a moment to adjust myself to the news that I was the husband of a Brownie leader.

"Boy, if this news seeps back to certain quarters of Manhattan, we will be put down as lost for good. The question heard most frequently in the market place will be, 'How corny can they get?' "

"Corny or not, it's going to shoot Tuesday afternoons for me," sighed my wife, "but what are you going to do?"

I got mine, indirectly, at least, through Florence's Wednesday activity. The Wednesday square-dance classes were provided free at Carleton Hall in Dennis by the Dennis-East Dennis Recreation Association, and not only all the little girls but all the little boys and all the big boys and big girls, too, attended them. They poured off the school buses into the ramshackle old hall and Dick Anderson, one of our Cape Cod square-dance callers, took it from there. Florence came home from the classes a square-dance enthusiast, which was more than she had been after the first Cape dance she attended. On that occasion she had been invited to go with neighbors who were taking their own children. She came home looking downcast.

"Well, how was the square dance?" asked her mother.

"Not very good."

"What's the matter? Didn't you get to dance?"

"No, I didn't dance once!"

"How come?"

"Well," said Florence indignantly, "Agnes promised me a dance with Herby, but he threw up and they had to take him home!"

The square-dance lessons seemed like a fine idea, one of many for which the Recreation Association was responsible. This association was an unofficial organization of the people of the community. Everybody in both villages was automatically a member. Money was raised at an annual auction, with Hadley as auctioneer. I had been one of his helpers at the latest one.

"This Recreation Association is a wonderful thing. I certainly hope it keeps up the good work," I remarked one day to Hadley.

"H'm," said he, and went away thoughtfully.

"I suppose I might as well serve on just this one more thing," I said to Elizabeth, "but let's draw a line from here on and not get involved in too much. I would open my big mouth to Hadley! How was I to know he was chairman of the nominating committee for the Association board, though? Damn it, I've been looking forward to things quieting down in the winter so we can finish some of our painting and wallpapering! I'm determined at least to get the upstairs hall papered.

"It's a disgrace the way it is—especially with that March

date staring us in the face. I should never have written that on the wall, but I thought at the time we'd get to it the very next week. Furthermore, I want to get down in my workshop and build those shoeshelves and a dozen other things we need. I haven't had a minute down there in I don't know when."

"What about some of the winter jobs I've got lined up?" asked Elizabeth. "I've got a sweater half-knitted that I brought with us from New York! At least I got my sewing done there. I never seem to here!"

We resolved to put aside two nights a week for household projects, and to let nothing interfere with those nights. Mondays and Wednesdays, we decided, would be dedicated nights.

A couple of days later Elizabeth came home from a Ladies' Aid meeting.

"They're planning a square dance. It's the first time the Ladies' Aid has ever sponsored a dance."

"Well! For a New England Ladies' Aid, that's getting pretty devilish. I hope you told them those suggestions we thought of after that other affair—you know, about making the refreshments end of things go more smoothly."

"I did," said Elizabeth a bit grimly.

"What happened?"

"They made me chairman of the refreshments committee!"

That cut into the next few days pretty well, and by that time our Recreation Association committee had got an art class organized. It seemed that through something called the State Aid Adult Education Program, money was available for adult classes involving such things as art, ceramics, hooked rug making, woodcarving, and furniture refinishing. Rug classes, for example, were popular all over the Cape, and had accounted for a great many fine hooked rugs.

"Well, I hate to tie up another evening, but I'd hate to pass up a chance at an art class, too," I admitted. "I've been wanting to take up painting for twenty years and never seemed to get around to do it. Being a member of the committee, too,

I want to see the class be a success, so I sort of feel that maybe I ought to support it . . . But on the other hand, it's going to meet on Wednesdays, and that's the night we've set aside—"

"Don't be silly. If you want to go, go. We'll pick another night. We'll make it Thursday."

"Well . . . if you really think I ought to. But Thursday for sure. How about you, by the way? Don't you want to go, too?"

"No, that would mean a sitter, and I don't really care enough about it."

A couple of days later Mabel Crowell called up and asked us to a rummy party Thursday night. When Elizabeth told me about it I squawked virtuously.

"Thursday night? Listen, the weekends are getting bad enough around here, but when they start creeping in toward the middle of the week— After all, we set aside Wednesday and that didn't work, and now we've set aside Thursday and if we let ourselves be pushed any further there won't be anything left. Monday's already down the drain—"

"Well, Mabel said she normally wouldn't have the party in the middle of the week, but it's for the Seth Searses and they're leaving for their trip Friday, so it has to be Thursday."

I threw up my hands.

"Okay, okay, we'll go. We'll just have to concede this week and make a new start next Monday night."

"But next Monday night," said Elizabeth, "is the first meeting of the P.T.A., and I suppose we really ought to support it . . ."

A few more weeks like that, and we stopped making resolutions. In the meantime, we had learned a little more about square dancing, and it had claimed us for its own. Naturally, then, when a group of enthusiasts got together and formed an organization called the Cape Cod Square and Folk Dancing Association, we felt we really ought to support it. We attended the first meeting and dance, and signed up as members. At this meeting it was announced that a beginners' class would be held every other Wednesday night at Lyceum Hall in Yarmouthport.

"Well, I don't see why you shouldn't," I told Elizabeth on the way home, in answer to the inevitable question. "This is a brand-new organization and we certainly should try to support its activities. It sounds like exactly what we need—I'm really sorry my art class is on the same night."

"It means a sitter."

"Well, we don't spend much money on entertainment up here. Anyway, it's only every other week, so that's not so bad."

Three weeks later the art-class teacher and the superintendent of schools had a squabble and the art class had to be suspended. Elizabeth urged me to finish out the beginners' square dance class with her.

"Besides, we can always use more men," she said. She and Mabel Crowell had singled out a couple of local men they felt should be doing more dancing and had taken them by the ear up to Yarmouthport. Neither of these gentlemen had had any previous intention of getting involved in any fool class, but they had been square dancing enthusiastically ever since.

"Well, as long as it's only every other week, and only has two more sessions to run, I suppose I might as well go," I conceded. "That's three more weeks and we'll be in the clear, and then let's set Wednesdays aside and get some of our household projects done. Forget Mondays. Forget Thursdays. They don't seem to work out. But maybe if we pick just one day a week and stick to it—"

That Wednesday the class voted to extend the course and meet *every* week.

"Well, that does it," I said to Elizabeth, after the extension had been voted. "Our weekday nights have gotten completely out of hand. The only hope now is our weekends. Saturday nights are out, of course. There's always something doing. But we're forgetting Friday nights. We don't *have* to make any Friday dates."

"All right," she agreed promptly, "we'll make Friday our stay-at-home night. And stick to it!"

"And stick to it!"

During that same evening Hadley Ransom clapped me on the back.

"Well, good to see you out! Where you been keeping yourself?"

"Oh, I've just been sitting home, wondering what to do with myself," I replied, but the tone of my remark was lost on Hadley as he tickled a passing girl and shouted some gay persiflage after her.

"Well, don't let it worry you," he said, turning back to me and rubbing his hands together in brisk anticipation, "things are going to pick up around here from now on. We're going to get our regular duplicate bridge started at the hall on Friday nights, beginning next week. *Everybody* turns out for that!"

18

CRANBERRY RED

"I have to go up to the bogs and I've got room for two in the car," said Mr. Sam's daughter, Mabel Crowell. "Would you like to go and maybe do a little gleaning?"

It was a fine October day, and we had been wanting to visit the bogs and watch the cranberry pickers in action ever since they had started picking a few weeks earlier. As usual, I had a day's work all set, and as usual I put it aside and went.

Mr. Sam owned more cranberry bogs than anyone else in our village. Lots of the natives owned small bogs and did their own picking with maybe one or two helpers, but Arthur Strong, who worked Mr. Sam's bogs for him, had to round up a crew of pickers every fall from among the Portygees over in Harwich.

This was perhaps the most difficult and worrisome task of the many and endless chores connected with cranberry growing. Arthur was an intelligent, conscientious, hard-working man, and it was a trial to him to have to beg and wheedle to get the Portygees to come and pick, and to stay on the job when they got there.

"Do you know what one of them said to me when I first went over to get a gang together?" Arthur asked Mabel once in tones of hushed horror. " 'To hell with the cranberries!' That's what he said!" To Arthur's way of thinking that was like saying to hell with America.

Three or four of the best pickers were conscientious and dependable men, but the rest, particularly some of the women, were afflicted with a gay, saucy, and scatterbrained independence that was wonderfully entertaining for an outsider to observe in operation, but which was nerve-wracking for Arthur, who had to put up with it. He was also hurt when they lapsed into Portuguese and discussed him in terms which—he could tell by the sound of their gibberish—were not only uncomplimentary but unprintable, especially in Portugal, Brazil, and the Cape Verde Islands.

Generally, however, their soft voices remained amiable and their dusky faces split frequently into white-toothed laughter, and they went cheerfully about the hard labor of cranberry picking and managed to pick an enormous amount of berries.

The cranberry-picking season lasted four or five weeks, and coincided happily with what was generally one of the finest periods of the year, from mid-September to mid-October. The vines were still green then, but where they had been combed by the pickers' scoops or the picking machine that Arthur ran they showed a tinge of the reddish-purple hue they would take on for the winter.

And now as Mabel drove us across the Cape on a side road we passed several small bogs, and she identified them for us as we passed. "That's Josh's bog there," she would say, or, "I understand George Hall sold that one to Pinkney Howes, at least I know George owned it once—anyway, Pinky bought it from someone. Pretty bad weeds there, take a lot of work to put

229

it in shape—if you ask me, Pinky got stuck, but then he usually does."

Presently we passed a small bog with a man and a woman working in it.

"Say, that looked like Nate Black," I said, craning around for another look.

"It was. That's his bog. That was Nate and his wife."

"You mean to say they do their own picking?"

"Yes. Aren't they something?"

It seemed so to me, considering the fact that Nate Black was eighty-six years old and Mrs. Black was about the same. Nate was also the proprietor and operator of the Black Hills Barber Shop, one of the most secluded barber shops I had ever encountered anywhere. It was located on his place in the hills not far from the little lost lake where we went for blueberries and beach plums. Nate was just a few months younger than D.H., who was definitely his oldest customer. He had been cutting David Henry's hair for more than sixty years.

"Here's where we turn off," said Mabel a couple of minutes later, and we left the pavement behind for a narrow sand road that wound out of sight through the woods.

It is easy sometimes, after exploring every two-lane road, paved or unpaved, that you can find in your own local area, to begin to think you know the region and what is in it. It is easy to lose sight of those large areas that lie *between* the roads. Even on Cape Cod there are many such areas, and we were entering one of them now.

What we were following was little more than two sandy tracks through the thick woods. Branches thrust out jealously from the sides into the narrow way and flailed the car as it passed. Similar single-width car paths confronted us from time to time at silent crossroads amid the trees where the vista was exactly the same in any direction. Mabel turned right and left and took this fork and that one, and the woods seemed to close in around us more and more. A cock pheasant sprang out of the brush beside the road, drummed away in multicolored glory to a bend in the road, and hung framed against the sky for an instant as he glided through a break in the trees.

"Maybe we'll see some deer, too, before we're through," said Mabel, wheeling nonchalantly around a corner. "Father and I often run into 'em through here."

"I hope you don't mean that literally."

"Well, not quite. Land, I'd hate to hit a deer. You know, if you smash up your car hitting a deer you're simply out of luck. You can't sue the State for damages, and what's worse you don't even get the deer! The conservation officer takes it."

"Well, don't hit one, then. I'm an old softie, I couldn't stand to see one hurt."

"I love to see deer," said Elizabeth. "I can't understand how anyone could shoot one."

"I love deer, too," said Mabel. "I'd hate to say which I love best, though—deer or venison." She took another turn and we could see open sky ahead through the trees. "Well, we're getting near to Bacon and Ellis now."

"Who are they?"

"Bacon and Ellis is a bog. That's the name of it." The trees thinned out ahead of us and the country opened up and there below us was a large bog.

"This one has been picked, all but one little section, and Arthur will do that with the machine," said Mabel. A good-sized square that had not been touched by the pickers could plainly be seen, as straight-edged as though it had been lined off with a ruler. We went along beside Bacon and Ellis for a moment, and could see another large bog off in the distance.

"That's Elbow. We'll be going past it in a few minutes," said Mabel, and then plunged us back into the woods again. We were in an old coupe that had been built in a day when high-crowned roads and deep ruts of the sort we were encoun-

231

tering still had to be taken into consideration, in a day before cars bellied the road the way they do now. For trips to the bogs a person needed either a car such as this or a jeep.

"Of course you don't get *too* much traffic on these roads, but once in a while I've met the truck bringing in the pickers," said Mabel. "Then there's always a lot of shouting and laughing and a big discussion about which car ought to back up. I'll bet I've backed half a mile sometimes before we were through. Tell you what, I'll drive you on over to Great Swamp first and then we'll come back to Elbow. That's where they're picking, at Elbow, and I have to take a check to one of the pickers."

We caught another glimpse of Elbow through the trees down a side track and then went on over a ridge and through some more woods to the largest of Mr. Sam's bogs. Great Swamp stretched away majestically below us, acre upon acre. A good sand road encircled it, and widened out at several points to provide places where the trucks could unload the empty boxes and pick them up again when they had been filled. We took the grand tour and then returned to Elbow.

The term "bog" had misled me. Most of my previous acquaintance with bogs had been through mystery novels. Bogs were dismal, soggy morasses in which Things stalked about on moonless nights; they were places where people, fleeing from a nameless terror, sank without a trace. Even though my better judgment told me that people could not very well pick cranberries on their hands and knees if they had to shove themselves through muck, I was still prepared to sink in up to my shoetops when first I set foot in a bog. I was not at all prepared for the dry, sandy soil which I found actually constituted the bottom of a cranberry bog.

Here was the prodigality of Mother Nature. Here were cranberries everywhere, so that it was not a question of picking all the cranberries but merely all that it was efficient to pick. It was not possible to take a step without crushing berries, even in sections that had already been picked. In fact, it was hard to believe they *had* been picked, so many were the berries that were left, until we saw the close profusion of berries in an area that had not yet been touched.

Water ditches ran in straight lines the length and breadth of the bog and divided it up into square sections. Over in the next plot the Portygees, about ten of them, were moving slowly forward side by side on hands and knees, rocking their scoops through the vines, covering the ground on each side and directly in front of them with half a dozen passes and then moving a few inches forward. In the section nearest us, Arthur was operating the picking machine, which was guided by two handles like a power landmower but which traveled at a much slower speed.

The combination of Mabel, pen, and checkbook drew the pickers as the flower draws the bee. She had come prepared, knowing that if one drew against the money he had coming to him the others would get the itch too. The pickers were paid fifty cents a box, which was a third of a barrel. Mabel had to keep a careful accounting of how many boxes each picker had picked, and stand ready to pay on demand any part or all of the money each had coming at any time. One by one they drifted over, grinned, and said they guessed they'd better have twenty, twenty-five, forty dollars—seldom more, as it was nice to have that one big check to look forward to at the end.

While Mabel was busy with her bookkeeping, Elizabeth and I sat down among the vines of a section that had been picked and began gleaning. Every time we lifted the low vines we would find a dozen or more shiny red berries that had fallen to the ground and eluded the pickers' scoops. It took very little time to glean a quart of top-grade berries.

Had anyone told me that sitting in a cranberry bog in October could rival and even surpass sitting on the beach I would have felt he had strange tastes indeed; but it was true. A breeze had sprung up that day which would have made the beach a trifle cool, but here in this low place, sheltered by the hills, the breeze left us alone and the sun warmed the sand through the vines just enough to make the ground temperature perfect for us.

The polished red of the berries and the russet-tinged green of the vines delighted the eye; the steady roll of the berries in the scoops and the soft voices of the Portygees pleased the ear. The warm sandy soil, the smooth round berries, and the delicate vines were a joy to the touch; the tart bite of an occasional raw cranberry, bitten but not chewed, gave zest to the sense of taste; and the sense of smell was invigorated by the light, special quality a field of healthy vegetation gives to fresh air. It was one of those magical situations in which all the senses participated and were alive, and it was good merely to be a two-legged animal close to the soil.

"Well, the cranberry has done it again," I admitted to Mabel.

Nothing on the Cape had handed me a greater surprise. Before Elizabeth and I arrived on its home grounds, we had considered the cranberry one of Nature's less intriguing small round efforts.

At Thanksgiving we would not have felt our turkey dinner was complete without the traditional cranberry jelly, but that was the only cranberry concoction we liked. Whole cranberry sauce was not allowed dish room on our table. According to my palate, it had a sharp, tangy, almost metallic aftertaste— or at least it had had when last I tasted it. I had avoided it for years.

As for cranberry juice, we thought that this was merely a case of the cranberry industry trying to start something. The only time we encountered the juice was occasionally on a menu when some tearoom went overboard trying to vary its appetizer offerings, and I for one never let curiosity run away with me.

We did not, therefore, look forward with any appreciable eagerness to being closer to the source of supply. The nicest thing about the cranberry, we felt, was the reddish-purple color of the bogs in winter. The subdued warmth of that color in flat, level stretches amid the gently sloped hills of the Cape had the pebbly texture of rich, handwoven, woolen cloth.

Wherever there were bogs tucked among the hills, they seemed to flow into every corner like a lake of vegetation. To add to their scenic charm, they were generally surrounded by woods and close to a lake or pond. Between the bog and the pond would be a weatherbeaten old shack—the engine house, for of course when a bog was flooded and drained the water had to be pumped either in or out, depending on whether the bog lay higher or lower than the level of the water.

It was enough, then, that the cranberry provided scenic attractions. It had done its bit. That its flavor left something to be desired was regrettable, but at least it was not a total loss.

We soon found, however, that the cranberry was not going to be content to cross our path merely in the great outdoors. It kept turning up under our noses on Cape Cod tables. The first time, during a midnight spread after a rummy game, I found myself confronted with whole cranberry sauce, and before I could pass it on and get rid of it my hostess said, "Oh, won't you try some of my spiced cranberries?"

"Spiced?" I weakened. Like most of us, I had certain illusions about food, and one of them was that I liked spices. All someone had to say was "spiced" and I was ready to take a taste. Spices were fragrant and exotic things; they made good reading, from the Bible on down; I liked the *idea* of spices, and so was always expecting to like spiced things. Actually, there probably were not half a dozen exotically spiced dishes I really liked; but the *word,* and the names of various spices, always intrigued me.

I was even willing to try whole cranberries, then, if they were spiced—and for once I was pleasantly surprised.

"Wonderful what a few spices can do for those things," I decided.

235

Then somebody fed us some "ten-minute" cranberry sauce, so called because it only has to be cooked that long, and it tasted even better than the spiced variety.

"Either my tastes are changing, or it's the sea air. But maybe these Cape Codders have a trick up their sleeves, or the commercial canners put something in that makes that after-taste," I said to myself.

After that the cranberry really began to strut its stuff for us. Mabel Crowell fed us Cranberry Crunch, and it became one of our favorite desserts. Then she fed us cranberry chiffon pie, and that was more than a dessert—it was a gala event. Then somebody gave me cranberry juice and ginger ale one evening and I, who would rather have a glass of plain water than most soft drinks, lapped it up.

When Elizabeth and I even gobbled up raw cranberries that had been sugared, mixed with pineapple, and served on shortcake, we knew the berry had signed us up.

It was pleasant to find we could enjoy cranberries so much, because nothing was more truly native to the Cape. Not only to the Cape, but to our own little section of it, for cultivated cranberries were first grown in Dennis. Wild cranberries were found and eaten by the Pilgrims, and in 1667 ten barrels of them were presented to King Charles II by his loyal subjects of the colony of Massachusetts, but nobody thought to try to cultivate them until about a century ago when a Dennis resident by the familiar local name of Hall cleared an old peat swamp and started experimenting. Cape Codders had been at it ever since.

Our neighbors not only put up their own cranberries, they also raised them in their own bogs—or if they had no bogs of their own, they had a relative or neighbor in the village who did and from whom they got their berries. We never ate a berry that had been grown more than five miles away, and some of them had been grown a lot closer than that. There was even one small bog right in the center of town, behind houses a couple of doors from the church, and we never knew it was there until we heard someone mention that it had yielded forty-five boxes!

I thought of all these things as the three of us busied ourselves with gleaning on that magical day, and I also got to thinking about how many Cape Codders had told me what hard work it was to handle a scoop and how they had all but said in so many words that a newcomer like myself would probably be yelling for mercy before he had finished filling one box. It occurred to me that it would be nice to have an excuse to stay in the bog for the rest of the day, and that it would also be nice, next time the subject of cranberry picking came up, to be able to take the wind out of some Cape Codder's sails by mentioning that I had once picked, say, a barrel of cranberries myself. A barrel—that was a good round amount to shoot at.

"Mind if I try my hand with one of those scoops along the edge of the ditch?" I asked Arthur. He picked me out a good one and gave me a brief lesson in how to hold the scoop, how to rock it back, and how far to shove the prongs into the vines before starting the lift.

"You won't want to do that for long," said Mabel, watching me indulgently as I assumed the proper hands-and-knees posture and made a few awkward passes at the vines.

"How would you like an extra picker this afternoon?" I countered. "I'm going to come back here after lunch and pick you a barrel of cranberries."

"That's three boxes, and if you do it I'll pay you a dollar and a half. That'll just about cover the rubbing alcohol."

"You've got yourself a boy."

We went home to lunch. While we were eating Freddie Barr came by to give us a couple of mackerel of his own salting and tell us all about the doings of the harbor committee.

"Honest to Gawd, that Asa," said Freddie, shaking his head. "I had things all set on a deal, and then he went and said

237

the wrong thing. I got things back under control all right, but it takes a lot of talking. I spend half my time smoothing things over!"

After lunch Mabel took me back up to the bogs.

"Maybe I ought to fix you up some kind of knee pads like the pickers wear," Elizabeth remarked before I took off. All the pickers—including the women, who wore slacks—had long strips of fur tied on each leg to make the going easier on the prayerbones.

"I'm only going to pick for a couple of hours at the most," I told her. "I won't need them."

When I got back to the bogs and told Arthur I wanted to pick for a while, he gave me a scoop and pointed out a section I could pick in.

"This doesn't feel like the same scoop," I commented.

"Try the others, then, and find one that feels right," he said in an approving tone of voice. "All the pickers have their favorites—in fact, most of them own their own. They pay as high as seventy-five dollars for a good scoop."

I took a box and went to work. After a while Arthur came by again. My box was about half filled.

"Well! You're going pretty good."

"I aim to pick a barrel of cranberries for Mabel if it kills me."

"A barrel? Why, I thought you just wanted to pick a few quarts for your own use. This is a thin spot here—come on over yonder," said Arthur, and transferred me to a better section.

I had got to the bog a little after two, and at four-thirty I was still enjoying myself, with my barrel picked and an extra box for good measure. By then the Portygees had departed, laughing and joking, some on a truck that brought in a load of empty boxes and some in their own cars. Arthur himself was about ready to call it a day. Because like sand anywhere, whether on the beach or the desert, the sand of the bogs grew cold the minute the sun began to drop low in the sky.

Arthur was still angry about the day's tally. Every day when it came time to count up the number of boxes each picker had picked, it was the same old story: the grand total claimed always exceeded in number the full boxes that dotted the swath the pickers had made.

"The same ones always chisel on their count, and the best picker of the bunch, a man with twelve kids to support, always takes the difference off his. None of the others ever offer to, even though they can see how many boxes there are on the field and know somebody has to be wrong."

Arthur had a notebook in which he carefully entered the tally of each picker, so as to report the figures to Mabel that evening. I asked him what was the most a good picker could pick in a day. Incidentally, about five and a half hours is as long as a picking day runs, since it is not possible to start in the morning until the dew has completely dried off the vines. Starting beforehand would injure them.

"Well," said Arthur, "I've seen 'em pick sixty boxes or better. In fact, you know that big woman that was picking today? She picked seventy-four one day, but she had a kid helping her—bringing her boxes, and so on. For a short stretch, now, there was a young feller who didn't get here till one o'clock one day because he had a flat up in the woods when he was driving in. Well, he went to work, and pretty soon he come over and said he had something to tend to and couldn't pick any more that day. 'How'd you do?' I said, and he didn't look much impressed with himself. 'Oh, only fair,' he said. 'I got seventeen.' I looked at my watch. It was three o'clock. 'Well, good Lord, you only been at it two hours!' I told him, and he felt better. They got no sense of time."

I looked at the four boxes I had filled in very little short of two hours and a half and decided I still had a few fine points to pick up on the art of handling a scoop.

239

Nevertheless, Arthur kept scrupulous account of every box of berries that was picked, so my modest contribution to the day's tally was not overlooked. Arthur never referred to anybody by name; his wife was always "she," Mr. Sam was "he," the pickers were all "he" or "she," and when he made his nightly reports to Mabel she had to guess whom he was talking about. The only time he went through the ordeal of mentioning names right out straight was when he read off the pickers' tallies.

When he had made his report that night, he hesitated in a manner that indicated he was not through.

"He picked four boxes," he announced.

"Oh, did he?" Mabel did not have to ask who "he" was. There was only one picker in the field who would have come up with a total like that.

"Yes. See, I entered him right here," said Arthur, showing her his notebook. Down in one corner of the page was a special notation. 'Picker—4,' it said.

By the time Picker had been home awhile, he had managed to forget about the fellow with the seventeen boxes and was feeling pretty good about his afternoon's work. In fact, he was a little hard to live with as he strutted about the house or lorded it at the supper table.

"Yes, sir, I guess I showed 'em. Nobody can say I can't go out and pick a barrel of cranberries, and furthermore I can still straighten up. All this talk about how lame I'd be!"

Along about the middle of our meal, however, I began to squirm around.

"Don't tell me you're getting stiff!"

"Certainly not. You know me—I don't stiffen up from a little workout like that. Never did. Ooh!"

"Well, what *is* the matter with you?"

"Get me some lotion!" I cried. "My knees are burning up!"

19

UP TO HERE IN ICE WATER

As we stood on the bank of Bass River and tried to master our goosepimples enough to take that first step into well-chilled water, we marveled at our own temerity. We were wearing sneakers, shorts, and flannel shirts, and carrying rakes and buckets.

"Isn't it amazing?" I asked. "Neither one of us would be caught dead in a cold shower, even in the middle of summer, and yet we're willing to wade out into a river in October just to get a bucket of oysters!"

"And I don't even like them!" added my wife.

"It's the thrill of the chase, I guess."

Actually, after our long confinement in the city, it was once again the realization that Nature's bounty was around us for the taking that drew us on.

I dabbled one toe in the water and withdrew it quickly.

"It's not so bad," I reported. "After that first moment of blinding pain you won't even think about how cold the water is. You'll be too numb to think."

"All I have to do is think about the price you used to pay at oyster bars for half a dozen oysters on the half shell and I can wade right in."

"Well, go ahead."

We waded in together, and the story was the same as it had been the last couple of times. At first we thought we could not stand it; then we found an oyster or two, and began to rake them in; and the next time we thought about the water, it seemed not uncomfortable at all.

"But I don't think we can stand it in shorts many more times," I said as we waded out into slightly deeper water to reach a patch of oysters that lay beyond the rakes of men limited by waders. "We can't afford to lay out thirty-five dollars a pair for waders, but we've got to do something."

There could be no question of mere hip waders in our case, because we could never quite resist the prize oyster or stray scallop that meant going in up to our waists. Our high-water mark in shorts was seldom less than belt-high, even though, as the water grew colder, we had entered it each time resolved to spare ourselves the frigid posteriors that went with wet shorts fanned by a fall breeze.

Today the water was clear, with only a slight ripple. We located the patch of oysters, edged into slightly deeper water to reach it, and suffered as the water inched up our legs. Some of the oysters lay on the bottom among the rocks but unattached. Some were attached to rocks, and some were in clusters of three or four, usually with a rock somewhere in the midst of them. Before we had gone oystering, we had been told that the oysters would look like stones on the bottom, but this was hardly accurate.

An oyster might be the color of stone, it might be partly hidden by sand, it might have a patch of seaweed growing on it, but an oyster looked like an oyster. We were soon able to spot an oyster which was only partly exposed or was camouflaged, and could generally tell by the color of its shell whether

242

it was a good oyster or a dud. There are other creatures besides man which enjoy a nice oyster cocktail and will go to extravagant lengths to get it; a dud is mute evidence that one of them has been successful. After an oyster has been eaten and its sprung-open shell left without life inside, the shell's colors gradually change.

Once in the water, I always got as much enjoyment out of exploring a stretch of river bottom and seeing the sights it offered as I did out of collecting a bucket of oysters. Sometimes a section of the sandy bottom would suddenly rise up and go swimming away, as a perfectly camouflaged flounder decided to take no chances on our thoughts turning to fresh fillets.

Occasionally a crab would wave its claw at my rake and go sidling away to some spot where it could dig in. Here and there patches of weed waved darkly on the bottom, and then it paid to take a close look for a scallop or two that might be sitting in their midst.

Raking in a scallop took a little more doing than did an oyster. Even when one was being careful, it was difficult not to stir up the bottom with the rake. If one missed bringing up an oyster on the first attempt—and the rocky bottom made this easy to do—it was only a question of waiting until the cloud of sediment settled down and the water cleared and then one could try again. If a person missed a scallop and waited until the water cleared, however, the scallop was nowhere to be seen, because scallops could move, and rather briskly. In fact, they were jet-propelled.

They traveled through the water by snapping their shells open and shut. When captured, they often expressed their displeasure and their wish to travel by snapping their shells the same way. Half a dozen of them all complaining at once in a bucket sounded as if they were scored for Spanish music.

Today, as usual, not only our shorts but our shirts were wet before we were through. Capillary action worked its way up my shirt tail and sent chilly fingers creeping along my spine. The deeper water was colder, so when I had half a bucket of oysters I waded in to shallower water to warm up my feet. The oyster quota was one twelve-quart pail per week for family use, and Elizabeth was good for her half.

I set my bucket down on the shore in order to putter around for a while free of its weight. Needless to say I came across four oysters and two scallops I could not resist. These being more than a handful, I slipped the smooth-shelled scallops into my shirt pockets and carried the oysters.

Scallops were one form of seafood the whole family liked. Their appearance helped. As an oyster lover, however, I resented hearing how much nicer scallops looked than oysters, because I happened to think oysters looked beautiful, whereas the actual scallop was quite a different story. Granted, the part of the scallop which was eaten was a nice, white little cylinder of firm, delicious meat—but what about the rest of the scallop, the part the general public never saw? What about the scallop's true personality? The edible "eye" or muscle of the scallop was all very well; the shell was a work of art; but the rest of a scallop was well calculated to make an oyster winsome by comparison.

"Wait'll you open one," said Hadley, the first time we went scalloping. "You've never seen a real mess until you've peeked into a scallop."

This whole aspect of seafood was occupying my mind when we called it a day and trudged slowly up the bank to our car.

"Say, are your teeth chattering?" asked Elizabeth.

"Oh, that?" I extracted the two scallops from my shirt pocket, where they had suddenly started clacking, and held one of them up.

"Say ah," I ordered. It obligingly clacked a couple of times and then remained partway open. I peered into it.

"H'm!" I murmured. "We'll have to operate at once. He must have lived a terrible life. You know, the thing that

244

amazes me most about myself is how liberal my attitude is toward seafood for a Johnny-come-lately. I never even ate a steamer clam until a few years ago, but I loved them right away. I like crabs, mussels, sea clams, quahogs, oysters, scallops —there's none of them I mind opening or cleaning. Yes, sir, I'm beginning to think there's no gop or gook Father Neptune can produce that wouldn't look good to me," I bragged. It was not far from suppertime, and wading around in cold water had a tendency to give me an appetite. "It's a shame you and Florence are so finicky and don't like so many of the good things of the sea, when they're right here under our noses," I added, harping once more on the old complaint.

Elizabeth glanced at me with hooded eyes.

"I understand that when the Hawaiian natives manage to spear an octopus, the lucky man who gets to it first always scoops out the eyes and eats them raw, because they're the best part. I suppose you're about ready to graduate to octopus eyes?

I swallowed thoughtfully.

"One more crack like that," I declared, "and I may skip supper tonight."

Something had to be done about the waders question, so after supper we got out the mail-order catalogue. Boot-foot waders, waist-high, were as expensive as we had expected—but another possibility presented itself. The picture showed a pair of vinylite waders with soft, stocking-like feet instead of expensive rubber boots, the idea being to wear sneakers over the feet of the waders. The price—about five dollars—was much more in our bracket.

"Let's be first with these smart new outfits," I suggested. "Get the order blanks."

The usual three sizes were available—small, medium, and large.

"Well, we're not exactly medium, and yet we're not what

245

you might call large people," I mused. "Which shall we be—snug or loose?"

"We'd better order the large size and be on the safe side. We'll be wearing heavy clothes under our waders, and we certainly wouldn't want them to be tight."

I shall never forget the night we first slipped on our new waders. When a mail-order house says large it means large, especially in circumference. Elizabeth looked as if she were standing in a plastic barrel. When she walked she looked as if she were being followed.

"Apparently the mail-order people have found that the average large man who orders waders is a beer drinker with a large pot," I declared. "They certainly have allowed plenty for it. Shall we keep the two sets, or both go in one pair?"

"We'd better send back both pairs and get mediums."

"And wait two more weeks in weather like this? No sir, you're not getting me out of these waders. What's wrong with having them a little roomy, anyway? Besides, I wouldn't deny Cape Cod a sight like this for anything."

The olive-colored waders terminating in blue-and-white sneakers quickly earned us the title of the Men from Mars in certain circles, and caused old Cape Codders, encased in traditional black rubber hip waders, to stare uncertainly and swear off New England rum. Nevertheless, the waders kept us dry, and they allowed us to wade out deeper than the others.

As winter came on, the worse the weather got the better we liked it. Amateur shellfishing tends to be an anti-social pursuit. Just as the fisherman's ideal is to be where the fish are but the other fishermen aren't, so it is the shellfisherman's pleasure to reach the oyster grounds and find the landscape empty of human figures. And if others appear while he is collecting his quahogs or oysters, his face breaks into no happy welcoming smile.

In this respect, I was soon as crusty as any Cape Codder. What I wanted when I went oystering was utter desolation.

The more deserted and desolate my surroundings, the more cheerful I became. What I wanted was to wade around collecting oysters, studying the various features of the river bottom through the clear water, meditating complacently on my sins, and enjoying large chunks of peace, quiet, and solitude.

It was a never-ending source of wonder to me to find myself knee deep and sometimes waist deep in ice water in the middle of winter, warm and comfortable, and know that only a thin sheath of vinylite lay between me and a very uncomfortable experience; to know that some extremely cold water was pressing constantly against every inch of its surface, seeking some tiny crack through which it might get at me. Eventually, of course, it did, now and then—but the patching kit that came with the waders worked very well.

Human contacts while shellfishing, though not to be desired as far as I was concerned, sometimes produced entertaining results. One day it fell to Mabel Crowell and me to do the oystering for our respective families. I liked to go shellfishing with Mabel, because she felt the same way about it I did. Once on the spot, we went our separate ways, gathered our oysters, and saved conversation for later.

On this particular day we hoped to find our latest special spot pleasantly devoid of mankind, but found instead two elderly men busily raking for oysters (*our* oysters—that's the way every true shellfisherman thinks of them). A woman with a basket on the bank picked up the oysters when the men tossed them into the grass.

We exchanged puckery, insincere smiles with these interlopers and went on farther down the line. When we had put sufficient distance—well, not sufficient, but it would have to do—between ourselves and those three nuisances back there, Mabel and I put about twenty-five yards between ourselves —just a good, unsociable space—and went to work.

I was just settling down to it when I was suddenly aware that a lean middle-aged woman, stringy haired and bespectacled, had appeared on the bank. She fidgeted back and forth along the edge of the water for a moment like some nervous shore bird, and despite the fact that she was only wearing galoshes she looked as if she were going to walk straight out into the water at any minute. She was hard to ignore—though, like a proper shellfisherman, I was doing my best. Finally she cleared her throat and spoke.

"I hope Bill Kennedy don't come around," she declared.

She was referring to our esteemed shellfish warden. I was tempted to say, "Don't worry, some of the boys put him on the train for Maine a couple of weeks ago and nobody's seen him since," which was true, according to the gang that hung around the drugstore; Bill was on vacation. However, on Cape Cod you learn that it is a good rule to listen, and not tell all you know. I was willing to listen.

"Why not?" I asked.

"Well, this area is closed for oystering, you know."

"What? Why, I've never seen any signs around here posting it."

"Well, they tell me there's a poster over in the Town Office says it's closed."

"Seems to me if that's so, Bill ought to get over and put some signs up here. Not many people are going to drop by the Town Office before they go oystering."

"If you ask me, the town seems to pay Bill Kennedy to ride around in a car to a lot of other places. We live up the hill here all year around, and I haven't seen him around here once."

"Well, if it's supposed to be closed it ought to be posted, all right," I agreed—and went right on oystering. My informant hopped around from one foot to the other for a while and blinked at me blankly, and then gave up her crusade for law and order. She walked up the shore, and I wondered if she was perhaps going to try her luck with Mabel and the others.

But then I began to find some nice patches of oysters and forgot to watch.

I could not help wondering, though, why it was people always picked me to try to scare off. Did I look that much like a timid soul? Maybe I did at that. Certainly there was a time not too long ago when I might very well have decided in the best Caspar Milquetoast tradition to stop oystering then and there until I could make sure I was not breaking any law. For many years I was the type to whom NO SMOKING, no matter where it appeared, meant NO SMOKING; who invariably walked, did not run, when the sign said WALK, DO NOT RUN; and who tiptoed and stopped breathing when the sign said SILENCE. Apparently I still looked the part.

My wanderings took me around a little point and into a small cove I had been meaning to investigate for some time. When I returned, only Mabel was still in sight.

"How did you like that woman's story?" she asked.

"It was quite a yarn. Where are those other people? Did she manage to scare them off?"

"I should say not. She was *with* them. They all went off up the hill together!"

The trouble with that day was that the weather was not bad enough. Later on we had some better days, such as the time we went oystering in a snowstorm, and another time when our favorite oyster grounds froze over and we had to break holes in the ice to get at them. We had plenty of elbow room those days.

In winter sea clamming, and summer as well, one had to be a bit more circumspect about the weather. It was one thing to be on the bank of a tidal river where the rise and fall of the tide was seldom more than two or three feet, and quite another to be out on the flats a mile or more offshore in the bay, with an eleven-foot tide due to roll in. To be out on those vast

249

empty stretches on a wild winter day when a wind was howling and the sea was beating against the outer bars was a strenuous, difficult, and indescribably exhilarating experience, and I went sea clamming more than once in the face of north and northwest winds which I knew very well would hold the sea in and keep the clams from showing. Sea clamming then was only an excuse for going out into that wild and exciting setting. But on such occasions I contented myself with the flats off Dennis, which were not too far offshore, rather than to try the greater reaches of the Brewster flats.

20

TEMPEST IN A COFFEEPOT

The quiet season on Cape Cod was a period during which nothing was supposed to be going on, but it seemed as if the deeper we got into it the more things went on, and the more complex and involved they became.

Of all the various tempests in a teapot which came along to enliven the quiet season, the finest was unquestionably the one which might be called the tempest in the Ladies' Aid coffeepot.

Actually, the pot was one of those large, cylindrical affairs generally called a coffee-maker, but we all referred to it as "the coffeepot." Indeed, for a while there, any reference to the coffeepot was immediately understood to refer to the forty-eight-cup aluminum coffee-maker whose normal habitat was the north kitchen of Jacob Sears Hall. The hall had two small kitchens, one on each side of the stage.

In complicated cases such as the Coffeepot Incident it is

251

difficult to present the background with absolute accuracy. One thing I can name with accuracy is the first occasion on which the Ladies' Aid coffeepot was taken out of the hall— because it was I who took it.

By one of those bits of irony which the gods are so fond of putting into these situations, it was after a Ladies' Aid affair that I took it, too. A history-making Ladies' Aid affair, what is more—the first square dance that organization had ever sponsored. The idea of the Ladies' Aid sponsoring a dance was a nine-days' wonder in itself, but after recovering from the first shock of the suggestion most of the old-timers moved stoutly with the times and decided it was all right. The dance was a great success.

As noted earlier, Mrs. Corbett was in charge of refreshments at this affair. After festivities were concluded there were still a great many sandwiches and a good deal of cake left over. These were divided up among all who cared to take some home with them.

We had asked eight people to come over to our house after the dance for coffee. Elizabeth went on ahead with a few of them to get things ready, while I stayed to help straighten up the hall.

In the course of straightening up we discovered that a second batch of coffee had been made in the big coffeepot and that it was still more than two-thirds full.

Naturally it would have been a shame to waste that much hot coffee, but it was also impracticable to split it up. The only thing to do was for all of us to drink it in one place.

A few minutes later, then, somewhat to Elizabeth's surprise, I entered the house with the coffeepot, followed by twelve more people all carrying sandwiches and cake.

In this innocent way—and with most of the officers of the Ladies' Aid present and accessories to the fact, for that matter —the seed was sown.

In the course of the summer several square dances were

held at the hall for the benefit of the heating fund. These were held on Saturday nights, and after these dances there was generally a gathering at somebody's house for a midnight snack. Since the group got to be rather large, it seemed a good idea to bring along the coffeepot upon leaving the hall so that the hostess could make coffee enough for the whole gathering at one time.

This borrowing was eventually noted by someone with a long memory who recalled that some measure or other restricting the use of the coffeepot had been voted once by the Ladies' Aid.

The minutes of previous meetings were searched, and sure enough it was found that a few years back the Ladies' Aid had voted not to allow the coffeepot to be taken for use outside the hall.

News of the existence of this rule got around, but the convivial group which had been using the coffeepot considered it a silly rule which should be rescinded at an early Ladies' Aid meeting. The coffeepot was not being harmed and might as well be getting some use. The only deference shown to the existence of the rule was in a custom which sprang up at about this time, a custom of returning the coffeepot to the hall that same night by the dark of the moon.

One of the summer people, however, a well-meaning girl anxious to do what was right, wanted to pay a rental fee, and let the cat out of the bag in her efforts to do so. Then the following week another hostess neglected to return the coffeepot in the shadows of the night, but did it instead in broad daylight the next afternoon.

She was seen!

The Ladies' Aid was not an organization used to having its rules flaunted. Sarah Josh, who had now succeeded Mrs. Luella as president, found herself in an uncomfortable predicament. Certain members complained indignantly about the flaunting, and the executive committee found it necessary to meet. It was decided that the Ladies' Aid should ask permission of the trustees of the hall to lock up the coffeepot in one of the kitchens—and while they were about it, their dishes, too, since their dishes had suffered some breakage through the years which was not all of Ladies' Aid doing.

As President of the Ladies' Aid, it became Sarah Joshua Sears' duty to telephone Asa Daniel Sears, Trustee and Clerk of the Board of Trustees of Jacob Sears Hall, and broach the matter. There were three Trustees, Ernest Everett Sears and Mr. Ezra Newton Sears being the other two, but Asa was able to speak for the three of them on all matters that did not require an actual vote.

While the Ladies' Aid Executive Council meeting which led up to Sarah Josh's call was taking place, it happened that Asa was finishing up a day's fishing during which everything that could go wrong had gone wrong. His motor had been balky. He had hooked bottom twice and lost one complete rig valued at $1.25. His worms were no good. The fish were not biting. He had broken his thermos before he had even had a cup of coffee. And he had slipped on the bank getting out of his boat and barked his shin. As he stalked into the house after that day's debacle, his black, beetling eyebrows were knit in such a terrifying tangle that it seemed unlikely they could ever be disengaged.

It was this ill-timed moment which Sarah Josh chose to pick up her telephone and call Asa.

The picayunish request which it was her unhappy responsibility to make was to a man in Asa's frame of mind exactly what a lighted match is to a roomful of explosive gas. Sarah Josh was all but thrown to the floor by the force of Asa's reply as it shredded the two blocks' length of telephone wire that connected their homes.

The gist of this blast was that the hall was for the use of any organization the Trustees felt it proper to rent it to or, in the case of genuine educational purposes, grant the use of its facilities free of charge, and that he would certainly not curtail those facilities by locking up one of the kitchens for any one organization. If the Ladies' Aid wanted to lock up its coffeepot and its dishes it would have to separate them from the hall's own dishes—which were also suffering breakage, he might add, and not alone at the hands of organizations other than the Ladies' Aid—and lock them up in a box in the basement.

This shattering experience left Sarah Josh ready to resign the presidency.

"I don't care about it myself one way or the other," she pointed out plaintively, "but the rule is there and it's my duty to see that it is enforced if the members say it should be. I don't know why I was foolish enough to be president in the first place!"

The news of this friction between the Hall and the Ladies' Aid soon spread, even to the other neck. About suppertime that night our phone rang. I answered.

"Hello?"

"What's all this gawdam stuff about a coffeepot?" It was Freddie.

"Just keep your paws off it, that's all."

"I never touched the son of a bitch."

"See that you don't. Did you hear about what Asa told Sarah Josh?"

"Yeh. I was just talking to Mabel. I guess I'll call up Ruth and see if anything new's developed. I want to talk to Asa, too. I want to ask him if he got any fish today, and see what happens."

"You've seen those flame-throwers the Army uses?"

"Yeh?"

"Stand well back from the phone," I advised.

The next regular meeting of the Ladies' Aid was but a week or so away, so the question of what to do about the coffeepot was put on the agenda for that meeting. In the meantime, the situation steadily worsened.

A small sign appeared on the coffeepot which read, "Not To Be Taken From The Hall, By Order Of The East Dennis Ladies' Aid, signed Sarah J. Sears, President."

Then two additional organizations indirectly added fuel to the fire: the Square Dance Class and the Young Couples Club.

The turnout for the Square Dance Class that week was unusually large, and the next day when he came by to inspect the hall Asa was appalled by the number of cigarette butts he encountered in the vestibule. He personally picked up and disposed of twenty-five butts, counting them carefully and wrathfully as he did so. In no time at all he was busy tacking up stern typewritten signs in all parts of the Hall which read, "Smoking *Strictly Prohibited* Inside The Hall, by Order of the Trustees, Jacob Sears Memorial Library, signed, Asa D. Sears, Clerk."

It was in this already nettled mood that he had occasion to visit the basement, in one end of which was set up a ping-pong table, with a chest nearby in which various athletic equipment was stored. The Young Couples Club of the church had put on a campaign the year before to raise money for the equipment—in fact, Asa himself had contributed substantially.

He had not had occasion to go near that section of the basement for some time. When he did now, he was rudely shocked by the condition of the equipment. It was scattered all over the place from Hell to high water. It was battered, it was bent, it was broken. Here was a scene which told of juvenile rowdyism, unsuperintended, allowed unbridled sway, and crying, Havoc.

Here was a disgrace the enormity of which one Trustee was not sufficient to absorb. Asa determined to summon Ernest Everett to the scene, and also to call forth the Reverend Oswald Blake, member and spiritual leader of the Young Couples Club, who also had charge of the athletic equipment, and a key to the hall to show for it. Asa marched straight across the street and knocked on the parsonage door with a stroke of doom, and, pausing only to use Oswald's telephone to alert Ernest Everett, marched Oswald back across the street to face the evidence of his club's neglect.

The Reverend Oswald Blake's Christian ability to turn the other cheek was given a brisk workout in that dark hour, for Asa had no more than got through with one cheek than Ernest Everett arrived and gave it to him on the other. In fact, for once Asa's efforts paled by comparison. Even he stood in awe. As a rule, Ernest Everett was a man of few words, but on this occasion he used them all several times.

When Oswald's broken and mutilated body had finally been flung into the alley, the Trustees went back upstairs and worked off some of their steam by putting the chairs back into some semblance of order. While at it they noticed that the fabric on a couple of them was torn.

"Everybody that has ten people coming to his house borrows chairs from the Hall, not to mention every organization's meetings!" snorted Asa, "and this is the way they come back!"

The situation, he felt, called for a full meeting of the Trustees, so a night or two later Mr. Ezra Newton was routed out and the three of them sat down to it in the library. Asa shouted into Mr. Ezra Newton's ear until his voice gave out, and then a vote was taken on a couple of questions.

Mabel was first with the news as far as we were concerned, having got it from Ruth Asa.

"All keys to the Hall are to be called in except for those in possession of the Trustees, and no more chairs are to leave the Hall!"

Everything seemed to happen in a way that heaped more coals on the fire. For example, this decision was reached two days before the Ladies' Aid monthly meeting. Most of their meetings were held at the hall, but as luck would have it the

257

meeting that month was scheduled for a private home. The Ladies' Aid was pretty miffed when it found its hostess could not borrow the usual chairs from the hall but had to go out and rent some for ten cents apiece. The hostess was even madder at being saddled with that unexpected extra expense.

Sitting on their rented chairs, the Ladies' Aid listened to certain of its members decry the rape of the coffeepot. They understood that even some of the summer people had been using it, and after all, they could not be counted on to take proper care of it. Strict enforcement of the coffeepot rule was called for, and a vote taken on the question. There were no dissenters.

One good reason why there were no dissenters was because Mrs. Corbett did not attend the meeting, which conflicted with the World Series. When she heard about the vote, she dissented plenty.

"Oh, I just wish I'd been there!" she fumed that evening.

"One thing about my good wife, she's never afraid to open her mouth," I remarked to Mabel, who had dropped by. Mabel had missed the meeting, too.

"Well, I don't care, I think it's disgusting. Half the women at that meeting had been drinking coffee out of that pot at private parties all summer and yet not one of them spoke up, not even when some of those women slandered the summer people. Plenty of them knew darn well that only regular summer people had used it—and every one of those particular summer people support the church, by the way—and every one of them took perfect care of it!"

The trouble was, that rule was there about the coffeepot, right in the minutes a few years back, legally voted on and made law, and even the members of the Ladies' Aid who were among the guilty coffee-drinkers felt helpless in the face of that *fait* long since *accompli*.

There the matter rested, then, for a couple of weeks. There was to be no taking out of the Ladies' Aid coffeepot. There was to be no borrowing of the Hall's chairs. There were to be no youngsters in the basement. There was to be No Smoking in the Hall. There was bristling on all sides.

Coffee-makers were priced. The midnight snack group talked about getting its own forty-eight-cup coffeepot and telling everybody else to go to hell. The Young Couples Club talked about getting *its* own forty-eight-cup coffeepot and telling everybody else to go to hell. (Seems they had been using it sort of quietly, too.) The Ladies' Aid talked about raising money to buy its own folding chairs and tell everybody else— well, never mind.

Then the reaction set in, and sounder opinions were heard. The regular meeting of the Ladies' Aid Executive Committee was held, and one member declared she was disgusted with the whole business, and that she would like to see the Ladies' Aid take its dishes and coffeepot and *give* them to the hall for the use of anybody in the community who wanted to use them . . . particularly since nobody really knew for sure any more which dishes were the Hall's and which the Ladies' Aid, they were so mixed up.

The Executive Committee voted to ask the Trustees to hold a joint meeting with them, and the Trustees promptly invited the Executive Committee to meet with them in the library on an early night.

A nice fire was laid in the fireplace. All the Trustees were present, and all members of the Ladies' Aid Executive Committee attended.

The most stirring speech of the evening was made by Ernest Everett, who had already decided that the decision made on the chairs in the heat of passion was pretty foolish. He declared that in a tiny community such as ours all halls and chairs and coffeepots and dishes should be there for the whole community. Members of every organization and committee and board in the village overlapped into every other organization and committee and board in the village, so when they

259

came right down to it who was fighting whom? When you stopped to think about it, what did it matter if the chairs got used and used until some of them started to go? That was what they were for. When they were worn out, we'd raise some money and get more—and who'd raise the money? The Ladies' Aid would hold a bazaar. The Young Couples Club would put on a supper. The hall would hold a square dance. Same way with the coffeepot, and the dishes.

At the next meeting of the Ladies' Aid, it was voted to rescind the coffeepot rule. By that time someone had recalled the fact that the only reason the rule had been made in the first place was because someone who was not even a member of the Ladies' Aid had been borrowing the pot for meetings in another village.

It was agreed that everybody would feel better about using it if a small rental were charged—which would also provide the fund for a new one by the time the old one was worn out— so it was agreed that a box would be placed by the pot for voluntary contributions and any user who cared to put fifty cents in the box could do so.

At this meeting, too, the oldest member of the Ladies' Aid, who was then ninety, rose and in her usual firm voice chastened the gathering properly. She declared that she had been present when the hall was dedicated, and she had been present at its fiftieth anniversary, and that never before had she witnessed the slightest friction over the hall. She hoped she would never do so again. She gave them all an admonishing look and sat down.

The little sign was removed from the coffeepot. Chairs were once more borrowed by anyone who needed them for a gathering, social or otherwise. The Young Couples Club promised to straighten up the athletic equipment in the basement. The No Smoking signs faded away, and the square-dance class put its butts in the sand bucket. The Hall became the hall again in everybody's thinking, the Trustees became the trustees, and the Executive Committee simmered down into the executive committee.

The center of all this strife had been a forty-eight-cup capacity aluminum coffee-maker the like of which could be bought for under thirty dollars. Because of it several regular meetings of various organizations had been extended by an hour or more, and two special meetings had been held, one of them involving fourteen persons. The total number of man-hours expended would have paid for six new coffeepots. The total number of woman-hours expended would have paid for a new hall.

From the standpoint of entertainment, though, it would have been hard to find a way they could have been better used.

21

WHO, ME?

"Ready?"

"Yes. You take the salad bowl and I'll bring the casserole. Janie, you bring the basket."

"It beats me how these covered-dish suppers work out so well," I declared. "Each woman turns out whatever she feels like—salads, hot dishes, desserts—yet it always comes out about even."

"It's the law of averages."

"Yes, but you'd think once in a while the law of averages would blow a fuse and everybody would turn up with macaroni and cheese, or we'd have fifty-five salads and no desserts. Come on—er—Janie, get in the car. And watch that basket." I sighed. Her campaign to be called Janie instead of Florence had gone so well that I had about decided to throw in the towel. It was easier sometimes just to call her Janie instead of having to repeat Florence three times before it registered.

We rounded the corner into Centre Street, and could see

the lights of the hall up ahead through the bare trees. A good many cars were already parked along the street and more cars were turning into it from both directions. When it came to anything involving eating, Cape Codders tended to be prompt.

Inside the hall, about half the places at the long tables were already filled by the early birds, their appetites well-sharpened by the December wind. If anyone wishes to know what a truly famished expression looks like, let him come and look into the faces of a Cape Cod group waiting to fall to at a covered-dish supper.

We found room at one of the tables and Elizabeth set up our places with the silverware and dishes from the basket while Florence and I took our edibles to the kitchen, whence they would be put on whatever table needed another casserole or salad. All around there was hustle and bustle, chatting and joking, smiling and waving, and that easy atmosphere which stemmed from the fact that everybody in the room knew everybody else.

For us to sit down to a supper with a hundred and twenty persons and know them all as friends and neighbors was a new experience, and a good one. The food was well cooked, hearty, and abundant. Those present had brought the food themselves, paid a small fee for the privilege of sitting down together and eating it, and lo! a sum of money had been painlessly raised for some worthy cause by whatever organization was running the supper.

George Landry came in with some friends, and it occurred to me it was almost exactly a year since we had sat together in Barnstable Courthouse and completed our transaction. Left at loose ends by the sudden death of his wife, George had sold his house to us, planning to move to Ohio. Now he was back again, as so many had predicted, and was building himself a new house on the hill across the highway.

The hall continued to fill up with men, women, and children, with families from all walks of life. The banker and the

263

carpenter were both there, but an outsider would not have known the one from the other. Both wore wool lumberjack shirts and old, comfortable suits. For that matter, the range of society was less than the city would have afforded. The poorer among us were not so dreadfully poor, and the richer were not terribly rich.

A hand touched my shoulder and George Landry spoke into my ear.

"Say, I'm on the nominating committee for the new church council, and I want to know if you'd be willing to serve if we put your name on the slate?"

George and his genial grin got a laugh out of me with that one!

"That's good! You want to get us both run out of town? Do you know, I was just thinking—it's about a year on the nose since we got together for the closing on the house."

"Say, that's right!"

"George! Didn't you bring a pound of butter?" One of the ladies on the supper committee exploded anxiously into our midst.

"Sure, and some rolls from D.H.'s," said George.

"We found the rolls, but we can't find the butter anywhere."

"C'mon, I'll show you where I put it." George slapped my shoulder and went off to locate the butter.

A day or two later, Elizabeth came home from the post office with a strange look on her face.

"What's this talk about your being on the slate for the new church council?"

"What? Who said so?"

"You mean you knew about it?"

"I forgot to tell you, George Landry said something about it to me at the supper the other night, but I didn't take him seriously. Judas Priest! He might be just woolly minded

264

enough to put my name up, but he won't get far with it. I don't know who else is on the nominating committee but they're not likely to take to the idea. A newcomer who hasn't even lived here a year yet, on the council of a Cape Cod church? That'll be the day!"

"This didn't come from George, though. It was Sarah Josh that mentioned it to me."

Sarah Josh! Wife of an Old Cape Codder! President of the Ladies' Aid! I was shocked.

"This is getting serious," I said. "They must be out of their minds. Why, I don't even approve of the idea myself! Are we going to have a real New England Cape Cod church here, or are we going to let every upstart that comes down the pike jump right onto the council?"

I cornered George at our next square-dance class.

"You weren't serious about trying to put me on the church slate, I hope!"

"Sure, why not?"

"Listen. You're a newcomer. I'm a newcomer. You're an old newcomer, but I'm a *new* newcomer—"

"Well, the nominating committee thought it would be a good idea," said George, "so it's all set. What are you worrying about? The worst you can get is three years."

I eyed him disapprovingly.

"What have you been doing, George—filling that committee of yours full of cocktails?"

"With Mrs. Luella on it?"

"I wish you'd reconsider. I'm not trying to be coy—I'll consider it a great privilege to serve—but it seems completely cockeyed to me to take somebody who's only been here less than a year and—"

It was a waste of time talking to George. He only grinned.

"Well, if I am put on the committee," I told Elizabeth worriedly when we got home that night, "then the only thing

265

I can do is make myself as inconspicuous as possible for quite a while—not talk much, you know, and—"

"I want to be there when Corbett doesn't talk much."

Preparation for, endurance of, and recuperation from the Christmas holidays occupied the next few weeks. In New York we had traveled a fairly brisk holiday pace from time to time, but our metropolitan experiences had never approached the week-long house-by-house observance of the merrie season that challenged our capacities in East Dennis.

With the holidays behind us, the next important event on the village calendar was the annual meeting of the church. It was to be an unusually important one, too, since we were to adopt a new constitution and set up a new church council.

The council was to consist of six elected members, the pastor, the Sunday School superintendent, and representatives of the Ladies' Aid and Young Couples Club.

The elected members were to serve for three years, with two new members to be elected each year. To get the rotation going, two one-year, two two-year, and two three-year terms were to be drawn by lot at the first meeting of the council.

The history of our church was in some of its parts the same as that of many another Cape Cod church—full of bickering and strife. Considering the character of Cape men of the past, it is small wonder. It might be fair to say that a hundred years ago the Cape was overburdened with leaders. It was heavily populated with men accustomed to command. One sea captain with unquestioned authority and an iron will might be a worthy and necessary fixture on a sailing ship; fifty sea captains stomping around in one small village were something else again. There were fifty of them living at one time along a one-mile stretch of the main street in Yarmouth. In the old days in Brewster every other man's stern eye and rolling gait announced him to be a sea captain. Yet of all the villages, some

266

say there were more sea captains per square foot living in East Dennis than anywhere else.

The adult male population of many Cape villages was thus heavily freighted with men accustomed to having their own way and not in the least used to having their opinions disputed. They took almost everything seriously, and religion particularly so. Hence, when it came to such questions as how a church should be run, and which way lay the path to Salvation, there were more squabbles and discord, more squalls and tempests, more red necks and jutting chinwhiskers, more horrendous collisions between irresistible forcefuls and immovable objectors, more feuding and splitting asunder, more getting up in Sunday meetings and stalking out of church, never to set foot inside it again, than could be chronicled in a lifetime.

These feuds were carefully preserved as treasured old family heirlooms and passed along from generation to generation, so that right down to the present day there were Cape Codders who stayed away from the local church because of the pew-to-pew exchanges Cap'n Ezra had had with Cap'n Joshua during church meetings of a century past. This attitude had helped to whittle the church down to the point at which Fred Underhill had found it, with about twelve souls attending on an average Sunday.

Old feuds meant nothing to newcomers, however, and as their numbers increased they gave a much-needed lift to the few Cape Codders who, headed by Mrs. Luella, had managed to hold the church together and somehow keep it going.

At first it was merely a question of attending and supporting the church. Actual membership increased slowly. Finally, however, after much private discussion, it was agreed that the time had come to go the whole way, and thirty-five of us, some natives and some newcomers, announced our intentions of becoming members. This more than doubled the actual active membership.

The old church had seen some mighty changes, then, and fairly sudden ones, too, but I still felt I would rather have been somewhere else when the night of the annual church meeting came and George Landry rose to present the slate of the nominating committee. Where there was hair, however, it did not stand on end, and no bald heads became noticeably red. The slate was accepted without incident.

The next night the new council held its first meeting. The members were mostly Cape Codders. There were a few newcomers, but none so new as I.

After a few remarks by Mrs. Luella praising the good job Mr. Landry had done as chairman of the nominating committee in choosing such a splendid group for the council, we settled down to the business of the evening, which was to determine how long each of us was to serve, and who was to be the first chairman.

Six slips of paper were numbered with 1's, 2's, or 3's and placed in our local electrician's hat. I drew a '1' and was vastly relieved. A one-year-term—not bad. Only twelve meetings in which to hold back my natural tendency to have a lot to say. Only twelve meetings in which to remain carefully in the background, and then I would be out again.

We all compared slips and announced what we had drawn. Doctor Rodgers had drawn the other one-year term and was looking as relieved as I. We quietly congratulated each other on our good fortune, and sat back contentedly to help pick out our new chairman.

"Well, now," said one of the men who had drawn a three-year term, "I've been thinking, and I wondered if we couldn't work it so we'd have a new chairman every six months. That way each elected member of the Council would serve once during the course of his three-year term."

Several people nodded, and Mrs. Luella said, "I think that's a splendid idea."

"It would avoid any question of personalities."

Mrs. Luella was already tearing two more slips of paper into precise sizes.

"That means, of course, that the ones who drew one-year terms will have to do their serving this year. Is it all right with everybody if we just let Doctor Rodgers and Mr. Corbett draw straws to see who's to serve first?"

I felt as though my chair had been pulled right out from under me. Doctor Rodgers and I exchanged a startled glance.

"Now, wait a minute!" I protested. "Let's not have any drawing. I hereby nominate Doctor Rodgers for first chairman. He may not be a native himself, but at least his wife's family are Old Cape Codders. I don't think it would do at all to have a raw newcomer the first time, of all times!"

I looked beseechingly at one of the Cape Codders for support, but he only grinned.

"I don't see it would matter any," he said.

"Never mind all that, just draw one of the slips, and the short one is *it*," ordered Mrs. Luella.

I glanced around at the true Cape Codders in the group— people with the proud blood of Dennis sea captains in their veins, and a couple of them able to trace their lineage back three hundred years on the Cape. The very house we were meeting in was steeped in Cape history: Capt. John Sears, who produced the first salt by solar evaporation in America in 1776 a few hundred yards from where we were sitting, had lived in this same house then; his room upstairs was still preserved almost exactly as he had left it. The church whose new council chairman we were about to pick had been founded by Cape Codders in 1814. In such an atmosphere, and with those thoughts in my mind, I reached out and prayed for the long slip.

Elizabeth was ironing in the kitchen when I got home. "Well, come on in and shut the door. It's cold," she said as I stood in the doorway cupping my hand around my ear.

269

I pointed to the east, in the direction of the cemetery.

"I just wanted to see if I could hear the Old Cape Codders whirling in their graves."

"Why? What happened? I suppose you had a lot to say after all. I thought you were going to keep in the background?"

"Well, I did, up to a point," I told her. "Kid, brace yourself for a piece of news."

22

THE WAITING LIST

"Hello?"

"Well, I understand they're going to have the meeting tonight about the turkey supper."

"That's what I hear. You going?"

"Jeezcrise no, I just finished setting out two hundred muskrat traps and I'm dead. You're not a member yet, are you?"

"No."

"Sent in your application?"

"Yes, but there's already a big waiting list, so God only knows what year we'll finally get in, if we ever do."

With the annual church meeting passed into history, the next important event was the annual turkey supper of the venerable East Dennis Social Club. As usual, very few members had either moved away or passed away during the preceding year. Prospects for those at the top of the waiting list were not bright; for those of us at the bottom, they were nonexistent. Mabel Crowell confirmed this when she dropped by that evening after the meeting.

"Well, it looks as if no new members are going to be taken in this year. We went over the list of old members, to see how many were likely to come, and even that's more than could sit down comfortably all at once in the hall. Of course, they probably won't all come, but they might. At any rate, then the waiting list was read off and there's about twenty names on it. Nobody could decide where we'd draw the line if we *did* take a chance and vote in a few new members, so it was finally decided that none should be taken in. It's a shame. The big mistake was made about twenty years ago when the membership got pretty low and some people from other villages were let in. They were all people with connections here or who lived here once, but even so, people who are actually living in East Dennis now can't be taken in."

"Well, we certainly can't complain, but it's too bad for some of those who've been waiting for years. Were many at the meeting?"

"I was surprised. It was really a good thing we met at the hall, so many turned out. In the old days when there weren't so many, the meeting used to always be at our house. I can remember listening to them when I was a little girl. Of course the big thing they had to decide then, same as now, was how many turkeys to buy, and who was going to cook them. Sometimes they were all cooked at some restaurant, and sometimes they were cooked by women all over town.

"There was one old man who always came to the meeting and always said the same thing. Every time he'd shake his head and look mournful and say, 'There's always one poor turkey in the lot!'

"I really wish you were going to be there, though, because you have to see it to believe it. Have you ever watched a hundred and fifty people eat a turkey dinner in twenty minutes? The platters never touch the table till they're empty. You'd think from the way they fill up their plates and fall to that there wasn't going to be enough to go around, when the truth of it is they always buy more turkeys than they need and everybody knows it. But still they shovel just as fast as they can."

Our discussion of the Social Club was interrupted by the telephone. I answered.

"Hello? Oh—how are you, Oswald? Good. What can I do for you? The what? Oh—won't stay on, eh? Who? Oh, is that how she broke her arm? I didn't know. Well, I'll come over in the morning and look at it, and see if I can fix it."

I went back to the ladies, who had been listening intently.

"Now what was all that about?" demanded Elizabeth, "and since when are you trying to fix broken arms?"

"Who said anything about fixing broken arms? Remind me in the morning I've got a Doorknob Committee meeting to go to."

"A what?"

"I've just appointed myself to the Doorknob Committee. The knob keeps coming off the parsonage kitchen door, so I'm going to see if I can fix it."

"Is it your job to fix doorknobs, just because you're the council chairman?"

"Don't forget, I'm also on the building and maintenance committee. Doorknobs come under my jurisdiction."

My wife swept her hand disgustedly in my direction.

"I wish he'd never got to be chairman! Ever since then Ozzie calls him up every time he wants to blow his nose. And he takes it. My little changed man. He used to lie in bed on Sunday morning and admire the nice lines of the steeple through the trees. Now he worries about getting it painted, and whether or not the clock is going to stop again. Instead of just sitting back in church and thinking a little about his soul, he spends his time counting the house."

"What was that about a broken arm, though?" asked Mabel.

"Well, I didn't know it, but it seems that when Miss Dolly broke her arm a few weeks back, it was because of this same

273

doorknob that she fell and broke it. She came across the street one day and started to open the parsonage door and the doorknob came right off in her hand and she fell over backward off the steps and broke her arm. If she weren't a good Christian member of the church she'd probably sue."

The next morning I visited the parsonage with my toolbox, which I had personally constructed and was very proud of. The parsonage was well over a hundred years old, and the doorknobs and locks went back a bit themselves. It was a serious situation to have the kitchen door out of order, since as with most Cape houses that was the door that got the traffic.

If it had been the front door, now, there would have been no problem at all—in fact, nobody would have known whether the front doorknob came off or not. Nobody could remember an occasion on which the front door of the parsonage had been opened. As a matter of fact, the front hallway was being used as storage space for all the articles the Young Couples Club had gathered for a forthcoming rummage sale, and was knee-deep in old hats, feather boas, scarves, and shirtwaists. I found this out when I went in to take the lock off the front door.

The reason I did this was because I had taken the lock off the kitchen door to see if I could put it in order while I was at it, and a spring had shot out of it when I opened it up. Fortunately the front door lock and the kitchen door lock were identical, so that by taking off the front door lock and opening it up I was able to discover how the spring should go back into the kitchen door lock. The only thing that was different about all this was that, being in the parsonage, I could not feel free to express myself in the terms I usually chose for such occasions. It was very inhibiting, being in such surroundings.

A lady was sitting with the children while Ozzie's wife was out shopping. While I removed the old homesteads of countless generations of spiders from both locks and oiled them for the first time in seventy or eighty years, she revealed the fact that she had been present at the time of the accident.

"I heard this thump sort of noise," she recalled mournfully, "and I looked out and there was poor Miss Dolly lying on her back with the doorknob in her hand." She tried to suppress a giggle. "It's terrible to laugh, but she did look so surprised," she said, and we both laughed guiltily.

"Well, we can't have that sort of thing going on," I said, recovering myself. "If I can't fix this, we'll have to get a locksmith or some kind of doorknob expert over here from Hyannis, or even buy new fittings."

However, I managed to get the doorknob fixed so that it did not seem likely to come off in anybody's hand again. As I walked home across the field next to the hall, a few snowflakes were beginning to dance in the cold air.

The snow kept coming thicker and faster, the wind grew stronger, and we began to make bets on how much longer it would be before the lights and the oil burner went off. We got out our kerosene lamps and filled them, and filled the kerosene tank behind the stove. Most of us had combination kitchen ranges—electric and kerosene, or bottled gas and kerosene.

When a power failure knocked out the furnace, it also knocked out an electric stove, and bottled gas was too expensive to burn for heat. It was a very comfortable feeling to know that the kerosene side of the stove was there. Between it and the fireplace, we would be warm enough downstairs, and could pile on the covers upstairs.

About nine o'clock the lights went out and the furnace stopped. We lit the lamps and the stove and wondered how long it would be before the telephone went out. The snow was falling so heavily that we could barely make out the mellow glow of oil lamps in neighbors' windows. We sat in the kitchen, close to the warmth of the stove, and talked by the soft light of our two hurricane lamps. We talked softly, and became conscious of the fact.

"Remember how it was that time the lights went off and we

275

all brought our lamps and got together at the Crowells'?" I said. The old house had somehow responded to the sort of light it had known in its younger days, and so had we. A gentle, leisurely, and very comfortable atmosphere had filled the living room and the little side parlor. "Remember how pleasant and peaceful it was? There must have been four or five different groups of people sitting around talking, but their voices were just a murmur instead of a clatter. And then when the lights suddenly went on, remember how people's voices immediately rose? Right away everybody was talking louder and faster. I think we were sorry the lights came back on so soon that night."

By the next morning, snow history had been made on the Cape once more. This time we had a couple of feet of snow, and in places the drifts were seven feet deep. One of these places was the stretch of highway between the post office and the little telephone office. The telephone operator was stranded there for twelve hours, until a relief party set out from the village and slowly dug a path to the building. Dame Nature was in a show-off mood. The high wind which accompanied the snow had also coincided with one of the highest tides of the year and had raised it to exceptional heights. We were provided with the unusual sight of cakes of ice floating around on our flooded meadow.

The Cape did not begin to have enough snow-removal equipment to cope with a snow of such dimensions. The highway remained impassable and we were on our own, cut off from the rest of the world except by telephone. Not only was East Dennis isolated, but each neck was snowbound.

As is usual when normal routines are upset, a holiday mood prevailed. With no school bus to threaten us, we had a leisurely breakfast. At nine-thirty Asa mushed over with such news as he had been able to gather by telephone. It was our biggest snow. This time we had not merely bettered the showing of

276

the past ten or twelve years. This time we had surpassed all existing records.

"They say we've made the front pages all over the country," Asa declared complacently, and we all felt very proud of our snow.

After Asa left, I still did not get going on a day's work.

"I still have the holiday spirit," I admitted.

"We never need much excuse."

"No. This is plenty," I agreed. I started upstairs and was trying to decide in which of several pleasant and useless ways I would spend my day, when we heard a clatter outside. I called down to Elizabeth.

"What's that noise?"

In the city she would have said, "It's some men shoveling the snow off the street," and I would have said, "Oh, that's good" and gone on upstairs. Here, however, she named off seven or eight of our neighbors, a roster of most of the able-bodied men available. This made quite a difference in my thinking. I got a shovel, reported for duty, and was accepted. Furthermore, it turned out we were working for the town and would be paid at the rate of one dollar and twenty cents an hour. Away we went, down the road toward the cemetery, in order to liberate my next neighbor's truck, which would help us greatly in the job of clearing the rest of the streets.

Someone had the foresight to bring along a bottle, and this flew back and forth at a merry rate, tossed from man to man and plunging into the snow for all the world like a magazine ad. Fortunately this vessel had been emptied and disposed of by the time our young minister, having located a pair of boots he could borrow, came striding down the road with a shovel on his shoulder.

"Well, Ozzie? Come to work on the wall?" I asked, referring to a text from Nehemiah III which he had recently used, and which told how everybody worked side by side with praise-

277

worthy community spirit to help build up the wall of Jerusalem.

" 'And after him repaired the priests,' " he nodded, turning III: 23 to good advantage, and began to put his shovel to use. It was not the first time Ozzie and I had labored shoulder to shoulder with our shovels, but it was the first time we had seen one dollar and twenty cents an hour come out of our efforts. Once, as duly-appointed members of the cesspool committee, we had shoveled together seven feet down in the bottom of the parsonage's new cesspool. Such rich experiences come seldom to those who are city pent.

This time we shoveled snow for the better part of two days before a bulldozer snow plow finally appeared, at which time a ragged cheer went up from a crew of men who did not care if they never handled another shovelful of snow. Some of us, curious to see what the storm had done to the beach, rode on the back end of the plow as it made its slow but steady journey to the end of Sea Street.

The cut through the dunes to the beach was clogged with drifts. The day was bright and sunny, however, and our expedition was provided with one experience which, to one of my inland background, at least, had the flavor of fantasy. We plodded through white and dazzling drifts which would have done credit to the Donner Pass—and then suddenly stepped out into a place where there was no snow. For one split second, it was like being one of those happy vacationers on a Florida resort poster who are shown stepping across the middle line of the poster from the dreary, snowy north onto Florida's warm sands.

The beach could scarcely have posed for a resort poster, however. It was a sorry sight. From top to bottom the tide had covered it with seaweed, old lumber and pilings, logs, empty casks, dead horseshoe crabs, and all the other usual litter of a storm, in quantities such as had seldom been seen. Huge logs had been carried clear to the base of the steep bank at the top of the beach, and several great semicircles had been scooped savagely out of the bank, far above the usual high-water mark. One beach cottage's fence hung in space, the sand completely cut away beneath it.

When I lowered my aching carcass into a chair that night, I was well pleased with my two days on the town.

"I never got a nickel out of the City of New York in all the time we lived there, and here we've only been in East Dennis a year and I'm already due to knock off $12.60 of the town's money," I remarked. "I'll say one thing, though—working for the town isn't the snap it's supposed to be!"

As usual, a little dinner under my belt fixed me up, and it being Friday night, we had a date to play bridge with the Underhills. We even decided to walk.

"Haven't you had enough of walking in the snow yet?" asked my wife.

"Yes, but there are a couple of beautiful little scenes along the way I want to point out to you, and we'll go by them too fast if we drive."

Actually, it was the kind of clear, cold winter's night which is wasted unless one takes a walk in it. Overhead, the greatest all-star revue in existence was giving one of its top performances. Orion strode majestically across the sky with the dazzling Dog Star at his heels. Capella gleamed like a pearl, and Castor and Pollux twinkled benignly down at Procyon. The great wheel of seven first-magnitude stars had never blazed to greater advantage, nor spoken more conclusively of the sureness of winter's grip.

It was, furthermore, the sort of winter's night that seems to encourage late hours. Florence had been invited to spend the night with a friend, so we had no sitter problem, and what with one thing and another it was almost four o'clock in the morning when we left for home. It was then that Nature provided, for the second time that day, a sight that stopped me in my tracks.

In the space of the hours we had spent in the Underhills' house a commonplace miracle, or miraculous commonplace, had occurred. We walked out under a preview of the soft summer sky of four months hence. Orion was gone. The Scorpion had risen in the east, and Vega was almost exactly where Regulus had been.

"What's the matter?" asked Elizabeth as I stood staring up at the lovely sight.

"I just got an inside tip," I told her. "Believe it or not, you're going to be lolling on the beach in a bathing suit before you know it!"

"Brrr!" said my wife.

"What is it about this East Dennis Social Club, anyway?" I said a few days later, marveling at my own interest. Once again Elizabeth and I were discussing that organization's waiting list. "As Fred Underhill said, it's nothing but it's something. And for some silly reason I can't analyze, it's one of the few things I ever came up against that I would really like to belong to. I guess it's because it's the one club that is uniquely of this village, and I've gotten to be sort of fond of the village."

"Tell you what," said Elizabeth. "You go out and make a pot of money and build us a bigger hall that will seat more people, and then maybe you too can be a member of the East Dennis Social Club."

"Nothing doing. I don't want to be a member in a bigger hall. I want to be a member in the *old* hall."

Hadley, needless to say, gave me a lot of trouble on this score when we went oystering the next day.

"Of course some of us would like very much to see you in the club, but after all we can't just take in *everybody*."

"I hope you choke on a turkey bone!"

A couple of men Hadley knew were already oystering when we arrived at the cove we had chosen for that day. We waded out to say hello. When he introduced me, one of them started fishing around inside his heavy jacket to get at the pocket of his wool shirt. It was a cold, raw day, with a keen wind that made our noses run and our eyes water.

"Oh, yes! I was going to look you up—didn't know you by sight, but I've got your name here on my list," said Jed Hall, finally producing a slip of paper. "You're on the committee that's going to write the minstrel show—you and me and Hadley and two others."

"I'll be happy to serve," I told him.

"I forget who the other two are we put on it. Let's see, now . . ." He tried to wipe his eyes enough to read the list, but then the wind whipped it out of his hand and away across the lake. "Damn! Well, I'll think of 'em, but anyway, we'll have to get together soon."

"I don't know," I said dubiously, "I'm beginning to get cold feet about this whole thing."

"Why?"

"One of my boots is leaking."

"Now, that's exactly the kind of joke we want to throw out of the show," said Jed. "Get to oystering, fellows."

A couple of days later I returned from the post office with further confirmation of the fact that the villages of East Dennis and Dennis were facing their annual threat of a blackface epidemic.

"The annual minstrel show is officially under way! Mr. Howard has sent out his postcards." Each year, when he began to get the minstrel show bug again and decided it was time things were getting under way, Mr. Howard Hall, the oldest minstrel, sent out postcards announcing that the first meeting of the Jubilee Minstrels would be held Saturday night to decide what the show was going to be about and then get to rehearsing. And I received one of the cards. I waved it importantly. "Us gwine hol' a meetin' at de lodge on Saturday night!"

"What are you planning to do in the show?" asked Elizabeth.

281

"I'm not going to do anything *in* the show, I'm going to help write it."

That same evening Asa Sears dropped by at about ten o'clock.

"Well, we got to discussing the waiting list again. There's quite a few people away in Florida and other places, so some thought we ought to take in at least a few more people to make up for them. But some others pointed out that maybe next year there wouldn't be so many go to Florida and then where'd we be? We went all over the whole list again and argued about whether or not each one would come."

"What was the final upshot of it? No new members?"

"No, sir. We finally got so completely confused that we all threw up our hands and decided to take in the *whole* kit and kaboodle and to hell with next year! We'll let next year take care of itself!"

"What? The whole list? Right down to the bottom?"

Asa's mouth puckered into a smile.

"You weren't at the bottom," he assured us. "You were *next* to the bottom."

It was all true. We had never seen so much turkey per capita, and we had never seen so much turkey disappear so fast. After the supper there was dancing. The traditional Grand March and Fore-and-Aft, or Portland Fancy, were followed by square dancing, and Freddie Barr popped the top button on his shorts right in the middle of a Texas Star. With his shorts falling down inside his pants, he uttered an anguished whisper to Hadley as they wheeled around, "gents in the center with a Texas Star."

"What'll I do?" he asked.

"Take shorter steps!" advised Hadley.

23

MINSTREL MAN

"The first meeting of this year's Jubilee Minstrels will now come to order," said Mr. Howard firmly and with noticeable satisfaction. He had managed to gather together fifteen men and Mrs. Savage, the minstrels' faithful piano player, and that was no mean achievement. We were launched. He could relax a little, because nothing could stop the minstrel show now.

Mr. Howard Hall of Dennis had been appearing in Cape minstrel shows for fifty years, but his knees still shook every time he got up on opening night to do his number. His specialties were singing old songs, and rattling the bones. First he would sing a chorus, and then he would do a chorus on the bones. The one thing a lot of the small fry remembered and looked forward to from year to year was those bones.

If there had been years when there was no minstrel show in Dennis, it had not been the fault of Mr. Howard, and now that an interested group had been formed again he saw to it that they produced. It was no easy matter to get anything done on Cape Cod, because time had a habit of whizzing by much faster there than any other place.

We all noticed it and often commented on the fact to each other. Gus Olsen, the plumber, for example, was interested in helping with our plumbing problems; Gus had every intention of coming by and looking them over for us; but he was a very busy man, and sometimes months would go by before he turned up. It was hard to be too critical, too, because in the meantime we had not got half the things done ourselves which we had intended to get done by then. We very much needed to have the time slowed down on the Cape, but nobody could seem to hit on a way to do it.

Each year the minstrel show was threatened by the element of time. The men who put on the show enjoyed doing it and wanted to do it, but they were busy with their garage work and drugstores, their kennels and restaurants, their fish markets and gas stations, their carpentry and contracting, and they were inclined to procrastinate. Because of that high-speed time system we had on the Cape, this tendency would have been fatal had it been allowed to exist unchallenged. Before anyone realized it, too many weeks would have slipped by, and a minstrel show would have been out of the question—for after about the middle of March it was hopeless to think of putting on a show. By then everybody was preoccupied with the all-important, bread-and-butter business of getting ready for the Season. The fact that the annual minstrel show ever got under way at all was largely due to Mr. Howard's determination that it should.

"Well, it looks like everybody's here. Everybody that's going to be, anyway," he said. "Two of the boys who couldn't make it tonight have said we can definitely count on them for the show, so that gives us fifteen men. Last year we had seventeen in the circle, but later on there was some little misunderstanding or other and three of the boys got mad— Did you call those boys, Nate?"

"Yes. They said they wouldn't care to be in the show."

"They're still mad," announced Mr. Howard. Being a Cape Codder, he respected the old Cape Cod custom of getting up and stalking out in stiff-necked wrath, to sit in a corner growling and licking one's wounds, every time something did not suit one. "Guess we'll have to get along with fifteen," he said.

The implication startled me.

"But, wait a minute, Mr. Howard," I protested. "I've never been in a show in my life, and I'm not planning to be in the circle—I'm only on the writing committee."

"Well, you'd better change your plans. If we've only got fifteen fellows, we need every man."

"Lock the door," said Hadley. "Nobody's gittin' out of here alive."

"Fifteen only gives us seven on a side," said Mr. Howard—Crow Hall, the interlocutor, being the fifteenth man, of course, "and we sure don't want any less than that."

"But I'm no performer," I declared anxiously. This was my first contact with an amateur show, and on top of everything else I brought to it a rather narrow concept of what it took to be a performer, due perhaps to overexposure to Broadway and professional actors and entertainers.

Whether performing became his profession or a mere avocation, a person with performerish tendencies started young, I had always understood. A performer got going at the age of four with clever imitations of Uncle Moe and other family characters at family gatherings and was in every show he could find time for from then on. He was not a person who waited until middle age was breathing down his neck to start being in shows.

Mr. Howard took a much broader view of things, however. He eyed me sternly.

"Can you carry a tune in a bucket?"

"Just about."

"Good. You're in the show. Now let's get on to the business meeting. All in favor of giving half the money to Carleton Hall and half the money to the Recreation Association like someone suggested say aye, opposed no. All right, it's so voted, and I guess that concludes the business meeting, so let's get to picking out the songs. If you fellows who are going to write the skit want to go in the other room and get to work, go right ahead. Mrs. Savage, would you mind running over 'Bill Bailey' for me? . . ."

"When am I going to learn not to listen to you?" I demanded of Hadley as the writing committee adjourned into the next room. "Now see what you've got me into?"

Hadley gave me a challenging stare.

"Don't you want to be up there in blackface behind those footlights, bringing down the house as you sing about Alabammy?"

"Bringing down the ceiling plaster, you mean. Listen, now—"

"Be honest. Aren't you ham enough to want to be up there on that stage?"

"Sure, I *want* to be—but I never have been, and this is too late to start."

Hadley's voice dropped to a resonantly reassuring tone.

"Don't worry, you won't have to do anything. We just need you to fill out the circle, is all. All you have to do is sing the choruses and laugh at the jokes. That won't always be easy, God knows, but at least you won't have to do it alone."

"And that's all I'll have to do?"

"Certainly! We'll break you in easy. Come on, let's get going on the skit."

Five of us sat down around a table decorated with five sharp pencils and two pads of paper and looked at each other. We had assembled in the home of Nate Howes, the undertaker's assistant, for that first rehearsal, and there in the dining room we were expected to get busy on the second half of the show while Mr. Howard and the others started shaping up the first part in the living room. Our job was to create the twenty-minute skit, or 'oleo,' which followed the minstrel show after a brief intermission.

"Well, let's see, now," said Jed. "What's Freddie Barr been up to lately?"

"Plenty—but don't forget, the skit *last* year was about Freddie," said Hadley. "We ought to spread it around and not put it to the same guy every time."

"I hear he took one of his horses to Narragansett last week."

"That so? How did Freddie make out?"

"Came in second."

"Not bad. How did the horse do?"

"Hey, that's pretty good! Write that down."

"Now, come on, fellows, let's get away from Freddie."

"Okay, who else could we hang the skit on? Anybody got any ideas?"

"Not me."

"Me neither."

"I understand Mr. Howard knows a place in Boston where we could rent a horse costume," said Nate.

"Stop tempting me," said Hadley.

"Say, that would be all right! We've never had a horse in one of our skits."

A horse! Certainly no amateur show should be without two men in a horse. Besides, I had never had an opportunity to see a horse costume up close and was curious to have a look at one.

"Seems to me a horse costume with a couple of local men in it would be a sure-fire laugh-getter," I said, "especially if we gave them a real workout. We could put them through all sorts of foolishness, like doing the conga and jumping up on a table and sitting in chairs—"

"Sure! All in favor of a horse in the skit—"

Hadley saw he could not hope to stem the rising tide of pro-horse sentiment, so he sought to deflect it.

"Okay, let's have a horse, but can't we hang the skit on someone else besides Freddie? Who plays the horses around this town?"

Three men spoke the same name.

"Gus Olsen!"

A horse-playing Swedish plumber. We were off to a good start.

"Sure! Somebody tries to sell Gus a half interest in the horse, and he says, 'No, I ban want a whole horse, or nothing—' "

"Write that down!"

"And then he tries to sell it to Freddie Barr—"

"How about it, Hadley?"

"Well . . . I guess we would have to bring Freddie into it a little," said Hadley, tempted beyond his strength, and the skit was definitely under way.

As we tossed our ideas around, the cheerful cacophony of a minstrel show's growing pains filled the house. Out in the other room, Mr. Howard had finished refreshing himself on "Bill Bailey," and two trumpets were blending tentatively in a Stephen Foster number. Brushes on a trap drum and cymbals indicated that the percussion department had been set up by our local kennels-master—"owner and operator of the only cat-house in East Dennis," as he called himself after he had built his new feline hostelry. Snatches of conversation that floated out from time to time from the living room suggested that the joke committee was not idle, either.

"How about this one? Lem Crowell is bowlegged—we could hang it on him. Lem goes up to Boston and gets a job as a floorwalker, see, and a woman comes in and says to him, 'My good man, can you tell me where I'll find talcum powder?' Lem says, 'Certainly, madam. Walk this way,' and starts off down the aisle. 'If I could walk *that* way,' she says, 'I wouldn't need the talcum powder!' "

"Write that down!"

"How about the one Hadley told a while ago there?"

"Pretty bad. But write it down, anyway—we might need it!"

"Here's a little joke magazine I picked up in the drugstore, but most of the so-called jokes in it are awful."

"Did you ever read a funny one in one of those?"

"No. Who the hell buys them, anyway?"

"Well, we had an afterdinner speaker down at Rotary the other night I think had been buying a few."

"Hey, I just remembered one we might use. We could put it on Fanny Hallett. Fanny comes into Goodspeed's store one morning—"

Over in one corner, Crow Hall was sitting by, a tall, thin, melancholy figure, making whatever inner preparations were necessary for the task of being interlocutor once again.

"How's life with Asa and Freddie on the harbor committee, Crow?" I asked him later in the evening.

Crow cleared his throat dolefully.

"Well," he said in his slow and cautious way, "I suppose it could be worse."

The life of amateur minstrel men was far from untroubled, I soon discovered. For one thing, my wife's reaction to the night that had been set for rehearsals was probably paralleled by at least ten other wives' reactions when we got home after that first meeting.

"*Saturday* night? Every Saturday night from now to the show?"

"Well, dear, Nate Howes goes to school in Boston five nights a week to study for his embalmer's license, and he's one of our end men. Besides, he has a piano."

"A fine thing! If I'd thought you were getting involved in something that was going to tie up all your Saturday nights,

289

I'm not sure I'd have let you out of the house. You've hardly been home two nights a week lately as it is, what with all these committees and things!"

"I know. Remember the good old days back in New York, the simple life we used to lead?" I put my arm around her and tried to coax her head onto my shoulder for a trip down Memory Lane, but it snapped up again.

"What are you going to do in the show?"

"Just help write the skit, and maybe do some special lyrics. After all, amateur shows are especially designed to take care of suppressed desires, and I've always had a suppressed desire to write some Gallagher and Shean lyrics. I got to thinking about it the night we came home from the minstrel show last year—remember, you asked me what was on my mind? Well, you remember that Gallagher and Shean business—Oh, Mr. Gallagher, Oh, Mr. Gallagher—only instead of Gallagher and Shean it'll be Sears and Crowell and other local names."

My lifelong designs on Gallagher and Shean began to bear fruit, especially at rehearsals, where additional verses grew out of the other men's greater knowledge of the local scene and its characters. Various highly slanderous little ditties quickly took shape. Only one stumped us so far as the question of whom to hang it on was concerned. It went this way:

"Oh, Mr. Crowell, Oh, Mr. Crowell!
With the women I am absolutely through,
For it is my firm belief
That they only bring you grief,
And so no more chasin' am I gonna do."

"Oh, Mr. Sears, Oh, Mr. Sears!
Now I'm glad to hear that you have changed your ways,
'Cause three gals just walked by slow—"
"What? Which way did they go?"
"They went thataway, Mr. Sears!"
"Lemme at 'em, Mr. Crowell!"

Considerable discussion went into the final selection of names for this one. We could not find any Searses or Crowells that fit. Various other local married men were named off, but the trouble was that the ones we might have used fitted the lyrics *too* well.

"How about Ed?"

"No! You never can tell— he *might* bring his own wife, and that would be too rough on her!"

"How about Jack?"

"We couldn't! That situation's explosive enough already!"

"Tom?"

"Huh-uh! *One* of those women would kill him."

I shook my head in frank admiration.

"I'll say one thing about you Cape Codders—you certainly haven't neglected sex!"

"It's something about the sea air. If we can ever build it into a tourist attraction, we're made."

Then after we named over a few more men, with no better results, Jed Hall finally came up with a solution. We hung it on the minister.

How to write an opening number just like they do it in one of those movies about songwriters was demonstrated that night, too. Of course, we borrowed the music from Irving Berlin, and that helped some.

"What are we going to use for our opening number?" someone asked. "Tell you one I like is that 'Show Business' number. 'There's no business like show business—' Could we use that?"

We all sat around humming and tapping our feet and thinking for a minute or two, and then an idea straightened Jed up in his chair.

"That's not the way it ought to go around here," he said. Jed ran a restaurant and inn during the summer and knew what he was talking about. "How would this be? 'There's no business, there's *no* business, when fall comes to Cape Cod!' "

291

About an hour later we had the complete lyrics, and they came from the heart. After all, the only thing that was really quiet on Cape Cod during the Quiet Season was the cash register!

After a couple of sessions on the skit we had it pretty well under way. Not that we really wrote anything more than an outline, as I learned when I naively asked if we should start getting the lines on paper.

"Hell, we never bother to write it out," said Jed, "we just explain our ideas to the fellows who are going to be in the skit and then they say it their own way!"

With the skit under control, Hadley was able to sit back and consider what contribution he was going to make to the minstrel-show part. He offered to do "Albert and the Lion," and the suggestion was declined with thanks by a vote of 14 to 1. He then fell back on the realm of song, choosing a ballad that seemed suitable to his meaty baritone, a tender, drippy morsel called "Too Young," with "Beautiful, Beautiful Brown Eyes" to follow for an encore.

This settled, he found time a few days later to turn his attention to me. We were at his house, having an after-dinner coffee and spending a few minutes talking over the skit before going on to the weekly rehearsal.

"Well, now, let's see if there isn't some kind of a little number you can do."

"What are you talking about? I'm not supposed to do a number."

Hadley's expression was not unlike that of a British colonel glancing at a junior officer suspected of showing the white feather.

"Well, I know all that, but at the same time there are only fifteen men in the circle this year, and I don't know whether you've stopped to realize it or not, but everyone but you is going to do *something*." A trail of sugar materialized on the table between the sugar bowl and his cup as he sweetened his coffee with his usual abandon. "Now, maybe you don't want to do a number alone, but I was thinking maybe we could do something together."

As usual with a Ransom proposition, I sniffed suspiciously —but nibbled.

"What sort of thing?"

"Well, I got to thinking, and I'll bet we could work up a swell magic act together."

Hadley, the magician, had often astounded us with some really impressive card tricks, but they hardly seemed suitable for a minstrel show.

"This wouldn't be card tricks," he said, anticipating my thoughts, "this would be some regular feats of magic. I know some sure-fire tricks that are foolproof. Even Corbett-proof. And the kids will love them. They'll be right down in the front row, and we ought to have at least one act aimed right at them. All you'll have to do is be the stooge and I'll do the rest. For instance, supposing I take scissors and a sheet of paper and cut out a rabbit, and tell you I'm going to make it disappear. The kids sit back and say, 'Aw, a paper rabbit! Nothing to that.' Then I tell 'em I'm going to make it reappear out of your coat—and I reach in and pull out a real live rabbit!"

"H'm. Well, I don't know. Sounds like fun, but . . ."

We continued to work away at the skit, and eventually had it in good enough shape to start rehearsing it. The part I particularly enjoyed was having the horse to put through its paces. I vied with Cliff, our drummer man, in thinking up new antics for it.

"You're going to run that beast ragged," Jed remarked.

"Well, if we're going to pay ten dollars' rent on a horse costume, we've got to get our money's worth."

"That reminds me, men. We haven't cast the horse parts yet."

"Say, that's right."

"Hadley and I were talking about it the other day, though," Jed went on, turning to me with a peculiar expression, "and it seemed to us that since you and Cliff had the most ideas for giving the horse a workout, maybe you two ought to be inside it."

A general cry of approval drowned out our protests. I glowered at Hadley, who was sitting by, whistling quietly, with every evidence of self-satisfaction. He had already promoted a rabbit into my tail coat. Now he was going to get me inside a horse! Cliff and I were elected into the horse by a vote of 13 to 2.

"And don't leave out any of those rugged gags you two were thinking up for somebody else to do, either," ordered Jed. "Now, who's going to play which end?"

"Well, if it's type-casting we're after—" began Hadley, glancing at me, but this master-stroke of his plot was thwarted by the fact that Cliff's legs were even longer than mine and therefore more suitable for the kicking end.

The weeks flashed by, and suddenly the Friday and Saturday nights on which we were to give our two performances loomed up black and menacing on the calendar a scant week ahead. We still had costumes to assemble and props to gather and Hadley and I had a white rabbit to get. The idea was to pick one up at the pet shop in Hyannis a couple of days before the show, so as not to have it on our hands too long, and then give it away after the second performance to any kid who wanted it.

Two days before the show we learned that the usual shipments of Easter bunnies to Cape dealers were late that year. We could not locate one anywhere, and by then it was unthinkable not to have the rabbit in our act. Without it, our big trick would fall flat. Without it, our act would have no high point. Mabel Crowell went off the Cape for us and chased up and down half the side roads of southeastern Massachusetts before she finally located and brought back alive a white rabbit. A *large* white rabbit.

"This was the smallest the man had, and I figured I'd better take what I could get," said Mabel, as Hadley reached into the cardboard carton and lifted out what looked like about a yard of rabbit. "As a matter of fact, he had one a little smaller that he almost sold me—it's just lucky he happened to get curious and ask what we wanted the rabbit for. When I told him, he took the other one right back. 'It's a good thing you told me,' he said, 'I hate to think what might have happened. There's two kinds of rabbits, and the other kind won't give you any trouble, but if your minstrel show feller got one of *these* near the seat of his pants I wouldn't want to be responsible. You get one of these stirred up and they can bite and kick and claw something fierce!'"

"Well, I don't know if you made the right choice, Mabel," said Hadley, "the other might have given us a funnier show."

Nevertheless he assured me that a rabbit would stay perfectly still as long as it was in a completely dark place. We tried it in the tail of my coat, and outside of feeling like a sack of flour, it gave me no trouble.

"Won't people notice a big bulge like that, though?"

"You'd be surprised. The whole secret of magic is distraction. People will be watching what we're doing—they'll never look at your coat. All you have to do is keep that side of it turned away from the audience during the act, and nobody in the place will notice anything."

Any show, I suppose, reaches the point where the whole experience involved becomes unbelievable. It was unbelievable to find myself, at long last and yet all of a sudden, back at Nate Howes' once again, this time to be blacked up for the show itself. By tradition, half the company blacked up at Nate's and half at Jed's. At our final rehearsal Mr. Howard sat down as usual and wrote out two lists of names. We were then each told where to report, and we did as we were told.

The Howes' kitchen was full of men in their undershirts, some with their faces and hands already blacked up, some being blacked up by others or by Nate's wife, Millicent, and some still waiting their turn. On the table were some brushes in a glass, a couple of flat cans of blacking, and the red paint for the lips. Grinning like a fiend, Hadley sat me down presently in one of the chairs and worked a brush around unstintingly in the blacking. The cold wet brush made me flinch as he began to paint.

"Hold still!" He glanced at Nate and his grin broadened as he turned back to me. "Know what these brushes are we're using?" he asked, holding out the brush for my inspection.

It took me a moment to recall that Nate Howes was an undertaker's assistant, and studying for a license of his own.

"The regular brushes didn't get here from Boston," someone explained.

"Ever been embalmed before?" inquired Hadley.

"These are out of my brand-new kit!" Nate insisted earnestly. "They've never been used!"

"Well, do a good job," I told Hadley. "When we get on that stage I want my family to look up at me and say, 'Don't he look natural!' "

When the only white face left in the Howes' kitchen was Millicent's, we put on our minstrel finery and drove to Carleton Hall. We stumbled our way around the back of the hall to the backstage entrance—nobody had thought to bring flashlights—and assembled onstage. The group from Jed's were already there. We looked around into each other's unfamiliar black faces, grinned nervously, and endured as best we could the long minutes that still stood between us and the rise of the curtain. All those weeks of easy-going rehearsals, which had given way to a general, desperate, last-minute buckling-down, had suddenly gone by in a flash, vanished, evaporated. We

296

needed more time! How could we possibly be ready to put on a show? The reek of demon rum was in the air as Dutch courage was passed from hand to hand.

Out in front, the shuffle of feet and the murmur of voices told us that people were arriving in numbers. The peephole in the curtain seldom lacked for a minstrel man's eye pressed to it.

"Looks like we're going to have a full house!"

"Here comes Asa Sears!"

"Gus Olsen is already here."

"How about Freddie Barr?"

"Yes, there he is."

The rabbit in my tail coat seemed to be gaining weight by the minute. My lips were dry, and the hand that clutched my notes was trembling as I strove to burn my lines into my memory—for by then I was in deeper than ever. Everybody in the show had a solo line or two in the opening number. Everybody had a Gallagher and Shean to do. Including me. Furthermore, what with the rabbit and certain problems I had had in connection with dressing for the rest of our act, I was far from comfortable.

My lines in the opening number came in the middle part, which went as follows:

The butcher, the baker, the grocer, the doc,
They all come knocking at our doors each day;
The banker, the lawyer, they've got us in hock,
Our wives keep telling them we've gone away.

I had "the banker, the lawyer, etc." In the past few days I had been over those two lines a thousand times; as a matter of fact, I had suggested them myself when we were thinking up the lyrics. But I was still fixing them in my memory as we fidgeted in our chairs waiting for the signal to start the show.

For once Hadley was nervous, too.

"Don't forget, now," he whispered anxiously, "when we sit down after the opening number, don't forget you've got a passenger. I don't want to get up in front of all those kids and pull out a dead rabbit!"

"Okay."

"Don't get flustered. Take a leaf from your old Uncle Hadley's book, and keep cool."

"You're not nervous, eh?"

"Me nervous?" Hadley's laugh would have been more impressive had it not cracked a little.

"Everything under control, eh?"

"Certainly!"

"Then where's your hat?"

Hadley clapped his hands to his wig.

"My hat! Hold everything! Where's my hat?" he cried, and rushed into the wings. I felt better.

Hadley's top hat was located and restored to him, and we took our places in the circle. The signal was relayed to us from the wings that everything was ready. Every seat in the house was filled, all one hundred and sixty of them. Mrs. Savage was poised at the piano. Our friends and neighbors were out there waiting to see what it was we had been up to all these weeks. There was nothing between us and them but an old curtain, and there was no court of appeal left anywhere to prevent it from going up now and exposing us to their view. We were trapped men, and we felt like it. Mr. Howard looked around the circle, just as nervous as he had been that first night in 1898. He cleared his throat.

"Well, men, if you're all ready, I guess we might as well get the show started."

Nobody was ready, but we went ahead anyway. We rose to our feet, staring straight ahead at the back side of that untrustworthy curtain, and our two trumpet men sounded those few lugubrious notes of Old Black Joe which had been chosen to herald its rise. When they had died away, Mrs. Savage's firm hands bullied the introduction into being. Bill Kennedy, the shellfish warden, hauled on the ropes and raised the curtain, and we gave the world "There's No Business, There's No Business, When Fall Comes to Cape Cod."

After the full chorus had sung the opening line, the individual lines began, each man stepping forward as his turn came. The music moved along measure by measure in its inexorable way, getting ever closer to that moment when I would have to step forward and deliver my bit. I took a final glance at the tiny typewritten slip held in the palm of my hand, and then put it confidently into my vest pocket. I was set. I not only knew those words, I would know them to my dying day.

"The butcher, the baker, the grocer, the doc," sang the man ahead of me, "they all come knocking at our doors each day . . ."

I stepped forward and sang out loudly.

"The banker, the lawyer, they've got us in hock . . ."

Blank.

The music moved on for a second, two seconds, while I stood frozen and mute before one hundred and sixty of my friends and neighbors and fifteen of my colleagues, including Mrs. Savage. Then:

"Ourwiveskeeptellingthemwe'vegoneaway!"

The words tumbled out in one frantic rush, and I stepped back into place with the dubious distinction of having got the first laugh of the show.

The opening number was dispatched with no further mishaps, and received hearty applause. Then came the traditional words of the interlocutor:

"Gentlemen, be seated!"

Fifteen of us sat down together, and one of us shot up again with a cry. I had sat on the rabbit! In my flustered state over having muffed my opening lines I had forgotten about the rabbit, and now I had sat on it! I had distinctly felt its soft body under me, and I had surely crushed the life right out

299

of it. The strange part of it all was that in parting with its life it had uttered a most unrabbitlike sound, almost a Bronx cheer . . .

While our audience roared, Hadley removed from the seat of my chair the jokester's delight he had placed there, an inflated rubber item called a "Poo-Poo Pillow."

"Just wanted to remind you about the rabbit," he whispered in a strangled voice. "Great work—you're stealing the show, boy. Two big laughs already."

The interlocutor and the end men exchanged a few introductory remarks which established the fact that they were all feeling fine that night, and then the first joke was unleashed.

"Mr. Interlocutor!"

"Yes, Sambo?"

"Mr. Interlocutor, you know Ted Crowell, that lives down Nobscusset Road there?"

"Yes, I know Ted."

"And you know that old car Ted's got, the one they call the Yellow Peril?"

"Yes, I've seen the Yellow Peril."

"Yes, well, you know Seth Sears, too, don't you, who has that early Chevvy—the one they put out just after the war?"

"Yes?"

"The Civil War, that is."

"Yes, I know Seth, and I've seen his old Chevvy. What about it, Sambo?"

"Well, awhile back Ted Crowell and Seth Sears got to arguing about who had the best car and which could go the fastest. Finally they decided to settle it by having a race to Provincetown and re-turn. So a week ago last Tuesday they lined up in the road by the Dennis garage there, and at nine o'clock sharp they started off."

"Is that so? Well, who won?"

"We don't know—they ain't got back yet!"

All the jokes were given a local setting, and some of them

had that same earthiness which had surprised me so, here in staid New England, the year before. The minstrels knew from experience, though, that people always claimed they wanted nice clean jokes—and were always disappointed when they got them.

"Mr. Interlocutor!"

"Yes, Snowball?"

"You know that drugstore down in East Dennis? It's one of the few down there."

"Yes, I've visited it, Snowball."

"Well, the other day the boss had to go somewhere, so he left that young Hall boy in charge—you know young Mervyn Hall?"

"Yes, I know Mervyn."

"Well, when the boss came back, he asked Mervyn if anyone had been in while he was gone. Mervyn said, yes, one feller had been in, but he took care of him all right. 'He wanted something to stop a cough,' said Mervyn, 'so I gave him a dose of castor oil.'"

"A dose of castor oil?"

"That's just what the boss said. 'Why, Mervyn, are you crazy?' he said. 'You can't stop a cough with a dose of castor oil!'"

"And what did Mervyn say?"

"He said, 'The heck you can't! That's him waiting across the street there for the bus, and he's got to ride all the way to Hyannis. He don't dare cough!'"

The first golden-voiced songbird was then introduced to render an old-time favorite, and the show rolled on its way. And during that next hour I learned things I had never really appreciated before about the keen satisfactions of performing. A group of amateur players are an embattled garrison besieged by an audience, and each man, in standing up and delivering as well as he can, performs an act of heroism that nobody appreciates as deeply as his comrades-in-arms.

301

"Professor Hambone will now entertain us with a few feats of magic."

I squirmed convulsively and sought to locate in my legs those tendons and sinews which, in a matter of seconds now, would have to get me to my feet and propel me toward the footlights. My God! I had not really stopped to analyze our magic act until now, but when you come to think of it, there were fifty different ways it could go wrong. It could easily be the sorriest flop that had ever embarrassed an audience. What if we—

Hadley had stepped to the footlights and explained that he had been taking lessons from a correspondence school.

"Now, to do these tricks I got to have an assistant," he said, looking around, "and the school says to pick the dumbest man you can find, so . . . Rastus! Come up here!"

The rabbit. I had to remember about the rabbit. I had to remember to sidle up and stand in such a way as to keep him on the side away from the audience. Matter of fact, I had to remember about a dozen things at once. I had never had any experience in moving around on a stage, and until I tried it I never knew how much thought had to go into every move to make it right. Right now, however, my problem was to cover the ten feet of stage between me and Hadley. I rose and mooched forward in a suitably halfwitted style.

It got a laugh!

This time the laugh was with me, and it was like a magic potion. Nothing could have put some backbone into me more quickly—hambone, to put it more accurately. How could the act fall flat? People were enjoying it already!

Hadley did a few minor tricks, building up to the rabbit, and through it all I felt as though I had a baby elephant secreted in my tail coat. I was sure one of those gimlet-eyed kids in the front row would notice the bulge. How could they help it? My own daughter was there, practically at our feet, trembling with excitement. Surely one of the kids would notice the lumpy condition of my tail coat, and spoil the fun by pointing!

Hadley was right, though. They never did. When he finally reached inside my coat and produced the rabbit, a shriek of astonishment went up that was worth everything we—and Mabel—had gone through. The look on his daughter's face when a rabbit is produced from Daddy's tail coat is something every father should see at least once.

The rest of the show was pure joy. One act after another went over well. The Gallagher and Shean lyrics made a hit. Hadley rubbed his hands together as we sat down after the entire company had sung them, two by two, and whispered, "Well, it looks like we've got a hit on our hands!" The horse costume was an inferno to be in, but our antics got laughs, and that was all that mattered. By the time the cast took a bow at the end of the skit, I knew that I had been a ham all my life, and that the experience I had had that night was one I would treasure for the rest of my days.

Here was one more new satisfaction for which I had small-town life to thank. Had we stayed in the city I would never have known an experience like that show. In itself, it was a minor thing—trivial, the serious thinker would call it—and yet the blood and bones of our little community were mixed into it. It was something in which nearly everyone in our two villages participated, on one side of the footlights or the other. It was something we created for ourselves, and only for ourselves. It was an expression of that surprisingly sprightly, entertaining, and warm-hearted life we had found among the allegedly frozen-faced Cape Codders.

It showed, too, how really good was the mixture that went to make up the Cape of today—that mixture of newcomer and native, of old and new. I liked Cape Codders, and I liked the kind of people who had taken a chance and moved to the Cape —people like Fred Underhill and Hadley Ransom. Every day was fun there, because the people were fun. Every day I had

303

the fresh pleasure of wondering—what was Asa Sears going to do next? What would Freddie Barr stir up next? What fool thing was Hadley going to involve me in next? What were all the others going to be up to?

We had been lucky, and the Cape had made us welcome. Yet why we had felt it was *the* place for us was still a mystery, something we still could not put into words. There were thousands of places we might have gone to live. Why had we moved to Cape Cod?

I could not say. The only thing I could say with assurance was that sometimes it pays to follow your heart.

24

DAVID HENRY'S BIRTHDAY

It was D.H.'s birthday. Eighty-seven years ago he had been born here in East Dennis. As I looked out the bedroom window at the church steeple that morning I thought about what his daughter, Gert, had said: "We've always had quite a celebration on his birthday."

We dressed with unusual care to honor D.H. that day. We decided to walk, and it was just as well we did. The cars were parked solid clear down the street. When we reached the church, we were lucky to find a seat, and very soon after that there were many people standing in the back.

The florists must have known David Henry, too, because the flowers seemed to have an extra touch about them. They filled the space behind the casket from one side of the church to the other. They were grief expressed in beauty and they surrounded D.H. with a soft and loving farewell of color.

The minister who spoke was the former pastor of the

church, a man rich in years himself. He looked around at all our faces and spoke, as he should, for us all.

"This is a wonderful gathering, because it is a gathering of friends. We all considered David Henry Sears a friend. I myself first met him sixty-five years ago . . ."

Elizabeth and I had known David Henry scarcely more than a year, and yet our sense of loss was also deep. I was not ashamed when tears unexpectedly came to my eyes as I filed past his bier with the others for a last look at his kindly old face. It was not merely because he was a man it would have been hard not to become fond of; it was because he was the finest link with Old Cape Cod, with the Cape Cod of the fast-dimming past, that had been left to us, and now he was gone.

We had already shared in our village's pleasures, its laughs, and its squabbles; now, for the first time, we shared in its grief. This was a gathering of friends, yes, and in death even as in life D.H. managed to fill our hearts with a sense of the value of friendship.

He lies now in our beautiful little cemetery. Cheerful and serene, it looks out over the marshes where the little meandering tidal creek flashes in the sunshine. From my window I can see a corner of that cemetery down the road to the east. David Henry is in good company. Jacob Sears is there, and the fabulous Christopher Sears, and Christopher Hall, and all the rest of them. There are fine old sea captains, and ornery ones, noble men and scoundrels, teetotalers and drunkards, good Christians who thought they were bad Christians, and bad ones who thought they were good; and just about every kind of woman you can think of, which will suit D.H., who never quite gave up the notion that he might marry just once more if the right woman were to come along.

They are a motley crew down there in our cemetery, but taken by and large they are as good as the next, and at least their goings-on would never give a person a dull moment. If I am able to hang on here until my time comes, I will be well satisfied to take my place there among Old Cape Codders and new ones, with that smug assurance so typical of the Cape resident that, whether he is dead or alive, the Cape is the best of all places to be.